out of Place

Rite out of Place

Ritual, Media, and the Arts

RONALD L. GRIMES

UNIVERSITY PRESS

2006

OXFORD
UNIVERSITY PRESS

Oxford University Press, Inc., publishes works that further
Oxford University's objective of excellence
in research, scholarship, and education.

Oxford   New York
Auckland   Cape Town   Dar es Salaam   Hong Kong   Karachi
Kuala Lumpur   Madrid   Melbourne   Mexico City   Nairobi
New Delhi   Shanghai   Taipei   Toronto

With offices in
Argentina   Austria   Brazil   Chile   Czech Republic   France   Greece
Guatemala   Hungary   Italy   Japan   Poland   Portugal   Singapore
South Korea   Switzerland   Thailand   Turkey   Ukraine   Vietnam

Published by Oxford University Press, Inc.
198 Madison Avenue, New York, New York 10016

www.oup.com

Oxford is a registered trademark of Oxford University Press

Library of Congress Cataloging-in-Publication Data
Grimes, Ronald L., 1943-
Rite out of place : ritual, media, and the arts / Ronald L. Grimes.
p. cm.
Includes bibliographical references and index.
ISBN-13: 978-0-19-530145-8

1. Rites and ceremonies.   2. Mass media.   3. Performing arts.   I. Title.
GN473.G75 2006
390—dc22   2005025826

Printed in the United States of America
on acid-free paper

To Bryn, making a place for himself
To Cailleah, out of place in a great place

Acknowledgments

In addition to colleagues, students, readers, and publishers thanked or acknowledged in the notes, my deep appreciation goes to Carolina Echeverria for envisioning the whole book in a single cover image. Thank you as well, Cynthia Read, for taking the risk, and, Susan Ecklund, for doggedly deleting the overdone dashes and ferreting out the misplaced commas.

Preface

Because I am a ritual studies scholar, the center of my attention is typically upon a boundary condition rather than a tradition. The theoretical and methodological commitments that ensue from focusing on religion and the performing arts require scouting disciplinary boundaries that separate and connect religion, theater, film, and media. These commitments require definitions of ritual that do not restrict it to religion. The presumed proper place of ritual—in temples, synagogues, and churches—is barely explored here. Instead, this is a book about ritual's out-of-place appearances: ritual hawked on television, ritual shot on film, ritual in the class-room, ritual in the wilds.

Ask anyone and you'll be assured, "Sure, ritual has its place." Like a dutiful servant, it should know that place and stay there. It ought not be springing up underfoot, as if its place were everywhere. But you can't just stash it anywhere either.

Ask people, "What's ritual's place?"

They'll tell you, "Someplace special." Their reply casts ritual in a role that is sequestered, if not sacred. Ritual, in this view, is not ordinary or public. On account of its curvaceous tendencies and circumambulatory ways, ritual would be out of place at work, rendering inefficient the great cultural machines that drive the workplace.

Jonathan Z. Smith, an eminent religious studies scholar, thinks ritual is about emplacement. Fair enough, but placement where? In a world of fast-paced globalization and market-driven economies, ritual seems awkwardly out of place, a clumsy, tradition-laden cultural activity. Nevertheless, it springs up underfoot, making troublesome appearances in unlikely places. Like a weed or pest, it resists being stomped out. Ritual can be surprisingly invasive.

These essays arise from having nosed around peculiar places that religious studies scholars don't habitually haunt. My usual research venue is "the field," which is to say, not the library (although I spend lots of time there too). This book doesn't arise out of ethnographic research any more than it is bound to textual research. Few informants and little data appear here, so the space occupied by these essays is not only not-the-library but not-quite-the-field either.

The simplest way to name the realm explored here is to label it "consultative." Whatever it is that I am doing when I consult, it is not ethnography, much less science. Ritual studies consultation is more akin to applied anthropology. This group or that institution is exploring an issue of ritual significance. I am invited to contribute a ritual studies perspective, sometimes to make recommendations or serve as a team member. Because of the brevity of my involvement, I have little time for sustained participant observation or protracted interviews, the two staples of ethnographic approaches to the study of ritual. However, insofar as I arrive on the scene a neophyte, the situation resembles fieldwork. Sometimes because I am asked to do so, sometimes because I choose to do so, I play the role of court fool. Lacking true expertise, I tease those who consult with me by tendering ironic critiques or reimagined possibilities.

Part I treats ritual in the media, largely television, but also the Internet, photography, video, and film. Chapter 1 addresses media scholars and producers interested in the roles that ritual plays, might play, or should not play in mass media. Chapter 2 examines a television production on sacred rites, offering a critique of the way it packages ritual for popular consumption and proposing an alternative way of handling ritual in documentaries. Chapter 3 contemplates the shooting of rites with still and video cameras, a strange but widespread cultural activity that can either disrupt, extend, or validate these rites. Chapter 4 proposes a method for studying ritual in film by applying various kinds of ritual criticism to the wedding scene from the film *Fiddler on the Roof.*

Part II examines ritual in the settings where university teachers most regularly present it, in classrooms and in scholarly debates over theory and method. Chapter 5 examines two undergraduate courses—neither of them on ritual—in which ritual nevertheless plays a significant but contested role. Chapter 6 tells the story of trying to integrate ritual theory and ritual practice in a university and a course caught up in the wake of 9/11. Chapter 7 reflects on ritual as a mediating process. It does so by examining ceremonial screens, barriers that create spatial hierarchies, thus distinguishing ritual leaders from ritual followers. Chapter 8 is the most overtly theoretical one. In search of the orientation that only a theory can provide, I lay out charts and tables in service of an argument with Jonathan Z. Smith over the nature of ritual placement.

Part III shifts from conceptual to geographical space, thereby initiating a discussion about ritual's role in the environment. Chapter 9 is a dialogue about two ritually significant places, a rural performance barn and an urban ritual studies lab. Chapter 10 is theoretical but not abstract. It is about survival, specifically about the role of ritual in shaping attitudes toward the environment. Chapter 11 poses an outrageous question: Can ritual help save the planet? Because the chapter amounts to an ecological poetics of ritual, it pushes the limits of the scholarly article as a genre.

Contents

PART I

Ritual in Mediated Space

I

Ritual and the Media

This chapter originated as a response to Media, Religion, and Culture, an international conference held at the University of Colorado in Boulder.[1] Recognizing that the notion of ritual was becoming important to media studies, Stewart Hoover, one of the organizers, asked me to attend the sessions and offer a response to their handling of the idea of ritual. So frequently was the term "ritual" used that tendering critiques of individual papers was impossible. Instead, I offered a brief primer of ritual studies terminology for use in media discussions, along with criticisms of the definitions of ritual implied by conference discourse. Later, I tracked down the scholarly sources that lay behind so-called ritual approaches to media and wrote brief critiques of them. Because these approaches were generalized and abstract, seldom treating actual examples of ritual's interaction with media, it was necessary to outline ways that ritual and media interact in actual practice. The result was this introductory invitation to ritual-and-media studies laced with some cautionary advice.

Media scholars as well as media producers have become interested in the idea of ritual as well as in the performance of actual rites. Not long ago, the terms "ritual" and "media" would have been regarded as labels for separate cultural domains—the one sacred, the other secular; the one term designating a religious activity and the other denoting tools and processes for transferring information. Media not only intruded upon but also profaned ritual. Since the two were segregated domains, an attempt to posit a significant connection between ritual and media would have seemed forced.

But things have changed. Now, media often validate rites. The presence of cameras announces, "This is an important event." Today, both notions, ritual and media, are understood quite differently, and the connections between them are remarked upon with growing frequency in scholarly writing. In some accounts ritual and the media are enthusiastically equated rather than fearfully segregated. The media, some claim, *are* ritual in contemporary form. However, when a metaphor (media *as* ritual) collapses into a simple identity (media *are* ritual), both terms can become useless. Either strategy—segregating or equating—oversimplifies the complex ways in which media and ritual interact, so it helps to identify some of the obvious possibilities:[2]

1. Media presentation of a rite
   Example: Film documentary of a rite watched by a spectator with little or no connection to the event
2. Ritual event extended by media
   Example: TV coverage of a papal mass witnessed by a faithful Catholic viewer participating electronically in the event
3. Ritual actions in virtual space
   Example: Cyberspace weddings resulting in legal marriage
4. Subjunctive (or "ludic") ritualizing
   Example: Myth- or fantasy-based games played on the Internet "as if" they were rites
5. Magical rite with media device as "fetish" (or "icon")
   Example: Putting one's hand on a TV set to receive healing power from an evangelist
6. Ritualized behavior toward electronic objects
   Example: The TV set as centerpiece of family gatherings; computer terminal as a locus of ultimate concern
7. Media-delivered ritual object
   Example: Presentation of a Torafax page on the World Wide Web.
8. Media document as certificate of ritual act
   Example: Funeral videos mailed from North America to Africa to attest to a death
9. Ritual use of media device
   Example: Amplification of Pueblo drumming during a ceremony. Christian worship services built around CD-ROMs produced by the American Bible Society
10. Mediated ritual fantasy
    Example: The initiation scene in the film *Emerald Forest*
11. Media as model for, or butt of, ritual activity
    Example: Hollywood gestures imitated, consciously or unconsciously, in liturgical space. Media-manufactured images as objects of homiletical critique

We most readily imagine the relation between ritual and media as a situation in which the viewers are on one side of a TV set and the rite on the other. The rite is elsewhere, and we viewers are here in our living rooms. The mediating device in the middle is doing what it is supposed to, mediating. Prone as English speakers are to using container metaphors, we imagine the ritual event as somehow miniaturized and coming through the TV set, like water through a pipe. The electronic device channels the action to us. The image on the set is not real, but the actions on the other side of the screen (and camera) are. We consume the images, the virtual realities, but not the rites themselves.

If we viewers are merely curious, just spectating, we take the moving images on the screen to be a kind of visual description (#1 above), a mirror, of reality. We spectate on that reality but are not really part of it. If, on the other hand, our lives are strongly implicated by the events on the other side of the tube, the events on the screen draw us in. We participate in those events (#2), even though we do so at a distance. In such cases, the event is not just described but made present. The rite reaches toward and includes viewers. No longer mere viewers, we are ritualists, congregants rather than audience members.

A different way of conceiving the situation is to imagine that the culminating ceremonial event is not on the other side of the screen and the camera but in media space itself. The clearest example is that of a cyberspace wedding (#3). The bride and groom are not physically in one another's presence nor that of a minister. Instead, all three work from spatially distant terminals. They say—or, rather, type—all the right words, in the right circumstances, with the acceptable intentions and proper qualifications. The result is a legal marriage, and the rite did not transpire behind the medium but within it.

A variation on this mediated wedding ceremony is the sort of virtual ritualizing that happens in myth- or fantasy-inspired games played on the Internet. Like the cyberspace wedding, the ritualized game transpires electronically, but unlike it, the framing of the event is subjunctive (#4). However much they may believe in it, they don't believe it. Such ritualists participate with playful or fictive intentions—sometimes advertised by the use of pseudonyms. Although the players may be utterly serious, they are also playing a game, so the seriousness is ludic, as-if. In reading a novel or going to a play, participants in virtual ritualizing can get *really* hurt, angry, or inspired; the virtual or fictive can have *real* consequences. It is not always easy to separate #3 from #4, especially if participants themselves are unclear about their frames of mind.

Ordinarily, one supposes that middle-class viewers think of the TV as an empty, inert box. When plugged in and turned on, it has power, but that power is comprehensible, at least in principle, at least by technicians. The power is not mystical; it has no will or purpose of its own. The box's power lies solely in mediating the rhetorical and psychological power of performers; their power is to persuade by argument and suggestion.

However, in some circumstances, the power mediated by the inert box accrues to the medium itself, transforming it into a ritual object, thus illustrating #5 above. Oral Roberts is praying for us—no, with us—and, following his guidance (as he is following God's), we reach out and touch the set, absorbing its power. Its power is, so to speak, borrowed from him, and his, Roberts assures his viewers, from God.

A slightly different alternative involves ritualization rather than magic.[3] Whereas magical rites assume a causal connection between symbolic manipulation and empirical outcome, ritualization is a tacit form of ritual. Ritualization involves what Erving Goffman called "interaction ritual," ritual-like behavior lacking the social recognition that would earn it recognition as a formal rite.[4] When a family focuses much of its energy and interest on a TV, so much so that its solidarity is maintained and negotiated in the space governed by the screen, the family members have ritualized their behavior around this "icon" (#6). Individuals can "iconify" computer screens just as readily as families "enshrine" TV screens. In both cases the interaction is a ritual substitute or analog. Surfing the Internet as a functional equivalent of drumming rhythm, or sitting in front of a video screen as a peculiar form of meditation are among the possible interpretations of human interaction with media devices.

Ritual objects, the Torah, for instance (#7), may be presented electronically on the Web without any attendant, media-presented actions and without rendering the medium itself iconic. In such instances ritual actions, for instance, reading and meditating on the Torah, are supplied from the viewer's side rather than the actor's side. In examples like this, an electronic medium presents the occasion for ritualizing but not the rite itself.

Asked what video does, we are likely to say that it records or documents. "Documentary" is a genre of both film and video. Conventionally understood, documentaries are description-like. If, however, they become suggestive and elliptical, they leap the boundaries of the genre to become art films. The standard documentary states; it declares. However, documentaries can do more; they can certify a ritual event (#8). I am told that Ashantis living in Toronto sometimes send videos of funerals back to their families in Ghana. Why? Because inheritance customs require participation in a funeral, and watching a video serves as a witnessing, therefore a certification, of a death.

One can think of the media as containing or mediating (that is, passing on) ritual, but the converse is also true: ritual may "contain" media and media devices. Since it is a cultural convention to think of ritual as traditional and old but to think of technology as new and nontraditional, we are sometimes surprised by the appearance of technological artifacts like amplified drums in traditional ceremonies such as Pueblo corn dances (#9).[5] Similarly, Bible stories now appear on video and in CD-ROMs, so multimedia devices and images are beginning to show up in standard, Sunday morning worship services. It may be that the world will witness not only media-assisted liturgy but also media-centered liturgy.

For some purposes, the difference between mediated fantasy (#10) and virtual ritualizing (#4) is probably not significant, since both are subjunctive. The difference is that the latter is overtly interactive; the game player acts in cyberspace. In contrast, the moviegoer who watches the film *Emerald Forest* is fundamentally a witness or consumer of initiatory fantasy, not a player in it.

It is conventional in middle-class religious institutions to be critical of the media, to make media the butt of homiletical polemics (#11). Such polemic is regarded as prophetic critique.[6] But it is just as likely that media also supply models for liturgical leadership, liturgical space, and liturgical imagery. Sometimes the appropriation of media models is witting, sometimes not. Although the influence may be mutual—media modeling rites and rites modeling media—I suspect that in practice mutuality is rare. In religious programming it is sometimes the case that TV programs are modeled after worship services, but this is the exception to the general rule, which I take to be: Influence of the media on liturgy is more pervasive than liturgical influence on the media.

Current Scholarly Writing on Ritual and Media

A summary of ways that ritual and media relate to each other does not constitute either a definition or a theory of ritual. The list is merely a reminder of the complexity of the relationship. Sensitivity to this relationship is often missing in research and writing on ritual-media relations. In the literature, implied as well as explicit definitions of ritual are insufficiently nuanced. In *The TV Ritual: Worship at the Video Altar*, Gregor Goethals does not distinguish between explicit rites and tacit ritualization processes.[7] Like her, I have argued that we should attend to the similarities between activities such as TV viewing and ritual, but, unlike her, I find it unnecessarily confusing if we obscure the distinctions. Goethals offers no formal definition of ritual, but she associates it with order, rhythmic patterning, and play, on the one hand, and with things mystical and supernatural, on the other.[8] In my view, it is a mistake to treat all rites as religious by definition or to identify them exclusively with order.

Bobby Alexander's *Televangelism Reconsidered* mobilizes the theoretical vocabularies of Victor Turner and Richard Schechner, approaches with which I am in considerable sympathy, but Alexander does not carefully distinguish between ritual and drama. Although considering ritual and drama as siblings can help us comprehend both kinds of action, equating them, like equating ritual with media, only confuses matters. Like his theoretical mentors, Alexander also makes ritual by definition a transformative act: "Defined in basic terms, ritual is a performance, planned or improvised, that makes a transition away from the everyday world to an alternative context, within which the everyday is transformed. . . . Ritual is transformative of everyday experience, especially everyday human encounters."[9]

Such a view is idealized. Not all rites transform, even those that are intended to transform. Vincent Crapanzano has provided the most compelling argument against the ideology of transformation.[10] His study of Moroccan circumcision rites shows that, although the ceremonial rhetoric in Morocco speaks of young boys as men, the ritual behavior, both during and after the rite, returns the boys to the domain of women. Transformation is announced but not really accomplished, so we need to question the received assumptions about ritual transformation. We should challenge the easy equation of patterned behavior with rites and resist too ready an identification of all ritual with religion.

Probably because of his influence in media studies, James Carey's few remarks about ritual in *Media, Myths, and Narratives* are widely cited.[11] His use of the notion of ritual is light-handed and undeveloped. For this reason it has little theoretical utility. Carey employs ritual only as an analogue, and phrases such as "ritual view of communication" make it unclear whether ritual is an activity in its own right or merely a point of view taken in studying something else.

Vivian Sobchack's treatment of genre film casts myth as content and ritual as form.[12] The function of ritual form is that of disguising conflict or avoiding contradictions. Her characterization of ritual—in my view, a distillation of popular attitudes toward it—identifies it with everything that is culturally conservative and anti-intellectual:

> Ritual is, of course, repetitive. Its power is also cumulative, action building serially upon action, gathering emotional weight as it grows. Ritual is symbolic and employs various simple objects to evoke complex associations. It celebrates tradition and the status quo. It is oriented toward the past, and what has been done before that ought to be done again: it is nostalgic. Ritual is simple, too, acting through patterns that are easily recognizable and often dualistic. . . . Most comforting, ritual is predictable. . . . It provides its audience with a respite from social anxiety, with a sense of belonging to a group that suffers the same conflicts and has homogenous goals.[13]

At the very least, authors who express views like this should say why they revert to an unchastened Durkheimian view of ritual, why they reject the Turnerian claim that ritual either is, or can be, socially critical.

Robert Abelman distinguishes among ritualized, instrumental, and reactionary television viewers.[14] He claims that 65 percent of the religious televiewing audience is of the ritualized sort. The portrait he paints of ritualized viewers is not complimentary. As with Sobchack's characterization, ritual is defined in a way that would likely inspire the scholars writing about it to avoid practicing it. For Abelman, ritualized viewers are habitual, likely to be church members, conservative in attitude, high consumers of television, demographically downscale, older, poorer, less educated, blue-collar, and allured by the personality of tele-vangelists. According to Abelman, highly ritualized viewers provide 95 percent of all financial contributions to television evangelism, and they were among those least shaken by the scandal surrounding Jim and Tammy Baker. According to Abelman, viewing does not evangelize or challenge ritualized viewers. It merely confirms the beliefs and attitudes they already hold. By contrast, instrumental viewers are more educated, less religious, and, by implication, more analytical. They seek information rather than confirmation, and the Baker scandal typi-cally caused them to stop viewing.

Abelman's ritualized/instrumental distinction may be momentarily useful, but it is also prejudicial. Not only does the rhetoric of his discussion make it plain that he himself disidentifies with the category "ritualized viewer," it pre-vents his seeing the ritual dimensions of the other two types of viewers. His understanding of ritual is a tacitly "protestant" view of it; it is not only value-laden, but negatively valued. In this view ritual amounts to habituated, unthink-ing action. Abelman feels no obligation to show that ritualized viewers display any of the qualities we normally associate with ritual. For instance, he does not show that they engage in stylized or symbolic behavior. Nor does he demon-strate that instrumental viewers do *not* engage in such behavior. He seems to assume his readers will not question the implied definition of ritual that equates it with mindlessness.

A more provocative, less biased attempt to think about the ritual dimen-sions of media is found in Michael Schudson's reflections on advertising as capitalist realism in *Advertising the Uneasy Persuasion.*[15] His discussion of ritual is not fully developed, but in treating advertising as a mode of hyperritualization, he grasps the similarities between ritual and advertising, namely, their manipu-lation of ideals. He emphasizes their dependence on hypertactile surfaces, their manipulation of typifications, and their capacity to shape attitudes without hav-ing to inspire beliefs.

The association between ritual and the media has begun to seem so obvi-ous to some observers that they posit an identity between the two. Quentin Schultze, for instance, declares flatly, "Television is ritual."[16] In a similar fash-ion, other writers declare that TV watching is ritual, negotiating cyberspace on the Internet is ritual, and attending genre films is ritual. The impulse to label media ritualistic is sometimes motivated by a conviction that their impact affects fundamental values, therefore they are religious in function. The implication is that ritual is by definition religious. Ron Burnett, for instance, says, "This theo-logical impulse continues to exercise great influence, but now the gatekeeper is the media. Power resides yet again in a place beyond the control of those who are proposed as its victims."[17] By "theological," he seems to mean "religious." But calling the media ritualistic when one means that it is religious is a mis-take. Ritual is not *necessarily* religious. We need to distinguish the general cate-gory ritual from specific types or dimensions of it.

The equating strategy (media = ritual) has limited utility. It turns heads, attracts attention, but the shock value is short-lived. If the two terms are not differentiated as well as connected, conversation between ritual studies and media studies is hardly worth pursuing.[18] If in the long run, there is nothing to say but, "Media activity is ritual activity," each idea loses its capacity to provoke interesting perspectives on the other, because there is insufficient tension between them. "Media *as* ritual," unlike "Media *are* ritual," reminds us that the claim is metaphoric, requiring a simultaneous predication of identity and difference: Media *are* ritual; media are *not* ritual. Metaphors provoke their users into noticing identity and difference simultaneously.

If media studies is to increase the level of its sophistication, the understanding of ritual needs to become more nuanced. For example, scholars should ask not just whether some aspect of media *is* ritual, but *in what respect* it is ritual. Do we treat something as ritualistic because it is formulaic? Because it is repetitive? Because it is religious? We need to assume the responsibility for specifying what definition of ritual we are implying by our claims.

Further, we need to ask not just *whether* something is ritual or ritual-like, but *what kind of* ritual it is like. Is it like pilgrimage? Like celebration? Like a rite of passage? Just as there are many different kinds of media, there are different kinds of ritual, and the differences among them are important. To ensure that we refrain from overstatement and overextension of our metaphors, we should also ask in what respects media are *not* ritual.

There is a tendency, perhaps best exemplified by Schultze, to multiply metaphors.[19] Television is not only "ritual," it is also "religion," "theology," "sacred text," "mythopoesis," "storytelling," "liturgy," "morality play," "soap opera," and "drama."[20] Like the equating strategy, the multiplication of metaphors soon discourages the critical thinking necessary for theory construction. However important metaphor may be to storytelling and poetry, if it takes over and consumes analytical prose, it discourages readers from taking it seriously.

Defining "Ritual" for Use in Media Research

The fruitfulness of considering media's relations to ritual depends largely on the understanding of ritual that animates the discussion. Too often the word "ritual" is an empty trope, a mere analogy or weak metaphor which is then mixed or overextended. Metaphors should be chosen with care and developed rather than multiplied. The word "ritual" functions too much like a badge of membership in the Current Discourse Club. It flags an author's intention of taking a broadly "cultural" approach, but it adds little or nothing to the analysis.

In media discussions clear definitions of ritual are rarely presented by authors who make it a key concept. On the few occasions when explicit definitions of ritual are used in media research, they can be as prejudicial as the older uses of "magic" were. Largely prejudicial or merely celebrative usages do nothing to enhance our understanding. Neither do conceptions that reduce ritual to one kind of ritual, say, liturgy or ritualization behavior. On the one hand, ritual is used as a synonym for religion and the sacred. On the other, it is identified with anything routine, patterned, or stylized. Defined too narrowly, its relation to ordinary life is obscured. Defined too broadly, its difference from ordinary interaction is occluded.

Like rites themselves, definitions of ritual have a history. In the late nineteenth century the idea of ritual was at the center of an *origin* question. In that era's evolutionary framework, religion was construed as primal, a cultural activity located at the beginning (metaphorically, the bottom) of the evolutionary scale. Ritual was taken to be religion's primary mode of expression: Primal religion was acted, not thought. The essence of religion was ritual, not theology, myth, or ethics. In some versions of this account, ritual was *the* primal cultural phenomenon, prior even to speech. Imagined in this way, ritual was the great undifferentiated action from which other cultural activities originally emerged and from which they differentiated themselves. Art, law, economic exchange, ecology, dance, drama, storytelling, and even city-building were descendants of the primal parent, ritual.

Ritual studies scholars no longer believe they can know the origins of either religion or ritual. However, there is still afoot a vague sense that the religiosity of preindustrial societies may be more deeply ritualistic than that of postindustrial societies. It is commonplace for anthropologists to maintain that rites of passage, for instance, have their proper home in small-scale, preindustrial societies.

Claims about the origin or primacy of ritual amount to scholarly mythmaking, a kind of abstract storytelling that can be provocative but which is in principle unverifiable. Its usefulness is in reminding us how complex rites are, how many kinds of cultural activity may flow into their planning and enactment, and how much latter-day twentieth-century North Americans long to participate in some synthesizing, whole-making activity. Such mythmaking also reminds us that the media are not only electronic, printed, or spoken but also enacted. Ritual, like television, *is* a medium of communication, an enacted one. Without resorting to origin myths, one can still say that ritual is a multimedium, a synthesis of drama, storytelling, dance, and art. There are definitions of ritual that take this fact into explicit account. M. E. Combs-Schilling, for instance, defines ritual as "a circumscribed, out of the ordinary, multiple media event—recognized by insiders and outsiders as distinctively beyond the mundane—in which prescribed words and actions are repeated and crucial dilemmas of humanity are evoked and brought to systematic resolution."[21]

In the early twentieth century the ritual question became largely one of function. No longer did scholars ask, "Where does ritual come from?" or "Which came first, myth or ritual?" Instead, they wanted to know, "What do rites do?"

The widespread, assumed answer was, "They provide social cohesion and personal consolation." The first, and dominant, part of the answer was borrowed from Durkheim; the second, from Freud. These two assumed answers to the function question remained intact until the late 1960s.

The mid–twentieth century witnessed a dramatic shift in ritual's scholarly and public image. No longer conservatively republican in its sensibilities, ritual became creative and potentially subversive. Inspired by Victor Turner, students of ritual articulated a new, or unrecognized, function to ritual's repertoire: social transformation. Turner did not deny that ritual could engender solidarity or bring about consolation, but he insisted that these were only part of a rite's real work. The other power of ritual was that of temporarily dissolving social hierarchies, remaking personal identity, and engendering cultural creativity. Communitas and liminality were the great forges, the formative social processes, utilized by ritual in exercising its transformative energies.

Presently, at the beginning of a new millennium, the ritual question is being conceived as a boundary issue. Theorists are engaged in debating the boundaries of ritual. Both ritual and the definition of ritual are understood to be acts of marking-off. For some, boundary maintenance is a way of protecting a preserve; for others, it is a way of bridging, of making connections between cultural or cognitive domains. Jonathan Z. Smith claims that ritual is "a means of performing the way things ought to be in such a way that this ritualized perfection is recollected in the ordinary, uncontrolled, course of things."[22] Ritual, as he characterizes it, is an idealized, controlled "space," making it different from the uncontrollable messiness characteristic of the extraritualistic arenas of human interaction. Recollection is the bridge between the "ought to be" of ritual and the "is" of ordinary behavior.[23]

Meaningful ritual-and-media discussion becomes possible when the two domains are neither equated nor segregated but rather differentiated and conceived as sharing a common boundary. In my view, performance-oriented theories offer the most provocative approaches to the interface of ritual and media. If performance is the "showing of a doing" or "twice-behaved behavior,"[24] ritual and media are species of performance having much to do with one another.

The notion of performance can be almost as slippery as that of ritual. There is the ever-present equating tendency: Ritual *is* performance; performance *is* ritual. And there is a reductionist tendency, which would make ritual a function of something more primary (performance, for instance). In performance studies, a discipline located at the intersection of drama and anthropology, the tendency is to make performance a superordinate category and ritual a subordinate one. In this view both ritual and theater are kinds of performance, the difference being that ritual aims at efficaciousness and theater at entertainment or that ritual arises from belief and theater from play or make-believe. Such claims, of course, provoke debates, but so far the ritual-theater debate has been more sophisticated than the ritual-media discussion. This is not the place to initiate a full-blown critique and reformulation of performance-oriented theories of ritual, but it is the place to suggest that performance theories of ritual are the most useful beginning points. The list at the beginning of this chapter was generated by asking performance-oriented questions: Who are the actors? What constitutes on and off stage? Where is the audience? What scripts dictate the performance? If nothing else, performance theories keep us from forgetting the obvious. They call attention to the surfaces upon which we humans inscribe meaning and on the basis of which we act.

2

Documenting Ritual

A producer working for FilmRoos, a California company, asked if I would consult on a film about ritual for A&E's series Ancient Mysteries. *She declared her personal interest in the topic and said with considerable gusto that she would fly from Los Angeles to Canada to conduct the interview. To refine the interview questions, a series of e-mail messages ensued. Since many media interviewers refuse to submit their questions to scrutiny, the emerging situation seemed to promise a discussion not driven by media's perpetual rush. In the end, however, no interviewer made the trek to Canada. Instead, I was interviewed through a black box by a pair of interviewers piped in from L.A. The interview was recorded by a crew flown in from Montreal. Since I was interested in public perceptions of ritual, as well as in interview processes, I asked a student assistant to videotape the interview session. The tape shows me facing the black box, behind which is a stand-in, a poor secretary drafted to sit in a chair so it would appear that I was actually talking to someone. Her job was to smile and nod approvingly. Eventually, I couldn't stand the scene, although she played her role well, so I relieved her of the onerous task and carried on, conversing with the black box. When "Sacred Rites and Rituals" finally appeared, it was, despite my admiration for Leonard Nimoy, who narrated it, a travesty, so I set out to reflect on what had happened by writing about the process.[25]*

The popular understanding of ritual is shaped less by scholarly debate than by media presentation. The media package rites into saleable, consumable products. Documentaries and other programs aired on television market not only the paraphernalia and performances of rites but also the idea of ritual. Because it attends to the full range of ritual, ritual studies must attend not only to scholarly definitions of ritual but also to popular depictions as well, since they help form the attitudes that participants carry into the enactment of rites.

The trouble is that media renditions of rites (as enacted) and ritual (as thought about) are seldom studied critically even by ritual studies scholars, since they are often preoccupied with physically and socially embodied rites, rather than virtual ritualizing. But media renditions of ritualized activity persist, for example, in *Survivor* and other so-called reality shows. So it is worth attending to the details of a specific example.

Sacred Rites and Rituals

"Sacred Rites and Rituals," produced by FilmRoos for A&E's *Ancient Mysteries* series,[26] was released in December 1996. It was aired and re-aired for several years, helping shape public attitudes toward the rites of others. In fifty or so minutes the film introduces viewers to ritual. The film's tenor and attitude are now echoed by other media presentations of ritual.

Since I was one of the scholarly consultants for the film, I know something about the process that lies behind the production. I kept drafts of the interviewers' questions and my responses to them. I also had the interview independently videotaped by a student so I could later reflect on the final film's editing and construction. Having subsequently worked with two other documentary series on ritual, one of which proposed to take the A&E production as a worthy model, I have arrived at a critical and comparative perspective on *Sacred Rites and Rituals*.

After agreeing to an interview by the FilmRoos producer, I received a list of nineteen questions that were to form its basis. There were three kinds of questions. One kind concerned the nature and definition of ritual (for example, Is ritual is an inherent need? Are we by nature ritual beings?). A second probed contemporary North American ritualized activities (for instance, Are mundane, secular events such as Super Bowl Sunday rituals? Can you comment on the lack of ritualized passage, particularly puberty rites, in contemporary Western societies?). A third sort asked about rites from ancient or non–North American cultures (for example, Could you discuss some of the oldest examples of ritual? Do you know what the origin of circumcision is and why it is such a widespread rite of passage?).[27]

I suggested deleting a few, adding one or two, and rewording others. All the suggestions were accepted. On the whole, the questions, as negotiated prior to the interview, were not naive; they were the work of inquiring minds. But a few of them were tendentious or leading: "Why are these ritual passages so critical, in your view, to a healthy society/individual?" "Do you feel there is a condescending, almost puritanical attitude toward the more physical, ecstatic, or theatrical rituals found in more primal traditions?" The answers were implied in the rhetoric and tone.

The actual interview, conducted long-distance with the interviewers in Los Angeles and the camera in Waterloo, Canada, was noticeably different from the e-mail questions. The interviewers posed many more leading questions than were contained in the written list. The interviewers clearly had an agenda to portray ritual in a particular light and to draft me into saying what they would like said. The questions, as actually posed in the filmed interview, had a distinctly psychological bias. The interviewers were largely uninterested in the political, economic, or ecological dimensions of ritual. They displayed intense curiosity about the ways rites heal and showed little interest in the ways that they abuse or exploit.[28]

To access the film's ritual dimensions, one should consider not only the *rites* depicted by the film but also the *ritualization processes* in and around it. Because "Sacred Rites" was part of the *Ancient Mysteries* series, there was considerable pressure to chant a kind of mystery mantra, not only to use the word "mystery" but also to cloak the idea of ritual in an ancient and impenetrable aura. Even though I protested that my field was contemporary North American religions, I was repeatedly pressed by the two interviewers to comment on ancient rites. I resisted, insisting that the producers find scholars with expertise in ancient ritual texts. They resisted my resistance, wanting to attribute a kind of expertise to me that I did not have. And the reason for doing so was not so much because they thought that I, in fact, possessed knowledge about ancient rites, but because they did not want to spend time and money locating yet another expert.

The result is a film that glosses contemporary rites with unexamined claims, made by the narrator, about their longevity. By implication, "ancient" includes not only things done a long time ago but also things that viewers would readily accept as having been done for a long time. For instance, there is a tendency in the series to count as ancient or mysterious things from non-Euroamerican cultures. Thus, exotic implies ancient; and ancient, exotic.

The implied definition of "mystery" in this film and other installments of the series is twofold. A mystery is any problem that filmmakers cannot quickly summarize for viewers. Even problems for which there are good data become mysteries if scholars have differing interpretations, if the data are incomplete, or if explanations are complex. A mystery is also anything that evokes a sense of great depth—anything uncanny or eerie. Both connotations are evoked regularly and indiscriminately in *Ancient Mysteries* programs. Asked to comment on the mystery of ritual, I replied that a mystery in the philosophical and religious sense has little to do with lack of information or human inability to explain a phenomenon. Birth, I said, is a mystery. A mystery is a mystery even when one can explain it genetically and biologically. A mystery is not something exotic but an event that implicates one's very being so profoundly that it evokes awe. The editors did not use the comment, probably because it questioned a key premise of the program. A noticeable difference between the two-and-a-half-hour interview and the final forty-eight-minute product was that the interviewers repeatedly sought explanations, especially popular psychological ones, of ritual behavior. I offered social or political ones not much to their liking, so the film itself chooses mystification over explanation.

Because the episode was called "Sacred Rites and Rituals," I inquired whether there was a meaningful difference between "rites" and "rituals." The question was ignored. The aired version uses the phrase only once and makes no meaningful distinction between the two terms. My suggestion that producers delete the redundancy by calling it either "Sacred Rites" or "Sacred Rituals" was also ignored. I have since encountered the phrase in the mouths of three other potential documentary makers. My guess is that its only function is to echo "death and dying," a phrase that sold, and continues to sell, books and courses. The qualifier "sacred" adds nothing substantive to the title or the film. It does not determine, for instance, that the focus will be on, say, worship rites rather than rites of passage or secular rites as distinct from those associated with religious institutions. The notion of sacredness is not explored or used in the film itself, even though the interview questions submitted to me had distinguished sacred from mundane rites. My inference is that the term "sacred" is rhetorical, calculated to claim importance for the film itself.

"Sacred Rites and Rituals" is divided into five, explicitly named parts: "Passages," "Journey of Faith," "Flesh and Blood," "Beyond Death," and "The Quest Continues." Although these sections are called "acts," their real function is clearly that of providing commercial breaks. Acts 1, 2, and 4 are largely organized around ritual types: rites of passage, pilgrimage, and ancestor veneration, respectively. No explanation is offered for choosing these kinds of ritual rather than other kinds to represent the whole of ritual.

Act 1, "Passages," focuses on Jewish circumcision and an African women's initiation rite, but it also includes the Hindu Agnicayana, which is not a rite of passage. Act 2, "Journey of Faith," is largely about two pilgrimage rites, the Kumbha Mela of India and the hajj of Saudi Arabia. In act 3, all pretext of the film's being a treatment of ritual types breaks down. Subtitled "Flesh and Blood," the section is also referred to by Leonard Nimoy, the narrator, as "Rites That Stagger the Imagination." The section is blatantly voyeuristic. Clips appear because they depict bizarre, bloody, or painful acts. Act 4, "Beyond Death," features an attempt in 1986 by Chinese actors to reenact Confucius's birthday ceremony. It is not so much a rite as an instance of "restored," or "re-behaved" behavior, that is, people pretending to be engaged in ritual.[29] This example is followed by an account of a South Korean businessman who venerates an ancestor and relates to his employees as if he were their patriarch. Act 5, called both "Rituals That Shape Our Lives" and "The Quest Continues," is a miscellany. It is vague in intent, and the film had not presented an earlier quest that this quest might be interpreted as continuing. The largest portion of the final act contrasts constructive and destructive, as well as religious and nonreligious, rites.

The choice of rites depicted in the film is driven almost exclusively by visual interest and the availability of footage and archival materials, not by how widespread or important the rites are, nor how well they illustrate a category, nor by how much is known about the rite. The implied criteria for visual interest are how much movement and color there is, the recording quality of the clip, and the projected ability to attract and hold viewers' interest. Among the aesthetic preferences exhibited by "Sacred Rites and Rituals" are largeness of scale (big crowds and wide vistas are preferred), scenes involving blood or pain, actions with no obvious explanations, culturally unfamiliar sites, and actions displaying ornate or minimal clothing.

Besides movement through five phases, the film alternates between the voices of Leonard Nimoy (who is seen on screen only at the beginning and end) and the talking heads of experts (whose authorizing biographical blurbs are superimposed on the screen). Scholars rarely speak for more than twenty seconds at a time. They do not interact with the narrator, much less the participants, and participants are never asked about the meanings of their own rites. Although it is never said, the film implies that one class of people acts, whereas another class understands. There is neither discussion nor debate over interpretation, since observers and participants do not interact, nor do the experts interact with one another.

Contradictions abound but are rarely commented upon. For instance, Philip Novak, one of the experts, speaks of ritual as action "that intends a transformation of state," whereas Nimoy describes a situation in which ritualists are "transported," that is, not transformed but elevated then returned to where they started.[30] In another example, the audience is shown the very concrete act of burning a ritual site, while Nimoy refers to it as an instance of "abstract mystical belief." The dissonance between things shown and things said, as well as between one claim and another, is considerable.

One of the most striking features of the narrator's script is its barrage of rhetorical questions: How original are these rites? Does pilgrimage change people? Which rites endure? Are all these rites related to one another? How did these rituals originate? Some of these questions are good ones, but others are nonsensical or unanswerable because of the way they are framed. Rarely is a question posed, pursued, then debated or answered. When answers are given, there is never more than one. Thus, ambiguity and conflict are edited out. Answers are either singular, authoritative, and implicitly absolute, or they are "mysteries."

As for the meanings of ritual symbols, there seem to be three possibilities in the film: What they mean is obvious; what they mean is a mystery; what they mean can be summarized in two or three sentences, usually concerning their imagined origin or supposed psychological function. Much of what is offered as interpretation is at the level of truism or supposed common sense, having little to do with either participants' or scholars' ways of speaking about the meanings of rites. "This simple ritual [Muslim circumcision]," the narrator tells us, is not threatened (as is the Agnicayana). Why? His answer to his own question is: Because it relates "so directly to the idea of a people's survival." How or why circumcision means survival is not at all obvious, but the comment is offered as if it were.

After a series of clips on weddings, births, and funerals, the narrator claims that there is "no doubt as to the meaning of these symbolic gestures," even though the viewers may have not the faintest idea what they have seen. They are shown, for instance, John Kennedy Jr. as a boy, saluting the flag. It would be hard to imagine a more familiar but more thoroughly equivocal gesture. How old would a viewer have to be to recognize the scene as that of a presidential funeral? Does the boy realize what is going on? Is this his declaration that he, the son, will carry on in the absence of the father? That he is playing soldier? Who taught him to salute? What does saluting mean to him? At the very point when one might expect a series of interesting but difficult questions, the film claims the meaning is obvious. The power of the famous photograph is due, in part, to its ambiguity.

Sacred Rites and Rituals is littered with tacit racism and sexism. Viewers are shown African women dancing bare-breasted. Judith Gleason, the expert who is credited with having shot the film, is shown saying that some of the dancers are Western educated and embarrassed. Despite this recognition, the camera continues to follow their breasts. White, American breasts would not be shown in such a manner on an A&E documentary. I overheard a woman watching *Sacred Rites and Rituals* mutter, "Wanna take bets on how many dicks we see!" She was right: The only naked male in the film is shot discreetly and momentarily from the side.

Viewers are shown some old drawings of the Lakota Sun Dance. The narrator speaks about it as a dead rite no longer performed. There is no awareness that the Sun Dance is, in fact, being enacted. In the final analysis, the film's producers do not use scholars to check the accuracy of their data, offer nuanced interpretations, or elicit undiscovered meanings from participants. Instead, the producers use the scholars as legitimizing agents, co-opting their names, institutional affiliations, and demeanor to enhance the saleability of the film.

The film includes old black-and-white footage of the hajj. A newsreel commentator refers to the pilgrims as "Mohammedens," and Allah as *their* god." The insensitivity and inaccuracy are blatant and dated. Viewers who hope the film will pull back out of this time warp and comment on the offensive, Orientalist ways Westerners *used to* speak of such rites are disappointed. The only revision of the picture painted by the old clip is that of updating the number of those attending from two hundred thousand to two million.

Although the narrator never directly accuses ritualists of being primitive or irrational, he implies as much by his rhetoric. He refers to rites as performances that "challenge logic." He asks his audience, "What belief is so strong that it has convinced these people to undertake this daring ritual?"[31]

Some of the film's basic assumptions are contradictory. On the one hand, it assumes an easy universalism. "Every culture fears disaster, disease, and death," claims the narrator, implying that people are the same everywhere. He suggests that *we* can understand *them,* even if they are "Stone Age mystics of 40,000 years ago." The universalist premise allows the narrator to offer commonsense interpretations when no interpretations by either participant or observer support his claim.

On the other hand, the film assumes a kind of evolutionary superiority: *We* can explain what *they* do (but not vice versa), so we are superior to them. Our rites, unlike theirs, are not logically challenged. This tendency to "other" is obvious in another way. When *Sacred Rites* offers examples of destructive ritual, it shows Hitler's Nuremberg rallies, not initiatory hazing in American marine boot camps. Implied critiques are usually aimed elsewhere, not at the heart of American cultural ceremony.

Ritual is made strange by *Sacred Rites and Rituals.* Its connection with ordinary life is severed. Both religion and ritual are reduced to one dimension: mystery. "Rituals obscure and mysterious," says Nimoy, "seem" to fulfill human needs. He, of course, does not pause to reflect: Do they, in fact, do so? Or do they only appear to? Ritual is rendered odd, in need of an explanation but one that participants cannot, or do not, provide.

If this television presentation of ritual were compared with a presentation of ice skating, for example, some of the peculiarities of *Sacred Rites and Rituals* might appear more clearly. One of the primary aims of sports interviewers is to engage, not avoid, athletes. Performers are consulted, as if their responses are more important than those of observers. Ice skaters, for example, are not asked *why* they engage in such odd behavior. Instead, the beauty or importance of ice skating is assumed. Skaters are asked how they felt during the event, how they prepared, where they are going to skate next. In contrast, ritualists are rendered absent from the ritual event. We do not learn their names or hear their voices. We gaze at their bodies, but their bodies are not real persons. We do not know or care what they think they are doing. The A&E narrator assures us, "The lives of billions on the planet are still affected by ancient rites," as if this were an amazing rather than an ordinary fact, and as if these rites had not changed across history.

At the end of the film, a pun is used to force the final transition. From a reference to ritual within *"family* space," we cut to Leonard Nimoy and a reference to *outer* space, the place that many viewers associate with his most popular role, Spock. Nimoy looks up at the stars as he links space with the future, implicitly consigning ritual to the past. In the film, ritual space, like outer space, is necessary to the health of the planet, but since ritual is not quite here in this world, not fully ensconced in the present, it is a mystery. By being rendered other, ritual, like Spock, is not quite human. By being portrayed as either more than human or less than human, ritual is made alien. Viewers are led to watch ritualists the way they watch animals in a zoo—with fascination at occasionally seeing their behavior aped but comfortable in the knowledge that they inhabit a plane of being that is different from that of the animals.

Rites, Ritualizing, and the Media

Strictly speaking, A&E's one-hour production was not a rite,[32] because the genre of action is not culturally recognized as such by either its producers or consumers. However, the film contains both semblances and representations of rites, and its production and consumption were marked by ritualized behavior.

The layers between viewers and ritualists, from the "inside" to the "outside," are (1) the rites as performed by ritualists themselves; (2) the observed, filmed, and edited rendition of those rites; (3) the film clips as selected for showing by producers and series editors; (4) the clips, films, or rites as written about by the script writer and commented on by the narrator and scholarly consultants; and (5) the film as seen, heard, and remembered by viewers.

Because of these multiple means of distancing, the transformations effected *by* the rites are overshadowed by the media transformation *of* the rites. Actual rites appear in level one, but the multiple transformations and distortions that occur between the first and final level effect a ritualization of the relations between viewers and ritual actors. Viewers undergo a process that resembles pilgrimage or tourism. Without ever leaving their seats, they are transported around the globe and returned home again. They participate not so much in the rites themselves but in the ritualization of television viewing.

The lure that leads viewers forward through the film is the implied promise that secret knowledge will be revealed. In this respect, the film is a quasi-initiation. Viewers are shown or told about mysteries. If we will but await their arrival, they will reveal something important. In the end, however, viewers return with mere souvenirs, the trinkets of pilgrimage, not the transforming knowledge imparted in an initiation.

Ordinarily, most viewers—and even some scholars—do not think of rites as products that compete on a market with other products. But on television rites become aesthetic objects and traded commodities. Producers of made-for-TV documentaries attend more to product recognition than to intellectual content. What will audiences-as-buyers recognize as, that is, "buy," as ritual? Some of the most saleable ritual commodities are blood, bodies, fast movement, masks, drumming, dancing, costumes, and, of course, "mystery" and behavior rendered strange.

The Tourist and the Contemplative Aesthetics

The A&E production *Sacred Rites and Rituals* illustrates much of what I do *not* like about media treatments of ritual. Besides the obvious fact that it co-opts scholarship, it neither increases human knowledge of ritual nor enhances viewers' felt sense of it. Asked subsequently by other film companies to consult in the production of two different series of films on ritual, I was later forced to think like a visual artist as well as a critic and scholar. How would I present ritual differently? What would it take to make me proud of the production rather than critical of it?

The table on page 24 summarizes the A&E aesthetic and an alternative one. The table contrasts what I call the "tourist" or "quasi-pilgrimage" style of *Sacred Rites and Rituals* with a style that I propose to call "contemplative."[33] The aesthetic of a film series *I would like to make* is in the right-hand column. What I am calling the "tourist" treatment of a rite is partly determined by subject matter. Like the tourist, the A&E film seeks out eye-catching phenomena. To warrant inclusion on the ritual tour, a certain size, scale, or grandeur is essential. Rites that are domestic, local, or improvised are unworthy of sustained media attention. In the tourist aesthetic, grandeur of scale is augmented with intensity of color and rapidity of motion. The filtered colors and accelerated pace are not meant to enhance a viewer's comprehension of the rite but to increase the capacity of the film to hold viewers' attention.

The tourist filmmaker assumes short attention spans, holding them by the rapid pace of the film's short clips. Rhythm is one of the most basic mechanisms of a rite. Rites do not merely use rhythms to *convey* messages; rhythms *are* messages. Rhythms are part of the content and effect of a rite. To overwhelm those rhythms is to engage in a counterritualizing act or, in some instances, even to show a fundamental disrespect for them. Like the tourist's eye, the A&E camera is busy, sometimes intrusive, sometimes distant. It seldom takes the time to dwell or participate, even momentarily. Often, in the A&E film, the most arresting movement is that of the camera, soaring over a crowd or zooming in on a face but not seriously attending to the actions of participants. The rhythm of the film's editing destroys the rhythms of the rites.

In contrast, the contemplative camera is less prone to express its distance from or power over what it shoots. It offers longer, fewer segments and attempts to honor at least some of the rite's subdivisions and rhythms. It follows rather than drives the action. It meanders and dwells. It is attentive to detail and color but does not artificially enhance or amplify them.[34]

All film de- and recontextualizes its subject matter, but the contemplative camera is wider in its angles, more circular in its attentiveness. It helps viewers grasp context, what surrounds or is behind a rite. However visually arresting a rite may be, much of its impact arises from the preparation that leads to it and the wake created in its aftermath. Ritual is ensconced in a social matrix that needs

TABLE 2.I. Tourist and Contemplative Aesthetics Compared

	A Tourist Aesthetic	A Contemplative Aesthetic
Subject matter:	Exotic dimensions of large-scale celebrations. Bigger is better.	Domestic dimensions of small-scale or marginal rites of passage. The small and local are worthy of attention.
Subdivisions:	Many, very short clips of the most visually arresting portions. The whole is broken into pseudodramatic "acts."	Longer, fewer segments showing preparation, crucial portions of rite, and aftermath. Formal subdivisions, if any, follow those of the rite.
Color, costume:	Major emphasis on intense color and unusual costume.	Attention to color and costume is incidental, not a major emphasis. Color is natural rather than enhanced. Costume is seen in relation to everyday wear.
Camera movement:	Camera is busy, peers in, then moves away rapidly. Camera is a tourist.	Camera is slower, more contemplative; sometimes dwells on small details. Camera is a participant.
Music, sound:	Music drives the action.	Music creates a space for contemplation or reflection.
Narrator:	Cinematic celebrity-actor-narrator who provides continuity and vocal emphasis but is not in the ritual space. Narrator is shot in an exotic space, the desert. He raises a host of unanswered, or unanswerable, questions to create a sense of "mystery." Narrator takes up considerable auditory airspace but neither challenges nor interacts with participants or experts.	The narrator reflects, converses, and sometimes participates. Narrator is seen in ritual space, as well as in other places, for instance, in domestic space. Sometimes takes issue with participants' claims or views. Raises questions that challenge both participants and viewers. Attempts are made to answer key questions, or to show why there is no easy answer to them.
Narration, explanation:	Explanations tend to be abstract and general—not about specific symbols or moments in the ritual process but about the whole rite or even ritual in general.	Meanings are local, rooted in the time and space of the rite. Explanations are negotiated among participants or between participants and the narrator.
Participants:	Ritual participants unnamed and uninterviewed. Pronounced tendency toward exoticism: the "others" are "over there" or "back" in time, and viewers need experts and narrators to make them intelligible.	Participants are named and interviewed. Emphasis on the here and now. Some actions are allowed to speak for themselves. They do not always need explanation or interpretation.
Experts:	Imported experts who engage in brief monologues. Those who ritualize are not the ones who know what the rite means. Those who enact don't know; those who know don't perform.	Participants are consultants. Those who perform also know. Scholars are inquirers, sources of a different kind of knowledge. Those who study rites have a different perspective, but they don't know everything.
Viewers:	Viewer feels, "I wouldn't perform such things, and I couldn't possibly understand them without expert help."	Viewer asks, "Why not do it that way?" Viewer feels, "I am like that too" or "I'd never do that, but it makes sense that they do."

to be understood. A rite, even more than a play, is seriously distorted by excision and dismemberment.

Rites do not typically have narrators, although there are exceptions such as celebrations and festivals in which public orators have an essential part. Because documentaries decontextualize, they require narrators, people who speak for or about the rites that viewers witness. It is possible, of course, to present a rite as if were an aesthetic object capable of speaking for itself. But even if one grants the necessity for narration when viewing rites from unfamiliar cultures, there are differing styles. The tourist style is "dramatic," whereas the proposed alternative is more "ethnographic."[35] The former is authoritative, imposing, and articulately declaratory. The latter is more interrogative—sometimes more sure, sometimes less sure—about what is being witnessed. The "dramatic" narrator does not take risks either with viewers or with ritual participants by asking real questions. The questions are empty, merely rhetorical; they are not the questions of a serious inquirer but those of a tourist.

Tourist-type narration, though often delivered with passion, tends to generalized and abstract, not about this rite enacted by these persons in this place but about ritual in general as enacted by "mankind." By contrast, contemplative narration is local and situational, an expression of this narrator's encounter with these people at this time.

Any filming can make participants seem other. Even family videos can "other" a family member, so a certain exoticism is inevitable in filming. But one can choose whether to heighten or dampen this othering effect. In the tourist aesthetic, participants are exoticized. Anonymous people are generalized into "others," "over there." There is local color but not local knowledge. On the rare occasion when local knowledge is presented, it is held by no one in particular. The participants, although they have faces, do not have names. They are cultural representatives, not persons.

An alternative is to present named, interviewed participants who, by virtue of their participation, are experts—of a kind different from the scholarly experts. Ritualists are allowed considerable headway in speaking for themselves. Their words do not always require interpretation.

The A&E film's experts are imported into the film and then carefully controlled. They are unable to question the rite, the participants, each other, or the narrator's interpretation of the rite. They speak in short monologues, not in dialogue. So, in effect, they authorize the film itself. Worse, they do so with little or no knowledge of the film's claims, and sometimes even with little of no knowledge of the rites presented or the ritualists who performed them. The questions to which they may have responded in preceding interviews are edited out, so that original dialogues are presented as monologues.

In a contemplative approach experts would emphasize the dialogical and tentative nature of their interpretations. They would be inquirers, people who do not know but are interested in learning. Experts, they nevertheless hold their expertise lightly. When they challenge or question, their challenges are open to question. They invite either dialogue or debate.

In the final analysis, viewers of a "touristic" documentary are rendered dependent on the film. They could not possibly understand performances so exotic and impenetrable without experts, narrators, and filmmakers. Viewers would not perform such rites, because they are too "mysterious," and viewers could not make intellectual sense of the rites without assistance. In contrast, the viewer of a contemplative documentary thinks, "Well, that makes more sense than I would have imagined. Why not do it the way these folks do it?" Or the viewer muses, "I would never do that, but now it makes sense why they do it that way."

I have summarized two possibilities, and for the sake of making the differences obvious, I have drawn a sharp line between them. My point is simple: There are other ways of constructing portraits of ritual for widespread media consumption, so we should reflect more fully on the ways that media transpose ritual enactments.

From Consumption to Production

I have helped produce mediocre, if not poor, films about ritual. The A&E film is the worst example. I worked on two other series in more substantial ways, serving various functions such as adviser, researcher, and writer, but in the end, making documentaries about ritual for television is a disappointing process.[36] There are better examples, but they are usually crafted for the classroom rather than television. *Gathering Up Again: Fiesta in Santa Fe*, another film for which I worked as an adviser, tracks real, named people both on and off the ritual stage. It captures performative failure as well as ritual success.[37] *If Only I Were an Indian*, by the National Film Board of Canada,[38] contemplates the problems of ceremonial appropriation with great patience, humanity, and insight. And *Kosher Valley* achieves the doggedly local and deeply humane qualities that ought to characterize films about ritual life.[39] So I am not advocating a style that is impossible, only one that is not likely to be lucrative for television.

Rites are among the most common occasions on which humans reach for cameras, but they are also one of the occasions during which cameras are most often forbidden. This double impulse, to display and to sequester, has long marked ritual events, and the introduction of media produces additional complexity and interpretive torque into this impulse. Mediated ritualization transposes the human body and human society in complex ways, making the mediated versions more difficult to study than the nonmediated ones. No matter how sensitively used, film and television, by transposing ritual enactments into aesthetic performances shown for entertainment and education, enhance certain ritual activities more than others. It is essential, therefore, that we invest time in studying media renditions of rites as well as rites themselves.

3

Shooting Rites

The occasion for the first version of this essay was an invitation to deliver the Kavanagh Lecture at the Institute of Sacred Music at Yale University.[40] *The ISM had just initiated* Colloquium, *a journal devoted to worship and the arts, and it was finishing its first DVD,* Work and Pray: Living the Psalms with the Nuns of Regina Laudis.[41] *Since I was already studying the problems of video documenting rites because I was designing a book-plus-DVD series,*[42] *I decided to identify some of the emerging issues concerning the visual documentation of ritual.*

Academic culture, like popular culture, is becoming strongly visual in orientation, but the camera—still or moving, professional or amateur—is a mixed blessing. On the one hand, it captures things so they can be studied. On the other, it can objectify, irritate, or even violate those at whom it is pointed. With DVD production in mind, scholars of various sorts are finding it increasingly necessary to have a camera in hand. Among their purposes are conducting field research, making classroom and conference presentations, supplementing written texts, and consulting with nonacademic organizations. They have little choice but to become adept at weathering the mixture of blessings and curses that beset camera-toters.

"Shooting Rites." Pacifists do not like the title. After Columbine, the gun metaphor rings violent, especially if the implied subjects in front of the camera are humans. Feminists would likely join the pacifists if the assumed shooter-photographer were leeringly male and the one upon whom the predatory photographic gaze rested were delectably female. The postcolonialists would undoubtedly join the feminists and pacifists if those shot were being objectified or patronized by either the shooting or the viewing of the shooting.

"Shooting," of course, is a metaphor. One could think of the act in other ways, for example, as "receiving an impression," but I say "shooting" so we won't overlook the possibilities of violation inherent in visual documentation.

One would think a ritual studies scholar could find a more venerable subject such as ritual and the sacred, ritual and political power, ritual and racism, or ritual and cognitive psychology. But the time has come for paying attention to the act of shooting rites. With its wry funerary voyeurism, the popular TV series *Six Feet Under* has created a cultural climate in which rites shot are au courant.

Pilgrims and explorers have long lugged home photographic souvenirs testifying to their presence at exotic scenes in foreign places. Rites are eminently photogenic. After tall mountains, bright flowers, and towering skyscrapers, what else attracts as much photographic attention as a wedding replete with flowing costume and energetic dance? Or an initiation stained with blood and climaxed with hugs and tears? What better way is there to package a culture for export than shooting people's ceremonies and celebrations?

Lots of people shoot rites. Tourists shoot them, hoping to import the local color (duty-free, of course). Family members shoot rites of passage, pickling collective memories in order to preserve a sense of belonging. Ethnographers shoot rites, aspiring to salvage indigenous practices before they are gobbled up in the maw of globalization. Documentary makers shoot rites to entertain television audiences (and perhaps, accidentally, educate them). Feature film makers sometimes shoot rites, usually as framing for more dramatic, nonritualistic actions. Journalists shoot rites too, but only on occasions when they serve as backdrop for local social dramas or global political events. Religious broadcasters shoot worship, song, and other ritual activities hoping to make converts of outsiders, extend sacred space into domestic space, and provide a visible product in return for donations. Even worship leaders and liturgy professors shoot rites as ways of teaching or evaluating liturgical skills. There are many motives for shooting rites.

But what does shooting rites do? What does it do to the rites shot, the people who shoot them, and those who enact them?

Shooting Documents

To shoot a rite is to render it an object of study. During my first field research in 1973, I took pictures. For one thing, tourists shot them, so a camera helped me blend into the crowd. For another, anthropologists are supposed to record what they observe, and I was then a religious studies scholar being adopted, under Victor Turner's tutelage, into the anthropologists' clan. So I shot the pageants, processions, and parades of the Santa Fe Fiesta as a form of quick, visual note-taking. The Fiesta was an annual, complex, multilocation event crammed tightly into a few autumn days. I shot its rites and performances because I did not have time to observe them carefully. Shooting was a kind of shorthand, as well as a substitute for really seeing.

Unlike texts and paintings, pageants and ceremonies do not sit still. Like all performing arts, ritual enactments evaporate in the doing. So shooting is a way of making them hold still so one can analyze them—turn them this way and that. Shooting freezes action, helping a scholar notice details after the action dies down.

My Fiesta slides, the visual documents created when I first began to study ritual, soon gathered dust, only a few of them making their way into *Symbol and Conquest*. In the book, the function of the photos was to testify that I had been there, taken it all down, and completed the anthropological rite of passage called fieldwork. The photos, ensconced in a proper book, were sucked into the service of what was then considered real, which is to say, textual, scholarship.[43] The pictures, never really valued in themselves, were put to work procuring tenure. So, in the end, the pictures were worth the investment in camera and film, although I never really studied them as people do today now that we have become serious about visual anthropology and material culture.

Shooting Reveals

In the early 1990s, almost twenty years after I had written about ritual and drama in the Santa Fe Fiesta, a filmmaker, Jeanette DeBouzek, went to New Mexico to make a video based on *Symbol and Conquest*. Her video, *Gathering Up Again: Fiesta in Santa Fe*, goes far beyond the book, and it captures a crucial behind-the-scenes event:[44] Randy, a Pueblo Indian, lives in Los Angeles. One summer, he returns to New Mexico, and one of his Hispanic friends invites him to play Chief Domingo in a traditional pageant that celebrates . . . well, that is the question. (If one believes local Pueblo people, it celebrates the conquest of Indians by Spanish conquistadors. If one believes certain bishops and clergy in Santa Fe, it celebrates the conquest of war itself by people of goodwill, regardless of race, color, or creed.)

Since Randy now lives in California rather than in one of the New Mexico pueblos, he does not realize that most Pueblo people have been quietly boycotting the Fiesta pageant, that no Indian has played Chief Domingo for several decades.

It is the day of the Entrada pageant, the ideological heart of the Fiesta, and, it seems, there has not been a full dress rehearsal. Randy arrives, greets his buddies, sees their ragtag, stereotypical "Indian" costumes, puts up with their mock threats about making "Indian" jokes, and prepares to perform. We witness

Randy as the meaning of the play and his part in it begins to dawn on him. He is humiliated and embarrassed. The camera notices him offstage crying. At one point it seems that an organizer is having to push him onstage to finish playing his demeaning part. Interviewed after the pageant, Randy admits that if he had known what was going on, he probably would not have participated at all.

The video *Gathering Up Again* threatened the local sensibility in a way that *Symbol and Conquest,* a mere book, could not. The video did not merely refer to ritual and interethnic difficulties, it reenacted them, making them present. The video had the capability of renewing the event over and over again. It could ritualize the revelation. Before our very eyes we could watch Randy awaken, his Spanish and Indian cohorts feel shame, and the pageant begin to unravel. The real drama is not onstage but backstage. We not only witness Randy's humiliation but also hear an utterance that one does not hear in Santa Fe: "I was ashamed of being Spanish."

When the state school board began to consider distributing the video to public schools, political pressure mounted in Santa Fe, so much so that the director felt she had to move to another city.

Shot rites, by revealing preperformance and backstage activity, can threaten or transform them, and the result is ethical and political debate.

Shooting Validates

Shooting a rite can amount to a declaration, "This event is really important; this is real." Think about weddings. Video documentation and portrait shooting not only disrupt them but also validate them. Norma Joseph, a friend and a religious studies scholar at Concordia University, once described a scene from a Jewish wedding that she attended in Detroit. The videographer was shooting the photographer who was shooting the wedding party, all of whom were carrying throwaway cameras distributed so everyone could help capture the fleeting, "precious moments." The reflexivity, Norma observed, was three layers deep.

"Capturing" sounds less violent than "shooting." The dancing, marrying, human animals in Detroit were not quite shot like game. Shots fired by a videographer are not bullets that kill. Perhaps photos are more like tranquilizer darts. They are for our own good, right?

Most rites of passage require witnesses. A fleshy, merely human, pair of eyes is a fallible witness, but the eye, amplified through a lens and dramatically followed up by a distinctive click or telling whir, creates "evidence"; it makes "memories." The act of shooting renders the one who wields the machine godlike, a manufacturer of eternity. Documenting a performance is no longer an act imposed on a rite by an outsider. Rather, shooting is part of the ceremony itself.

Like Kabuki theater performances, the scenarios of contemporary Japanese weddings are laced with dramatic freezes, pauses built into processions so viewers, including those with cameras, can take in the costumes and postures—the whole scene—without being distracted by the mere busyness of bodily movement. To the Japanese eye, the stilled photographic moment is more sacred than the moving cinematic one. The Japanese wedding performance is constructed to facilitate the shooting, and the shooting validates the ritual act.[45]

Of course, it is not only in Japan that photos and videos have come to possess the validating power usually ascribed to marriage licenses and tombstones. Because shooting itself can become ritualized, the co-opting of scholarly visual materials is always a danger.

Shooting Publicizes

Did you watch Princess Diana's funeral? That day, my son and I were in the Bay, a Montreal department store. There, for all the world to see, was a homeless woman surrounded by a circle of big-screen TVs. She was weeping shamelessly. We watched her watching them.

Not to have shot Diana's ceremony would have deprived royalty of an opportunity to be publicly contemplated; *not* to have shot the ceremony would have deprived the world of a moment of togetherness. *Not* to have shot and disseminated Diana's funeral would have been to cheat the bag lady and the rest of us of a chance to grieve and, yes, to gawk. Without the shooting, the funeral rite would have lost most of its public accessibility. Without the shooting we fathers would have lost an opportunity to discuss dying princesses with our sons and daughters.

A Ghanaian graduate student conducting field research on funeral rites in Toronto discovered that they were regularly shot and that the videos were being shipped back to Ghana.[46] Why? Because tradition requires inheritors to participate in funerals, and video participation is one way of discharging that duty across an ocean.

Like Kodak, Microsoft now capitalizes on the fact that even in ritually inept cultures, rites of passage must be shared. The "share this folder on the network" command now provided by Windows XP enables you to discharge your kinship duties. No sooner do we return from a wedding or funeral, having shot it on a digital camera, than we can share the entire folder, in an electronic album no less, with all the distant relatives, and even the entire Web-watching world, if we are so inclined. Why? Because shooting validates as it publicizes.

Shooting Mystifies

A shooter looks through a viewfinder, screen, or lens and, by doing so, focuses on some things while cutting others out. The right and ability to define which things are out of bounds and which things are central is an enormous, mystifying power.

Since I work more often with artists than with advertisers or scientists, most of the photographers of my acquaintance regard their instruments as aids for contemplation. When they walk the streets or prowl the woods with the intention of shooting, they slow down, attending to the details of things. They contemplate what most of us hurry past. For them, shooting is an act of selection, and selectivity helps them attend to what appears—to attend fully, as one does in meditation practice.

But selectivity and focus cut both ways. They also blind the beholder. Shooting hides countervailing activities and disguises blemishes. With digital editing, one can now disguise and manipulate right down to the pixel level. Consequently, most of us are unable to tell which things were "really there" and which things were edited in, or out.

Rites, like photos, enable participants to contemplate what is really real, to encounter mystery, but they also mystify. Rites, like photos and film, cloud the sources of authority, shielding them from criticism. Ritualizing, like shooting, is one of the primary ways of constituting authority. Those with ritual and photographic know-how have more authority; those lacking such knowledge have less. If you don't use Powerpoint, you are not a real scholar, maybe not even a real person, right?

Authority is not only constructed *in* ritual and *by means of ritual* but also *about ritual*. In the television series *Ancient Mysteries*, A&E presented an installment called "Sacred Rites and Rituals."[47] Leonard Nimoy, the narrator, exudes the cool Vulcan rationality that he embodied as Spock on *Star Trek*. He frames rites as examples of exotic violence. These rites, the script has him say, "challenge logic." Ritualists' actions are made weird by the process of cinematic decontextualization. Naturally, these ritualists have no names.

As an interviewee in the series, with the albatross of attributed expertise around my neck, I was sucked into the vortex along with the other scholars and with Nimoy. I was shot into complicity with the script's interpretive strategy, even though I would have dissented vigorously from much that Nimoy said and the film did.

For the last decade, I have been involved, as on-screen expert and behind-the-scenes adviser, in the production of films and plays dealing with ritual. My protests notwithstanding, I am presented in television documentaries as knowing everything about rites, ancient and modern, Eastern and Western.

Behind the scenes, my job, as two producers put it, is to keep them honest. Often, when I see the results, I am sure that I have failed my task. The "honor" of being inflated into an authority figure for documentary television is itself a kind of ritual dismemberment. Hours of interviews and advice, along with pages of notes and bundles of research, are sliced paper thin, salami for fast-food visual consumption. Scholarly work is used to warrant producers' and advertisers' values. Producers may listen dutifully, even enthusiastically, but when the editing starts, most of the advice is ignored. In the end, the genre, television documentary, falling prey to the prevailing cultural images of ritual, determines the outcome, the presentation that the public watches. The television genre and the cultural prejudices exert canonical force.

Almost none of this made-for-TV shooting leaves me happy with the final product. So, inevitably, I follow up the supposedly creative filmmaking task with a critical, scholarly one. The airing of a film usually necessitates an article—just to protect myself, if nothing else. Being shot into the stratosphere of expertise, one is forced to ask questions that neither theology nor ethnography prepares one to ask: As public intellectuals, are we responsible for the pap that airs in our names? Are we morally obliged to traffic with television image-makers? Should we not lock ourselves into ivory towers and write responsible books instead?

Shooting Constructs

The *Harlem Book of the Dead* is a beautiful, disturbing volume.[48] From the 1920s through the 1960s, the funerary photographer James Van Der Zee shot the African American dead of Harlem. Photographing them was both a sign of respect and a way of engendering hope. When it became technologically possible to superimpose images of Jesus on a coffin lid or a band of angels above a corpse, the bereaved found it easier to embrace the evangelical opportunities lurking around death.

One photo from the *Harlem Book of the Dead* that stops me in my tracks is of a mother, a father (smiling, no less), and a child sitting for a family photo. Nothing unusual is going on, except that . . . the child is dead.

Novelist Toni Morrison says of Van Der Zee's photos and of this tradition of mortuary photography, "How living are his portraits of the dead."[49] The right photograph not only memorialized the deceased, created an ancestor, and preached a sermon but also painted an icon, an aperitif of the resurrection. Shooting was a way of constructing sanctity.

Of course, only a little reflection is necessary to recognize that the eternity afforded by shooting devices is a little less enduring than that promised to Muslim and Christian faithful. Photos, after all, fade. Even CDs and DVDs, across time, deteriorate. The "never" in the claim "The image and sound quality of DVD never decline with age" is like the "never" in "I'll never get pregnant," or "We will never attack another country first." It is a pious aspiration, not a fact.

When my children were younger, I interviewed them on video, hoping to discover and capture what was behaviorally sacred to them. I would ask, "If the house were on fire and you had time to grab only one thing before running out, what would it be?" One afternoon, they turned the tables, asking me what I would snatch. I heard myself answer, "The videotapes of your birthdays, holidays, trips, and these interviews."

My kids are adolescents now, and interviews are harder to extract, but the family watches the aging childhood videos over and over again. Each new round of sibling wrangling, each little bit of kid metaphysics is met with hoots, laughter, and the ritual utterance: "Here it comes, the part where . . ."

One does not have to be a ritual studies scholar or even a dad to understand why a family Bible or a crucifix would be left to burn while the family photos would not. Even flawed family shooting rites can produce icons, constructions that embody the ultimacies to which they point.

Shooting Dramatizes

The anthropologist Victor Turner taught a generation of scholars that ritual is nothing if not dramatic.[50] He made the claim not as an observation of a fact but as a matter of definition and theory. Many scholars continue to echo his assumption. I no longer share it. Although ritual and drama may be first cousins, and rites can be photogenic, we are not well served by the assumption that rites are *necessarily* dramatic. Many rites are sedentary, repetitive, and boring—marked by a rhythm quite unlike the climactic actions that the Euroamerican West expects of drama. Try to make a film of a rite, and you will discover how undramatic ritual can be.

But never mind. By shooting it, one can make it dramatic. If the drama is not there in the actions of participants committing acts liturgical, you can, if you are adept at video editing, put some drama there. You know . . . the way Ken Burns makes moving documentaries about the Civil War, baseball, jazz, and New York City by constantly panning across or zooming into manuscripts and relics. Never mind that the historic actors are dead, or that the objects were never living, the camera and narrator are alive. By their shooting and zooming and panning and storytelling, they can dramatize the inert into the lively and engaging.

Of all the shooters of ritual, Leni Riefenstahl, unfortunately, was one of the most talented. Utilizing thirty cameras and 120 assistants, and pioneering documentary innovations that are remarkable even today, Riefenstahl, in *Triumph of the Will*, dramatized the 1934 Nuremberg party congress into a national coming-out ceremony.[51] Then in 1938, in the *Olympiad*, she transformed the 1936 Olympics into Greco-Germanic religion.[52] *Triumph of the Will* and *Olympiad* are masterpieces, studied by documentary makers everywhere. The loop of ritualizing and dramatizing is so effective that each process feeds the other. Consequently, the films continue to exert canonical force on their viewers, even those who dissent from Riefenstahl's ethics and politics.[53]

Shooting Violates

Tourist photos seem innocent enough until you are pulled up short, instructed by indignant locals that not all rites are fair game. Shooting a rite can disrupt it, or, if sustained, even destroy it. Shooting rites causes trouble in situations where rites are regarded as holy and cameras profane. You can understand the consternation of the locals. If *your* grandmother's funeral were disrupted by a bunch of handycam-carrying strangers, the expanding and contracting phallic lenses of their electronic gadgets trained upon *your* grieving uncle, profanation would seem to be the *only* possible outcome. Even scholars, dedicated to analysis, would protest the photographic rape of a memorial service.

Feminist scholars have launched the most thorough critiques of "the gaze," with its voyeuristic, objectivizing, violating possibilities.[54] On some occasions, shooting amounts to what in the Spanish American Southwest was called a "rite of reduction," an enactment formally imposing a subordinate status on Indians. Therefore, like women, indigenous people have become wary of the camera, since it has served too often as an instrument not only of sexism but also of racist colonialism. Late nineteenth-century photographic projects such as that of Edward R. Curtis not only rendered Indians iconic but also functioned as a form of trophy-taking, the white man's peculiar form of head-hunting.[55] Shooting was a means of packaging the booty of conquest so it could be traded back east. As a consequence of photographic and cinematic intrusion, many native groups now consider shooting an intercultural rip-off, so they forbid it during their ceremonies, or else they make camera-toting white folks pay dearly for the privilege.

Shooting (Dis)embodies

What shooting seizes upon is bodilyness, and if ritual studies is about anything, it is about the embodiment of meanings in social contexts. The study of ritual is not primarily the study of ideas in people's heads or feelings in their hearts but about meanings embodied in posturing and gesturing. Film and video are methodological necessities for studying postures and gestures. Shooting the surfaces of things, bodies included, has analytical, and not merely expressive or entertainment, value.

However, there is another side to photography's peculiar way of embodying. Some years ago, my wife and I were studying Spanish and boarding in a local home in Salamanca, Spain. One afternoon we noticed on the mantle several pictures of people, their mouths wide open. Something—we did not know what—was being deposited on their tongues. Later, when we inquired, we were instructed in a mixture of Spanish and English. "Pan," they said, then, "S*agrado, sagrada. . . .*" They were trying to teach us the language we'd come to learn.

Eventually, we pieced the meaning together. They were talking about bread, holy bread. Communicants had been photographically frozen in the act of consuming a communion wafer. Like a bloody sheet at a Moroccan wedding,[56] the framed photo was proof that the definitive act had been truly committed. Friends and relatives relished such photos. We saw them everywhere, so Spanish clergy were obviously complicit with the practice.

Such scenes give one pause. Many of the reigning theories of ritual, religion, and liturgy ill equip us to deal with such practices. The first impulse of many who study religious rites is to object to shooting them at all; doing so is either in bad taste or a violation of sanctity. If we ask ourselves what reputable liturgical theologians might say about the act of shooting a host as it greets the tongue, the answer is not difficult to imagine.[57] What could be less dignified or more crassly literalistic than bared teeth and salivating tongues? The Spanish photos could be used in liturgy courses as illustrations of the evils of popular religion and photographic imperialism. Why? Because shooting disembodies in the very moment that it creates a tactile or visual surface that the senses can grasp. Shooting embodies by disembodying.

Shooting Complicates

The shooting mind can be a profoundly suspended, if not disbelieving, mind. Theologians and liturgists sometimes complain that the detachment attendant to the act of shooting is a prophylactic to faith. Several years ago I was shooting the Toronto Towneley cycle of mystery plays. It was raining, and most of the audience, not up to the ordeal of redemptive suffering, had gone home for supper. A bedraggled, university-age Jesus was lugging a cross down the *via crucis*, which is to say, across the quadrangle of Victoria College. A few persistent photojournalists were still weathering the scene, their cameras trained on the savior. A photographer in a yellow poncho boldly approached the dripping Jesus on his way to Golgotha, which is to say, toward Bloor Street. The photographer drew surprisingly close to Jesus' face. A few of us gasped. The shooter snapped a shot. Then, suddenly, he fell to one knee and began to weep as he clapped his hand over his mouth. At that moment, I, having stepped back rather than in, shot him shooting "Jesus."

What is one to conclude from the photojournalist's actions? Certainly not that shooting obviates the possibility of faith. And certainly not that being deeply moved requires one to believe. Just as Huichol shamans can swallow hundreds of peyote buttons and still organize pilgrimages and know where baskets and bows should be placed, so one can simultaneously shoot and revere. Just as Hopi children learn to hold simultaneously the knowledge that kachinas are spirits as well as their relatives dressed up in masks and costumes, so one can ritualize in a fictive, or even ironic, mode. It is possible, simultaneously, to shoot and to revere, to embrace fictionality and to have faith. The only caveat is that you have to practice.

Not only does shooting complicate things psychologically, it complicates them socially. The social complexity of a feature film can be staggering. *Titanic*, for example, lists fourteen hundred names in its credits; the number of hands stirring the pot was enormous. Socially, cinema is the most complex of contemporary artistic acts. If for no other reason than this social complexity, cinematic art remains largely intractable to the few religious studies scholars and theologians who have tried to analyze it. Who is "the artist" in a movie? Whose responsibility is the shooting? The convention of crediting or blaming the director or the star is just that, a convention, and it has little analytical value.

The psychological and social complications give rise to conceptual ones. Conceptually, the relationship between shooting and rites is not as simple as it may seem. We cannot, for example, merely equate the profane with what a culture will shoot or the sacred with what it will not shoot. Nor can we unequivocally claim, for instance, that shooting desecrates funerals but sanctifies weddings. The conceptual conundrum faced by students of ritual is not merely the result of machines, of digital cameras and such, but also of faulty theorizing. With only one or two exceptions, theories of ritual have not attended very fully to the seam between the subjunctive and the declarative, between fictive and ordinary reality. Too easily we have accepted a polarized cluster: On the one hand, we clump ritual with sacrality, believing, and not-acting. On the other, we cluster profanity, the suspension of disbelief, and acting. But the fence that generates this easy dualism is, in practice, breached coming and going, from both directions. Since both insiders and outsiders now have cameras, since ethnographic outsiders now participate, and since participating insiders quickly learn how to observe, the conceptual Berlin Wall between ritualizing and dramatizing, two utterly constitutive kinds of human interaction, is crumbling.[58]

Even in contemporary Christianity, where the relationship between ritual and theater is typically nonintegral, the boundaries can bleed. Robert Duvall's film *The Apostle* contains two revealing behind-the-scenes outtakes.[59] In both, we see the insider/outsider, actor/nonactor boundary being breached. Not only do real preachers and a real congregation act in the film, but an actor and a technician, both members of the crew, are seized by the spirit during the making of the film. Duvall not only has to direct and act the part of Sonny, who is leaving his fictive congregation, he also has to negotiate with actual church members to keep the real congregation from dividing over the issue of being shot by "Hollywood." They worry that Hollywood will reduce them to caricatures.

In the film, real pastors must not only preach and court the spirit, they must perform their preaching and spirit-courting for the cameras. So everyone, it seems, is crossing and recrossing the seam between fictionality and ultimacy. Whereas Duvall the director-actor has to perform toward believing, the evangelists believe toward performing. In the last analysis, perhaps the difference makes less difference than our theoretical postures would lead us to believe.

Whither?

I have now created a conceptual tangle and uttered a mouthful. Big though it is, it could be uttered in a single sentence: Shooting documents, reveals, validates, publicizes, mystifies, constructs, dramatizes, violates, (dis)embodies, and complicates. The sentence may be a little dizzying and this romp through shooting contexts too much like a roller coaster ride, but conducting field research and working among performce and media artists is like that. If you feel disoriented, you have done a good job of stepping inside the zone inhabited by field researchers and media consultants. As if rites, by themselves, were not confounding enough, I have multiplied the complexity by considering rites shot photographically and cinematically. But to what end? With what implications?

I conclude with several brief provocations—the beginning, not the conclusion, of a conversation or debate:

1. Shooting, and all that it has come to represent here, is not going away. Not only religious rites but virtually everything on the planet has, or will have, a recording device pointed at it, for good and for ill.
2. As scholars and teachers we should learn to think and act not only *in* or *with* media and art but also *between* the media and *among* the arts.
3. This between-space is infested with a thick knot of issues not neatly separable into ethics and aesthetics, economics and religion, or any of the other tidy compartmentalizations that usually give us comfort.
4. Because an orderly, sectored model of culture is no longer viable, neither are curriculum models that overvalue departmentalization.
5. Because shooting now regularly appears on both sides of the line that once separated practitioners and researchers, the models for research must necessarily be collaborative, interdisciplinary, and reflexive.
6. The false split between those who perform or participate, on the one hand, and those who think or theorize, on the other, is a major deterrent to good scholarship.
7. So let it be said: Scholars, rise up and seize the means of production. Forget television and shoot for the classroom. Learn to shoot and edit as you once, in the far-distant past, learned to use word processors.

As a famous starship captain could have said, "Go where no book-toting scholar has gone before." Or, as Martin Luther ought to have said, "Shoot bravely."

4

Fiddling with *Fiddler*

This chapter insistently pushed its way out of a first-year course called Religion and Cinematic Culture. My colleagues and I taught it together, with faculty working on films linked to their own areas of expertise and with students submitting written work in dialogue form. One evening, hoping to provoke a debate, I took an overstated position by saying in class, "During the wedding scene in Fiddler on the Roof, *I am delighted when the rope separating the men and the women comes down. I'm a boundary-hopper. Lots of boundaries that other people consider sacred I regard as arbitrary, even destructive. If we'd do away with all religious, national, and ethnic loyalties, we'd be a lot better off. Wouldn't we?"*

Probably a better strategy for provoking debate would have been to take the opposite position, "Not only should the rope have stayed up, but Tevye should never have left for America, nor should his daughters have loved and married in ways that contravened Jewish tradition."

More of the students would have argued with me. In any case, I was seduced by the choreography and cinematography of the wedding scene, so I labored on it for months, both during and after the course. After several consultations with Jewish colleagues, a series of presentations, and multiple revisions, the outcome was this chapter.[60]

When I first began field research on ritual in 1973, I was surprised to discover how entangled it is with drama. No longer surprised, I continue to study ritual's interactions with its performing arts relatives. Theater, music, dance, and even film share certain family resemblances with ritual. All are constructed from carefully selected, highly condensed, strongly framed activities. Details matter. Every gesture, from large to small, must be enacted in the right way. Everything that counts must appear in the designated frame. Nothing appears in that frame unless it counts, and if it counts, it is likely to be foreshadowed or echoed elsewhere.

In addition to selecting, condensing, and framing, there is another family resemblance. Ritual, like other kinds of performance, evaporates in the doing. The usual scholarly response is to render a ritual enactment a text, specifically, as a field notebook or ethnographic description. The irony, of course, is that scholars often seek out enactments as ways of circumventing texts.

In any case, there is growing recognition that prose descriptions of rites are impoverished, so film, video, and audio recordings are becoming essential tools for studying ritual. Film, then, is not only formally akin to ritual but also useful for studying it. Whether a film of a rite is best considered yet another kind of text or another kind of performance is a question scholars debate.

Even though performances are framed, they are not necessarily captives of their original frames. They can be reframed, transposed from one genre to another, hence the possibility of a rite out of place. To document a rite on film is to transpose it. A filmed rite, however much it may seem like a rite, is not a rite. The differences are as important as the similarities.

An ethnographic film grants us access to rites that may be otherwise inaccessible; a film is a way of knowing. An ethnographic film makes present the reality to which it was a witness, enabling viewers to participate in both films and rites. But ethnographic films also insulate viewers from rites; film testifies to an absence as well as a presence. At its worst, a film is a simulacrum, a stand-in, even an appropriative rip-off, because when we shoot something, a rite, for example, we remake it in our own image.

Video documenting a rite is not as simple as pointing a camera at ritual activity. As soon as you pick up even a home video camera and point it at your son or daughter frolicking in the back yard, cinematic conventions come into play. Family videos are shot with eyes and hands nourished, or undernourished, at the movies and in front of TV sets and computer screens. Movies set the production standards by which we are prone to judge home videos wanting and even professional documentaries boring. Movies and television shape our expectations, determining what is deemed real or interesting. The visual ethnographer, as surely as the dad in the back yard, is culture-bound—more precisely, movie-bound and television-bound.

Why study rites in movies? Because movie conventions and practices shape the way all of us, ethnographers included, view and construct the world. Movies shape not only filming practices but also ritual practices. The person sitting in the movie house or in front of the TV screen is the same person who worships and weds. The attitudes carried *to* ritual scenes are carried *from* the cinematic scenes.

Another reason for studying ritual in feature films is that movies are assuming increased pedagogical importance. A growing number of teachers, from primary schools through universities, are incorporating films and film clips into curricula. Often teachers are untrained and unreflective about media, assuming that films get students closer to reality, thereby holding their attention more effectively than lectures.

Here, we will consider a single film clip, not an entire film, and then, by unpacking that scene, illustrate a method for studying ritual and film more generally. My question, then, is methodological: What can ritual criticism, applied to a single scene in a feature film, teach us about the transposition of ritual into cinema and cinema into ritual?

The clip consists of the wedding scene from *Fiddler on the Roof*.[61] The 1971 film, based on a 1964 Broadway musical, tells the story of a Jewish family forced in 1905 by a Russian pogrom to abandon Anatevka, their home. For most of the movie, the forces of global antisemitism loom in the background. In the foreground are local relationships, the love lives of three daughters, and the responses of their parents, Tevye and Golde, to the daughters' marital choices. In the wedding scene, the oldest daughter, Tseitel, marries Motel, a poor tailor, rather than Lazar Wolf, an aging, wealthy butcher with whom she has been matched.

Later, the second daughter, Hodel, will pair up with Perchik, a revolutionary and educator, eventually having to follow him to Siberia. The third daughter, Chava, will marry Fyedka, a Russian Orthodox peasant, putting her family in the position of having to shun her as if she were dead. All three daughters' choices force Tevye, their father, to renegotiate the traditions that have governed the lives of Orthodox Jews in Russia.

At the heart of the film is Tseitel and Motel's wedding, which is disrupted by a pogrom. How does one study such a scene?[62] At the very least, any interpretation must be cinematically cogent, socially aware, and religiously educated. We must work diligently both *in* the film as an aesthetic structure and *around* the film as a social process and consumed product. An adequate method must take the film *as film* seriously, attending to the fact that it is a feature film and a musical rather than a documentary or ethnographic film, but the method should not ignore the fact that the film refers to and instigates actual ritual practices. An apt method would enable us to understand how these practices are transfigured by the cinematic process, and it would attend to the twin processes of the film's production by a crew and its consumption by diverse audiences. In short, the method requires mimetic criticism of the rites to which the film refers, formal criticism of the rite in the film, source criticism of the representations on which the film draws, expressive criticism of ritualization in the production of the film, and reception criticism of ritualization in the consumption of the film.

Mimetic Criticism: Rites to Which the Film Refers

When religious studies colleagues visit RE105, a university course called "Religion and Cinematic Culture," to make presentations on films such as *Fiddler on the Roof, Daughters of the Dust, Kundun,* or *Jesus of Montreal,* uncoached, they will spend most of the class time talking about the beliefs and practices of the traditions to which the films refer. Since religious studies scholars usually study religions rather than films, scholars springboard to arenas they more effectively control, namely, the religious systems themselves. This interpretive strategy is referred to by literary and drama theorists as *mimetic* criticism because, implicitly or explicitly, it treats cinema as a representation of nonfilmic, social reality.

A tacitly mimetic inquiry from a student might sound something like this: "Did traditional Russian Jews in 1905 really separate males and females with a rope to keep them from dancing together at wedding celebrations?" The "really" is a cue that the query arises from mimetic assumptions about the relationship between the film and Russian Jewish weddings.

An astute faculty member might reply to the student's query, "Yes, just as men and women sit separated in synagogue services, so in wedding celebrations, they danced in the same room but not together, and certainly not as couples. Is couple dancing what you take to be normal at weddings?"

Mimetic criticism concentrates on the presumed real rite that the cinematic depiction supposedly reflects. The filmed rite is construed by the interpreter as a mirror—sometimes accurate, sometimes distorting—but nevertheless, a reflection of the real rite. "The real rite" is a construct that glosses over the differences among three things: ritual texts, ritual performances, and ritual memories. Because texts, enactments, and memories are plural, they are potentially—I would say, inherently—inconsistent and conflictual. So a production researcher or film student who speaks of "the" Jewish wedding is engaged in imaginative construction, and a historian of religions would be quick to point out the diversity of actual Jewish weddings. When historians of religion talk about the Jewish wedding, they know it has a complex history and that their target is both moving and plural.

From a referential, or mimetic, point of view, what do we need to know about Jewish weddings? There is substantial scholarship on Jewish weddings, so I will present only a few points germane to an interpretation of the movie's wedding scene.

For most of Jewish wedding history, agreements were primarily between parents or families, not brides and grooms. In modern times the agreement has become more bride-and-groom focused. This shift is the key historical change driving the *Fiddler* wedding scene.

In ancient times the wedding ceremony was not followed by a feast, as is the case in our film. Rather, the feast *was* the wedding, with a single blessing addressed to the groom. Weddings were not held in synagogues any more than early Christian or Muslim ceremonies were held in churches or mosques.[63] Like the early Christian wedding, the ancient Jewish wedding was largely a civic affair, only later becoming a liturgically sacralized event.[64]

The classical rabbinic wedding consisted of two phases. The first, betrothal, was called *erusin* or *kiddushin*. *Erusin* means "to be bound or joined." *Kiddushin* means "to set aside or sanctify," as when sacred property is consecrated for ritual use. During *kiddushin*, a groom uttered to a prospective bride, "Behold, you are sanctified unto me." This act of declaring her sacred, that is, set aside, made it so.

Whereas in ancient times, the betrothal ceremony typically preceded the marriage rite by a year or so, by the twelfth century, betrothal had become merely the opening phase of a single wedding rite; betrothal was no longer a separate ceremony. In both periods betrothal was sealed by a properly witnessed act of transferring property–today, a ring—from the groom to the bride.

A key part of Jewish wedding rites during the time in which the film is set was the *ketubah*, the wedding contract. The *ketubah*, which maintains the fiction that a husband purchases a wife, was a second-century innovation giving women limited legal recourse. The contract, written in Aramaic and signed by two witnesses, was read, at least in part, and then presented to the bride during the wedding ceremony. The document ensured that a husband had assets that could be transferred to the bride in case he died or broke the agreement, or in case she launched a successful divorce claim against him. A second wedding document, *shiddukhin*, specified the arrangements. Both documents were signed just before the wedding.

The second phase, *nissuin*, is also named *huppah* after the canopy beneath which it occurs. In the wedding's early history the two central actions of this phase were (a) the transfer of the bride from her father's house to that of the groom and (b) the sexual consummation of the marriage. In the period of the film, the central action was that of blessing the marriage. It was not, for example, saying eternal vows or expressing personal sentiments.

Weddings, even among Orthodox Jews, vary by region and social class, but it is worth risking a historical reconstruction. An early twentieth-century eastern European Jewish wedding might have looked something like this:[65]

1. Negotiations, with or without a matchmaker
2. Meetings of parents
   a. Agreeing on arrangements
   b. Gifts from the groom's father to the family of bride
3. An engagement interim, the length of which varied
4. Aufruf (the groom's being called to the Torah on the Sabbath prior to the wedding)
5. Mikvah (the bride's ceremonial immersion)
6. Hasan's tisch (the groom's gathering with male friends and relatives)

7. Procession
8. Erusin/kiddushin (betrothal phase)
   a. The groom makes a marriage declaration, "Be thou consecrated unto me according to the laws of Moses and Israel."
   b. The bride accepts a token of the commitment, e.g., a ring
   c. Ketubah (reading of the marriage contract written in Aramaic)
9. Nesuin/huppah (canopy phase)
   a. Bridal circumambulation of groom
   b. Seven Blessings and shared cups of wine
10. Transition
    a. Glass breaking (conventionally interpreted as a reminder of the destruction of the Temple)[66]
    b. Yihud (private time for bride and groom)
11. Celebration
    a. Circle dancing
    b. Games and dances to entertain bride and groom
    c. Meal
    d. The Grace after Meals, including the Seven Blessings
    e. Gift-giving
12. Sheva berakhot, week of celebratory wedding feasts that include the Seven Blessings

Even this brief hypothetical sketch illustrates how selective a swath the film cuts. The wedding scene is twenty cinematic minutes long, but it implies something like a six-hour wedding. As mere audience members, we would likely experience a full-length documentary shot at a real-time pace as interminable rather than moving. In the movie, we hear no reading of the contract, which would remind us that marital trouble is possible. We see no escape of bride and groom for a bit of private time, which might make us think about sex. We hear no man declaring, "Behold, you are sanctified unto me," which might leave a non-Jewish audience wondering about the relationship between sanctity and male possessiveness. In other words, the *Fiddler* wedding is a "perfect" wedding—but only for a movie. Even the ways in which the ceremony is deliberately fractured contribute to its cinematic perfection.

Formal Criticism: The Rite in the Film

If film studies colleagues were to visit RE105 to discuss *Fiddler*, they would make choices different from those made by religious studies colleagues. Film scholars identify crucial turns in plot, point out editing choices, discuss camera angles, and track character development. Their approach is more formal in the sense that it concentrates on the art form itself. Engaging in formal criticism, an interpreter suspends disbelief, enters the movie world itself, and acts *as if* the world outside the frame is either irrelevant or nonexistent. Approached formally, what matters is not historical Jewish weddings or an audience's responses. What matters is the film itself—its structures and processes.[67]

In creating a work of art, artists make choices. Feature film makers do not merely document weddings. For that matter, not even documentary film makers do so, because they largely serve television audiences who demand to be served only the juicy parts. Even ethnographic film makers rarely show entire ceremonies. Just as the rabbis selectively scoured a vast array of customs, choosing to ritualize one but not another,[68] so the director of a musical selectively depicts only what contributes to the cinematic agenda, for example, the advancement of a plot line, the development of a character, or the generation of a mood.

In *Fiddler on the Roof* male-female love relationships, which promise (or threaten) to result in a wedding and thus a marriage, serve as microcosms of the major themes of the film: religion, community, ethnicity, and politics. In the film, we witness only the one wedding that transpires between Tseitel and Motel, but it is a metaphoric compression of the entire film. In other words, the wedding scene, along with the married state it effects, is, formally speaking, designed to be the crux of the movie. One may enjoy the dream sequence, for instance, but it does not carry the filmic burden that the wedding does.

The *Fiddler* wedding scene is cinematically marked as especially sacred. It compresses time, thereby constructing a scene that is moving rather than labored. It assumes a vocal POV ("point of view") that is parental, alternating with a visual POV that is sometimes communal, sometimes "divine." The elevation of the wedding moment is also signaled by another remarkable feature: The bride, groom, and rabbi are also reduced to silence. The film eliminates the traditional words of the ceremony and superimposes a song, using the voices of participants but without having them to mime the words. We do not hear the words that solemnize the marriage. What we hear are the words of "Sunrise, Sunset," expressing the sentiments of the parents:

> Is this the little girl I carried?
> Is this the little boy at play?
> I don't remember growing older.
> When did they?

The parents' sentiments echo the feelings displayed on other characters' faces. By cinematic means the historic Jewish wedding of interfamilial contracting has been transposed into the modern romantic wedding of sentiment. We in the audience gaze affectionately at the community and family, who are affectionately gazing at the bride and groom, who are gazing at no one in particular—except for loving sideways gazes at each other:

> They look so natural together
> just like two newlyweds should be.

Together, we are all transported into life's mating cycle, which fits neatly over nature's seasonal cycle:

> Sunrise, sunset,
> sunrise, sunset,
> swiftly flow the days.
> Seedlings turn overnight to sunflowers,
> blossoming even as we gaze.

The rite naturalizes the highly cultural activities of pairing and of gazing at pairing. As surely and naturally as the sun rises and sets, so people fall in love, marry, and procreate, replacing their parents and grandparents.

Gone are the matchmaking, bartering, and contracting.[69] Parents no longer decide; lovers do. Romantic, couple-love cinematically displaces the supposedly heavy hand of eastern European marriage traditions. Even so, ritual is co-opted into sanctifying the emergence of romantic love and generating a wedding ethos appropriate to it.

Formalist critics would be dissatisfied with an interpretation that merely scissors out a scene. Like every other kind of criticism, formalism is implicitly holistic, insisting on the interpretive importance of context. The part—in this case, a scene—should be construed in the context of the whole, the entire film. For instance, the wedding dance asks to be played off an earlier dance. In both instances, groups that are initially divided (first, Jews and non-Jewish Russians, then Jewish men and Jewish women) are united. The divide between them is transcended, only to be reestablished later.

Another point at which our scene benefits from integration with other scenes is the appearance of Fiddler himself (he has no proper name). When he appears in other scenes, he either actively leads or strategically follows the other characters. Bending, stepping, and bowing, he animates transitions, marking major liminal moments. In marking the transition from procession to canopy, there is a notable difference between his appearance here and elsewhere. Here, for the first and only time, he does nothing. He does not fiddle. He just sits on the roof, doing nothing, contributing not a single, solitary, sweet note to the marital festivities.

One might interpret Fiddler's inaction as a way of assuming the passivity of a spectator, a moviegoer, but it is better read as the marking of an especially elevated moment. By ceasing his usual activity, he honors the marital act as worthy of awe. The wedding is flagged as a sacred moment by the director's having Fiddler stop fiddling around. The wedding rite is elevated beyond other activities that might be considered competitors. For instance, Fiddler doesn't even show up for the Sabbath liturgy. Although utterly constitutive of Jewish life, the rite is, perhaps, too routine for Fiddler. To take another example, at the exodus from Anatevka, the most catastrophic social-political event of the entire movie, Fiddler behaves more or less in his usual way.

A third example of our scene's entanglement with the rest of the film consists of intrusions upon the wedding scene, which are foreshadowed elsewhere. Simplified, the Jewish wedding has four phases: agreement, procession, betrothal-wedding, and celebration. The cinematic strategy, however, is to disrupt this continuity, making a very basic anthropological point, namely, that religious, social, and political realities are inextricably tangled. Social drama inevitably feeds into, and breaks in upon, ritual drama.[70] The writers and director refuse to indulge the audience with an unsullied wedding. Conflict is required to drive the film forward and hold our interest.

The wedding rite is disrupted five times. It is crosscut by poverty, intravillage quarreling, modern ideas about love, and the political realities of Russian anti-semitism. A minor disruption arises when a beggar approaches someone for a handout. Two midsize disruptions emerge from the squabbling between Tevye, father of the bride, and Lazar Wolf, to whom the bride would have belonged if the agreement had not been breached. Their acting out only makes sense in view of previous scenes.

The disruption most directly related to the marital metaphors of the film is introduced by Perchik, who verbally muscles into the second round of the alpha-male tussle. He challenges the segregation of the sexes during the wedding festivities. This moment too has been set up by his previous manner of teaching the girls in the family. He reestablishes order, but only by effecting a scandalous ritual innovation, couple dancing.

The final and major disruption is instigated by Russians who set the local pogrom in motion as they ride their horses into the celebration, upending tables and gutting the wedding pillows.[71] This last disruption, which has been repeatedly foreshadowed, presages Holocaust violence, terminating the first act and making it exceedingly awkward to sip cocktails or crunch popcorn during the intermission. This disruption is marked by what one might call a prolonged "gestural theodicy." Tevye's open-armed, heavenward query is that of a man stunned by God's permitting the desecration of his oldest daughter's wedding. Not even the forced exodus from Anatevka precipitates such a dramatic gesture.

Interrupting a cinematically sanctified rite five times keeps the drama high so the rite doesn't drag. It emphasizes the humanity and fragility of ritual, and it facilitates the intrusion of ritual innovation. But notice one thing: The wedding itself, the moment under the canopy, is not disrupted; it is kept intact, virginal.

Source Criticism: Representations on Which the Film Draws

Just as films borrow from life, so they borrow from other works of art. Because source criticism examines interactions among works of art, it is inherently comparative, casting a wider net than mimetic criticism. However difficult it may be to distinguish one art from another or the art world from the social world, source criticism is carried out by both audiences and filmmakers. Like film-makers, audiences learn to recognize conventions, genres, and recurrent themes that link separate works of art. If people experience these recurring patterns as revelatory, they may dub them archetypes.[72] If they find them oppressive, they may label them stereotypes or clichés.

No North American ritual action is more movie- and television-conditioned than the act of marrying, and that conditioning is increasingly global in scope. No rite compares with the wedding for either its Hollywood attention or its sustained spending. The occasional funeral—that of a pope or president—may garner a large television viewing audience, but Vatican and state funerals do not generate hundreds of thousands of imitators. The so-called white wedding, evoked by the royal wedding of Victoria and Albert in 1840, has its imitators the world over, including Asia and Africa. Seven hundred fifty million people watched Prince Charles and Lady Diana Spencer marry on television in 1981. Weddingchannel.com claimed between three and four hundred thousand brows-ers in 1999. In 2002, $50 billion was spent on weddings and wedding prod-ucts in the United States, an average of $22,000 per American wedding. Figures from other countries show as large or larger figures.[73]

Since 1890 there have been over 350 films containing the words "wedding" or "bride" in the title. Neither feminism nor changing statistics on the hiring of women have lessened the box office power of wedding films. In fact, Otnes and Pleck, authors of Cinderella Dreams, dub the 1990s "the decade of the wedding movie."[74]

Like brides and grooms, Fiddler's directors, actors, set designers, and cho-reographers carry to the filmmaking task not only information about Jewish weddings but images and attitudes formed by a host of other cultural resources that are neither eastern European nor Jewish.[75] Source criticism makes clear that cinematic creativity is more like editing than it is like magical creation from nothing. The wedding scene in Fiddler depends not only on rites, ritual texts that prescribe them, and memories that eventuate from them but also on other artistic representations: photographs, paintings, literary works, plays, and other films. Among Fiddler's key sources are the short stories of Yiddish writer Sholom Aleichem, the Broadway stage play, and the paintings of Marc Chagall.

By comparing the film with Sholom Aleichem's stories, we find some re-vealing differences. For example, in the stories, Tevye prays a lot more. The lan-guage of the stories is much more explicitly religious than that of either the play or the film. In fact, producers worried whether the play would be "too Jewish." Whereas many of Aleichem's cultural symbols were allowed to stand, only a few of the religious ones were. Onstage, Tevye, his family, and his village are reli-gious, but not "too."[76]

It is something of a surprise to discover that Sholom Aleichem's short story "Modern Children" contains no wedding scene, only the single line, "The next day they were engaged, and not long after were married."[77] The story, unlike both the play and the film, is neither ritually driven nor wedding-centered. The story is marriage- and choice-centered, working through questions such as: Who should choose one's marriage partner? What are the right motives? Whose pledges and desires should be honored? What are the financial and emotional consequences of marriage-partner choices?

In Aleichem's stories, Motel, the groom, dies early, and Tevye, who has outlived his wife and wants to retire, must now raise his grandchildren and nurture a grieving, destitute daughter. Furthermore, Tevye and his family do not leave for that other promised land, America. Instead, it is the place "where all unhappy souls go." Rather, the goal is Palestine, but Tevye's responsibilities keep him from ever getting there. This Tevye, unlike the one in the movie, is stuck. A musical, especially one designed for Broadway, cannot end on such a dire note, thus its exodus, though tragic and bittersweet, is also humorous and hopeful—the stage play more so than the film. These and other such changes have led to the interpretation of *Fiddler* as representing or even effecting the Americanization of Judaism.[78]

Another difference between the stories and the film is that there is no "fiddler on the roof" in Sholom Aleichem's stories about Tevye and Golda's family.[79] Writing a wandering, rooftop fiddler into the story as a transition-marking character and primary symbol of the Jewish soul was the work of several people, perhaps most obviously Joseph Stein, who wrote both the stage play and the screenplay.

Fiddle-playing was widespread among turn-of-the-century eastern European Jews, and one fiddler, Stempenyu of Barditshev, is enshrined in Sholom Aleichem's story "Stempenyu: A Jewish Romance," but this story had little influence on the movie. However, some think Marc Chagall knew Stempenyu's music as well as this story by Sholom Aleichem.[80] And Chagall's paintings were well known to several of the American artists responsible for both the stage play and the film. Chagall's paintings depicting shtetl life are replete with fiddlers, many of them playing at weddings and a few perched atop roofs. Two or three fiddle over a corpse. Boris Aronson, *Fiddler's* set designer, had worked with Marc Chagall and was a key source of Chagallesque visual and spatial influences in the play.[81] So there are fiddlers among *Fiddler's* sources, but no there is no Fiddler on the Roof who is a prototype for the Broadway invention. The fiddler, like the movie named after him, is a repository of enough artistic influences to make the study of him a scholar's paradise.

Expressive Criticism: Ritualization in the Production of the Film

When one is working with a single poet or film auteur, the resulting interpretation may be accurately labeled *expressive* or *auteur* criticism, but since *Fiddler* is a movie by a notably collaborative director, *production* criticism may be a more appropriate term. Whatever we call it, expressive criticism, which treats works of art as the expressions of their creators, takes us behind the scenes, redirecting our attention off-camera.

Without participant observation it is usually difficult to know much about the ritualization of production, but the recent inclusion of deleted scenes, filmmaker interviews, and documentaries about the making of films helps critics know more than they would have known a few years ago. Happily, the current DVD edition of *Fiddler* includes commentaries by director Norman Jewison and Chaim Topol, the Israeli actor who played Tevye. In addition, Jewison has recently published an autobiography that contributes to the understanding of his directorial intentions.[82]

However much the viewing public identifies films with lead actors, scholars and film professionals conventionally attribute artistic creativity to directors.[83] Because of Jewison's last name, it is often assumed that he is Jewish. Because the play was first staged in America, and Tevye leaves for America, it is also commonly assumed that Jewison is American and the film, likewise, American. The executives who hired Jewison as director were shocked when they found out that he was not Jewish. United Artists executive Arthur Krim recovered from his shock by declaring, "We don't want a Seventh Avenue [Yiddish] production. We want the film to play everywhere in the world, regardless of religion."[84]

Norman Jewison is a United Church Canadian, and the cast was international rather than exclusively, or even largely, American. One of the reasons Jewison did not cast Zero Mostel as Tevye—he had played the part on the Broadway stage—was that he "seemed so American, so New York."[85] When Jewison and his family left the United States for London, the Canadian director was so angry about American presence in Vietnam and about the Kennedy and King assassinations that he turned in the family's work permits.[86] Leaving the United States to shoot *Fiddler* in Europe was, among other things, an act of protest against American policies and practices, so one could argue that in certain respects *Fiddler on the Roof* is more Canadian than American and at least as Christian as it is Jewish. The fact that *Fiddler* is never interpreted as either Canadian or United Church (even though Alfred Hitchcock films are now being interpreted as Catholic) tells us something important about the relationships between Americans and Canadians, as well as Christians and Jews. Jewison aimed to make a very Jewish film, not a Canadian or an American film. He exercised great care to construct a work that would be historically realistic and ethnographically authentic. Because he was a goy, an outsider, he spent the first six months doing research on Jewish religion and culture.

Just as it is very Canadian *not* to advertise one's citizenship (especially when wanting one's products to be consumed by Americans), so it is very United Church to play down one's denominational identity in pursuit of interfaith activities that hold out the promise of restorative justice. Social justice was, and is, an important theme and motive in many of Jewison's films. With *Fiddler* he clearly felt the burden of a being a Gentile creating a movie about a people subjected to genocide. One Jewish scholar thinks Jewison the Gentile was actually freer to draw more fully on Sholom Aleichem's stories and characters than were the Jewish-American stage play producers, who had to worry about being "too Jewish." The irony is that Jewison's Canadian United Church earnestness about his task may have led him to miss an important dimension that is uniquely Jewish in the stories, namely, their humor. But this is a minor caveat. For the most part, Jews responded enthusiastically to Jewison's film.[87]

Fiddler's fictive Anatevka, Russia, of 1905 was shot in 1971 in Lekenik and Mala Gorica, Yugoslavia; therefore, many of the faces we watch in the wedding scene are not Russian Jews but Yugoslavian Christians. Jewison and Topol, in their running commentary on the DVD edition, relish this fact. The production transaction with the villagers was not merely economical, it was also an interfaith activity of sorts.[88] Jewison would delight in this story sent to me by Rabbi Sheldon Zimmerman:

> To my amazement and enlightenment when I served as a rabbi in Dallas I attended weddings of the children of Christian colleagues and friends, and "Sunrise, Sunset" was the wedding song of choice. When I inquired further, I was told by Christian colleagues that it is one of the favorite Christian wedding songs. Somehow *Fiddler* is far more American than it is Jewish, and the play receives far greater production in churches around this country than it does on any professional stage. I was further reminded of this when my colleague at the neighborhood mega–Baptist church had one of his congregants ask me, "How does one dress a rabbi?" When I inquired as to why the question, he said that they were putting on *Fiddler* and needed to know how to dress a rabbi. I loaned out more prayer shawls to my Christian friends than I ever did to my own congregants.[89]

Jewison's next film following *Fiddler* was *Jesus Christ Superstar*. The chapter of his autobiography that treats both films is called "The Spirit of Chagall," and it bears the opening lines of "Sunrise, Sunset" as its epigraph. *Fiddler*, it seems, touched Jewison more deeply than *Superstar*. The first line of the first chapter opens, "For as long as I can remember I've always wanted to be a Jew."[90] Although his English Christian roots can be traced back to the year 1216, Jewison feels that his family must have been Jewish at some point in time. Being beaten up as a kid because of his last name and sneaking off to synagogue with a friend also reinforced his Christian identification with Jews. Although steeped in the United Church—specifically, its Methodist strand—Jewison is Jewish in sentiment, although not in fact.[91] Jewison is a wannabe.

Because newspaper criticism of *Fiddler* tends to focus on the lead males who have played Tevye, it is easy to forget others whose sensibilities the film expresses. For instance, the entire movie, except the dream sequence, was shot through a silk stocking, mere pantyhose, donated by a secretary "with a very good pair of legs."[92] The textured sepia tone transports moviegoers into the Old World, coddling them with warmth and intimacy, the mystical source of which they would never have imagined. Similar ingenuity was exercised on the dust cloud fuming beneath the bottle dancers' feet. It was fuller's earth on an indoor wooden floor. The dance, which would otherwise have seemed slick, now plays as earthy, grounded in the close-to-the-soil ethic imagined to be typical of eastern Europeans.

One other behind-the-scenes fact is of ritual and theological interest. Tevye talks directly to us (a technique borrowed from theater) and to God. The audience and the divine are both positioned outside the movie frame. Since camera heights and angles change throughout a movie, Tevye could not locate God as simply as he had done onstage, namely, in the upper right corner of the rear of the theater. So in the movie, a god-stick was erected. Painted with a white bull's eye, it was posted at the proper height so Tevye would know where to look. In this way, God becomes spatially reliable, therefore cinematically convincing.

Reception Criticism: Ritualization in the Consumption of the Film

No art form is more audience-driven than a movie. Reception criticism considers a film as it is viewed and utilized by audiences. It concentrates on personal and collective movie-consumption processes such as marketing, distributing, viewing, and reviewing.

The reception of *Fiddler* was rapid and widespread. The first Broadway run of the play, which began in 1964, lasted 3,242 performances, breaking all previous records.[93] The movie, released in 1971, won three Oscars. *Fiddler* has been performed live the world over, not only in Israel and America but also in France, Germany, the Netherlands, Czechoslovakia, Austria, Argentina, Finland, Greece, Norway, South Africa, Mexico, Sweden, Iceland, Spain, Yugoslavia, and Japan. By addressing key issues—the negotiation of tradition, the fragility of intergenerational links, and the trials of diaspora religion—*Fiddler* initiated a new awareness of ways in which Jewish preoccupations were also universal concerns. Jews who felt distant from the old ways could reconnect with their roots, and non-Jews could see that Jews were "just like us." Doing things "my way," the American way, and the Jewish way did not have to be opposites. Tevye became universal, Everyman, every father, the model for resisting just enough while adapting at just the right time for just the right reason, love.

Ritual includes not only its enactment but also its preparation and after-math. Blockbuster films are now designed to reach well beyond the movie house with toys, video games, T-shirts, and other merchandise. This big commercial splash was not programmed in 1971. Even so, *Fiddler* rippled well beyond the stage, cinema house, and wedding parlor. In the aftermath of the film, Sholom Aleichem's characters became well known around the globe, an impact no col-lection of stories or stage play, even on Broadway, could have effected. In Japan, the play has evoked its own kind of ritualization quite different from that of North American Christian and liberal Jewish weddings. Having adopted *Fiddler* whole-heartedly, the Japanese wonder how North Americans and Western Europeans can understand such a "Japanese" play.[94]

Movies sometimes have quite direct ritual impact on audience behavior. However derivative, a ritualized allusion to a film or other work of art elevates the occasion, in much the same way that citing authorities authenticates the writing of scholarly books. "Sunrise, Sunset," is on almost every wedding music list. To hear it or sing it is to footnote the movie, enacting a bond with not only the wedding party but also the moviegoing audience.

Songs pierce the heart faster than words. (How can a wedding or a funeral be felicitous if no one cries?) People go to movies for a good cry. Faydra Shapiro, a Jewish colleague and religious studies scholar, visited RE105 to lecture on *Fiddler*. She told students how, as a teenager witnessing her parents grow misty-eyed during "Sunrise, Sunset," she found the song schmaltzy. Now that she is a parent, she confessed, the song brings tears to her eyes as well.

On final exams for RE105, students, including non-Jews, say they "just love" the *Fiddler* wedding scene. Not only are students taken by it, so is Norman Jewison. He sang "Sunrise, Sunset" at his own daughter's wedding. "Everyone cried."[95] The good-cry movie is no less ritualized than the rural Greek wedding led by professional mourners.[96] The stylization and predictability don't neces-sarily make movie tears and funerary wailing inauthentic. However, they are ritually rather than literally real, so a reception critic shouldn't equate the movie-induced good cry with weeping any more than a ritual studies scholar should equate liturgical blood and body with literal blood and body.

The song "Sunrise, Sunset" is now showing signs of age, and its popularity is declining. Scenes from the movie play in fewer heads. Only about 10 percent of the students in RE105 say they have seen it. Even so, the song still appears almost universally in the "Jewish wedding" slot of wedding planners' repertoires. In addition, you don't have to be Jewish for *Fiddler* to have ritualistic impact, because it is also categorized more broadly as "processional," "nonliturgical," "father-daughter," and "groom-and-his-mother" music. "Sunrise" is Jewishly nondenominational in the way that commencement prayers are Christianly nondenominational.

In the movie, "Sunrise, Sunset" is sung overtop the actual blessing of the marriage. In a real wedding, such a superimposition would likely be experienced as a violation of decorum, if not an actual desecration, so at post-*Fiddler* weddings, the song is played during the procession or reception. It is not used at all in Orthodox communities resembling the one in the movie.

In the late twentieth century, "Sunrise" enshrined the Judaism that non-Jews loved to love. Even in the twenty-first century, when the song is becoming the music everyone loves to hate, it has the status of a tradition despite its being the invention of a lyricist and a composer, Sheldon Harnick and Jerry Bock.

In post-Protestant and secular cultures a film that becomes too obviously sacralized as a tradition will soon be lampooned. In January 1973, only three years after the film, *Mad* magazine published a comic book–style parody. A big-bellied, balding, heavily jowled, thoroughly American Tevye no longer has to wish that he were a rich man. He is a fat cat with a spoiled dog and an expensive house in the suburbs. His daughters are pampered, under the care of that famous Jewish psychiatrist, Sigmund Freud. "Sunrise, Sunset" provides the tune for a song about pushing fifty, dyed hair, and antiwrinkle cream. However much *Fiddler* was received as a Holocaust movie in the last half of the twentieth century,[97] in the first decade of the twenty-first century it is becoming something else. The *Mad* magazine article was prophetic.

Alisa Solomon, a *Village Voice* reviewer writing about the revival of the stage version of *Fiddler* in 2004 at the Minskoff Theatre, berated the play for its nostalgia. Violating the so-called eleventh commandment ("Don't [mess] with *Fiddler*"), she writes:

> The primary audience to whom *Fiddler* originally spoke—American
> Jews in the throes of upward mobility and dispersion from concen-
> trated urban communities into the goyish suburbs—no longer needs to
> stake a claim to an ethnic past nor be assured of being fully American.
> The grandchildren of Tevye no longer dream of becoming rich men.
> . . . In vast numbers, they're there. And more and more of them
> are voting Republican. A few even have a hand in shaping Bush's
> bellicose foreign policy. . . . The image of Jewish powerlessness
> represented—even celebrated—in *Fiddler* was turned on its head only
> three years after the musical's debut, when Israel captured the West
> Bank, the Gaza Strip, and other territories. Tevye's tenderness, comi-
> cally puffed-up patriarchalism, and clash with modernity take on a new
> kind of nostalgic appeal: *Fiddler* works to remind Jews of our bygone
> innocence.[98]

So having a movie assist in generating wedding sentiments isn't a foolproof tactic, because movies, like rites, age, and it is far easier to retire, parody, or pan a movie than it is a rite, even one buttressed by Tradition.

Rabbi Jeffrey Stiffman deals with the aging of "Sunrise" in a gentler and more humorous tone than that of Alisa Solomon.[99] He sent me this note:

When my daughter and son-in-law were to be married, they made up a humorous pre-marital ketubah. Among the things that they wrote were: "We will not have an accordion playing at our wedding. We will not have 'Sunrise, Sunset' played at our wedding." After the wedding dinner, I got up and announced that I had a special gift that I wished to give to my daughter and son-in-law. I sat down at the piano, the orchestra leader pulled out an accordion, and we proceeded to play the song. Everyone had tears in their eyes except my daughter and son-in-law who were almost on the floor with laughter.

Performance theorist Richard Schechner locates theater's primary ritualizing in actor training workshops rather than rehearsals or performances. I would locate film's most pervasive ritualization more in its reception than its production. One religious studies scholar describes his youthful moviegoing experiences this way:

> I regularly participated in the weekly Saturday ritual of going to the movies. This event was one I shared with a wide variety of folk: young and old, farmers and townspeople, men and women, Catholics, Protestants, and non-believers. For two hours the cares and demands of everyday were set aside as we entered the magical world of the cinema. Seated in the darkened theater we allowed our private fantasies, fears, and aspirations to meet the drama enacted on the screen. We gathered to watch the reenactment of the primordial conflict of good and evil. . . . The drama on the screen moved us, and shaped us. . . . As we sit and watch a film, we are participating in a central ritual of our technological civilization. . . . The act of going to the movies is a participation in a central ritual of this culture's spiritual life.[100]

Darrol Bryant is not merely talking about obviously ritualized "cult" films such as *The Rocky Horror Picture Show*, a film to which audiences go in costume so they can perform in character along with the film, or about the live performance of the musical *Hair*, which sometimes eventuated in audience members' dancing, singing, smoking up, and even making love with actors. Bryant is talking about grade B westerns.

The ritualization of a film's reception is no different than the ritualization of anything else. Ritual is not "digital"; it does not operate with a simple off/on, yes/no logic in relation to ordinary activity. Rather, ordinary activities become more or less ritualized; ritualization takes place by degrees and in many forms. A film's reception can be ritualized by:[101]

- taking it as a charter for action, thus identifying with the characters or actors and aspiring to act like them or avoiding actions that do not accord with the film's values

- blurring the boundary between cinematic and noncinematic reality by elevating actors into stars or imagining directors as having special insight, as if they were oracles or diviners
- meditating on a film's revelation, awaiting its healing, or expecting inspiration from it
- re-viewing a film; treating it as classical, canonical, or required viewing
- assuming the truth of a film's generative metaphors (e.g., marrying is as natural as sunrise and sunset)
- amplifying a film (e.g., by dreaming about it, praising it, retelling it)
- defending a film; endeavoring to dampen critique of it
- associating with others who love the film
- treating a film artifact (e.g., DVD, first edition) with extra care, for example, lining up to purchase it upon release, keeping it in a special place, or having it bound in expensive materials
- turning viewing into a cult event with parties and merchandising
- naming one's children after characters or other such mimetic activities

We have now made our five interpretive passes, so we return to the question: What does this model of ritual criticism, applied to the single case of *Fiddler*'s wedding scene, suggest about the transformation of ritual into cinema and cinema into ritual? One could present the answer as a myth, a wry chartering story:

> Once upon a time, after many centuries of arguing and bargaining, some rabbis began to ritualize selected parts of weddings. In doing so, they borrowed from European Christian neighbors who had been borrowing from them.
>
> Later, a couple of Jewish artists attended numerous weddings in eastern Europe. They loved the celebrations and couldn't stop the violin music in their heads, so they told stories about wedding negotiations and painted brides and grooms floating over the tops of roofs.
>
> Not so long ago (but still quite a while ago), some American Jews who had never been to the Old Country read the stories, saw the art, and decided to make a play—actually, several plays—by adding some music, subtracting some stuff they found embarrassing, and playing up a wedding. The play became what is known in America as "a big hit on Broadway."
>
> To make the big hit bigger, some magnates hired a Canadian, thinking he was Jew. This internationally minded, justice-hungry wannabe hired an Israeli actor and shot the film in Yugoslavia using lots of Christians dressed up like Jews. He made a film that people thought was utterly American (even though there were few Ameri-

cans in it) and utterly Japanese even though there were no Japanese in it.

Some Jews, along with their Christian friends, went to the play. Then, there was a big rush, together, to the movie houses. Jews and Christians went to the film, several times over, sitting side by side. People the world over bought the CD and, later, the DVD. They liked the music so much that they learned the lyrics and began to marry each other to its joyous rhythms. Marrying, they felt like movie stars, having overcome fairy-tale adversities. By falling in love they could keep the sun rising and the sun setting.

With passing time, Jews like Tevye and Golde and their children and their children's children found themselves, once again, living in ghettos, only this time, suburban ghettos, where they were walled in, richly but less than happily, with their neighbors—Greeks, wannabes, Muslims, males, females, gays, Christians, and non-.

The story could have other endings, of course, but enough already. The story doesn't really end anyway; it's still going on. Readers are likely to want the result not as a tale told by an idiot but as a set of conclusions. Here they are:

- Rites, especially rites of passage, especially weddings, permeate cinematic culture.
- Ritualization is found in all aspects of cinema, not only in its form and content but also in its production and especially its reception.
- The ritualization of reception has a life span; how a film or scene or song is received changes across relatively short periods of time.
- Cinematic weddings are consumed in ways that condition movie viewers to carry expectations into actual rites, for example:
  - an insistence on dramatizing ritual. Rites themselves are often not very dramatic, so drama is instigated by playing offstage conflicts against onstage ritual enactments.
  - a desire for ritual compression. Rites must not be long or boring; they must entertain, holding participants' attention in the way movies do.
  - an expectation that rites highlight individuals, their feelings, and their decisions. This expectation casts families and communities as supporting rather than lead actors.
  - an insistence that rites should mark triumph over adversity.
  - a recognition that rites, even those marking triumph, also foreshadow the onset of further trouble.

Why should ritual studies attend to a rite in a feature film, especially one suffused with the razzmatazz of a Broadway musical? The main reason has to do with the nature of culture itself. Like mycorrhizal fungi beneath the soil, cultures are systems of exchange. People who engage in ritual activity, as well as people who observe or theorize about it, are nourished or depleted by non-ritualistic cultural processes that engender formative attitudes. Without our necessarily being aware of them, attitudes wrapped in sentiments pass from one cultural form to another. Cultural currents flow in and out of ritual. Even if words and actions are deliberately held constant by authorities and traditions, ritual meanings flow. However much the meanings of symbols may be prescribed and codified, contexts change, and because they change, so do meanings. Nothing exists in a bubble—not film, not ritualizing, and not theorizing about ritual. All are shaped by their ambient cultural and historical situations. In sum, movies, fictive or not, exchange nutrients with ritual traditions, intellectual activity, and moral behavior.

Do people believe in this exchange, this movie ritualizing? Most would likely say no. But under the spell of cinematic magic, they act as if they do. If you think musicals and grade B westerns don't matter just because they are not great works of art, then you do not understand the presidencies of Ronald Regan and George Bush Jr. War-making is one of the most ritualized activities on earth, and films are one of the most effective ways of ritualizing, even sacralizing, the process of becoming a citizen, inventing a hero, or destroying an enemy. How we ritualize acts of imagination declares whom we aspire to be and what costs we are willing to pay to enact this aspiration, so how we imagine ritual is as important as how we enact or theorize about it.

PART II

Ritual in Classroom and Conceptual Space

5

Ritual in the Classroom

I teach ritual studies courses. Sometimes I teach them ritually, sometimes not. However, even when I teach courses without "ritual" in the title, I occasionally teach them ritually. Ritual is not only a phenomenon that scholars turn into subject matter, it is also a way of engaging things. One can ritualize teaching as surely as one can ritualize sitting or eating.

One year, when I was on leave, a Zen monk taught my course "Zen Meditation, Zen Art." Still robed as a monk, Victor Sogen Hori created a stir among students. He spoke with authority that I could not muster, given my checkered history with Zen and my sparse writings about Buddhism in North America. Much later, after he began teaching at McGill University, Hori organized a conference on the teaching of Buddhism in North America. I was invited but did not attend. After all, I do not claim to be a proper Buddhism scholar. Despite my obvious lack of qualifications, Hori persisted and eventually convinced me to write a piece on teaching Zen even though I was not at the conference. He pressed me, knowing that I sometimes brought ritual studies perspectives into my courses, including the Zen course. I finally yielded to his pressure after he agreed that I could tell the stories of two actual courses rather than reflect in a more theoretical or prescriptive way about teaching Buddhism.[102]

For twenty-odd years I have taught a course called "Zen Meditation, Zen Art." When I first proposed it, darts arrived from several directions. A colleague at another university assured me that I was less than qualified to teach it, my several years of Zen practice notwithstanding. My Japanese was nonexistent; so was Sanskrit.

Chinese we didn't talk about. And I was no Buddhologist. What did I think I was doing?

I said I was not teaching classical Buddhism on the basis of classical or canonical Buddhist texts. I explained that the bulk of the course was on Zen and its acculturation in North America. I poked back by asking how qualified he was to teach the last leg of Buddhism's historical journey, the one that culminates in contemporary North America—my field, not his. I asked: Would we require that a course on Christianity in North America begin with Jesus and the New Testament? I doubt it. There are roots courses, I said, but there are also fruits courses. One is not better or worse than the other, just different. My colleague was unmoved by my quips even though he knew I meant what I said.

Then there were members of the university's Arts and Science Council, who, never having seen a course description involving Buddhism, read it with a mixture of bewilderment and bemusement. The first question was tossed out by a testy professor of English: "Why isn't this course being offered at the community college, where they teach bricklaying and underwater basket weaving and god knows what else? Surely, the so-called arts in this course description—can you believe it, flower arranging and martial 'arts'—have no place in an arts and science curriculum of a modern Western university."

Fortunately, a Japanese-sword-collecting colleague from the School of Business and Economics (quarters from which I did not expect support) sparred with my colleague from English and won straightaway. My only entry into that fray was to remind another inquirer that, no, I had not been hired to teach "theology and literature," rather "religion and the arts in North America," and that "the arts" were variously construed in different cultures and that, no, I did not think a course on Milton's *Paradise Lost* and Christianity would be a better alternative; the English department, thank you, was doing that.

Despite initial faculty skepticism, students liked the course. It was the mid-1970s, and Zen was in sync with the cultural mood. "Zen," the word rang mystical, if not true. Consequently, the first time I taught "Zen Meditation, Zen Art" it flew. The students said so, and I knew it. By the second and third times around, I realized that it was the most revision-free course I'd ever taught. Students arrived in droves eager for enlightenment and willing to practice zazen on the floor, chant sutras, or visit Zen centers in Toronto. Although students exited the course unenlightened, they developed a sense for the practice and its cultural ramifications. The only complaint was that the course was not *more* experiential. Why not practice zazen in the Ritual Studies Lab twice a week, they asked, and why not more tea ceremonies, a makeshift sesshin, and encounters with a few visiting Zen masters? Some years I relented and offered zazen outside class.

A few students from that era, especially those who sat, stay in contact some twenty-five years later. One is now a Buddhist priest; others have spent time in Zen centers and monasteries. Testimonies arrived, unbidden, extolling the course's life-changing, life-enhancing qualities. I did not set out to make converts, only to convey or evoke the sense of Zen. I believed—and still believe—that if students do not sense, as well as think, a topic, they will not understand it. Education is of the senses and emotions as well as the brain.

After those initial, successful years there was an interlude created by several converging forces: the requirement to teach other courses, sabbatical, my own struggles in a Zen teacher-training program, and the availability of part-time faculty with impressive credentials. For a decade or so I did not teach the course even though I sometimes wanted to.

Then came the academic year 1999–2000. Once again, I was scheduled to teach the Zen course. Fondly remembering the early days of the course, I anticipated it. But when students stopped by to sign up for the course—it had a waiting list—I found myself tipping backward rather than looking forward. The students talked about Zen in a tone that struck me as different, not what I remembered. They were mildly curious, hoping to be entertained. They were not looking for masters or expecting to be enlightened.

By midterm it was evident to both my teaching assistant, Barry Stephenson, and me that something was not taking, that we were failing to cultivate a sense for Zen among the students. So we resorted to more dramatic means. We arranged a debate. Students were to come to class in the persona of a Zen teacher; they could pick which one. They didn't have to dress up, but they were to maintain the demeanor, attitude, and speech of a Zen master they had read about. In an attempt to have them encounter Zen as embodied in named and located persons rather than as a set of generic ideas and practices, the course had introduced them to half a dozen practitioners whom they now got to "be."

In class Barry and I provoked debate among the dramatized Zen masters. If we couldn't inspire them, then we would tease them into crawling into someone else's skin. Two Zen teachers, themselves the spiritual offspring of a common master, were pressed to take up their differences in public. An entrepreneurial teacher was confronted with students who thought he had lost touch with the point of the practice. Marginalized and exploited female Zen students confronted marginalizing, cavorting American male teachers.

Even though students playing the roles had absorbed few of the details of the lives they were representing, once they loosened up, they did enter into the spirit of dharma-horsing-around (however unlike dharma combat it may have been).

Later in the course, we tried another performance strategy. When it became all too obvious that the students did not understand koans, that, in fact, they were not even intrigued by them, we resorted to acting out. Barry became the Zen master and I, his student. He got to slap me, publicly, and, coached by our rubrics and texts, we stood on desk tops, acting the fool in search of the oxlike self. But the best we could do was titillate a lethargic, slightly bemused audience. They marveled that we would make such a desperate spectacle of ourselves.

A key component of the course was the final "Zen and the art of" project. The number of "Zen and the art of" books is large. Many of the books are junk, but they reflect North American ways of selectively adapting and distorting historic Zen. A major aim of the class is to attend to the values that determine patterns of adaptation and modes of distortion. And the populist artsiness of the American "Zen and the art of" industry is a good example for study. My aim in having students study this motif is partly to incubate their creativity and partly to inculcate a healthy iconoclasm. Doing so successfully requires a delicate balancing act.

I had remained foolishly hopeful right up to the very end, even though the course was one of the flattest I had taught in thirty years. But the "Zen and the art of" projects set me back. With each new paper I was faced with my own failure to teach even the most basic ideas, attitudes, and practices that I had set out to inspire in the Zen course. The students wrote as if they had not taken it.

Students were allowed to write on an Asian art traditionally associated with Zen—haiku, tea, Noh, sumi, and so on—or on a Western art such as photography, sculpture, literature, poetry, or dance, provided they first conducted research on a traditional Asian form. If students chose to pursue a project on a Western art, they were to read about Zen's relation to the traditional arts of Asia, particularly Japan, as well as study some of the "Zen and the art of" literature that saturates the North American market. Then they were to ask, for instance, What would it mean to engage in photography as an extension of practice, as if it were a Zen art? Photographers were advised to look at the Zen Mountain Web site for examples.

In addition to discussing ways a specific art and a distinctive religious tradition interact, students were invited to submit their own art and to describe the process, for instance, of shooting and developing. In the "old days" of the Zen course students had begged to be allowed to experiment and practice with Zen and art. But this time the requirement was met with incredulity and indifference, with only an occasional flash of interest.

The papers written about Asian arts inevitably emphasized form, content, or technique, and they stuck closely to the scholarly texts they had read; largely they summarized sources. Those written on Euroamerican arts emphasized spontaneity and personal expression. Despite repeated lectures and discussions on the Western acculturation of Zen, students inevitably settled on flow or spontaneity as *the* Zen quality and then wrote entire papers showing how their photographs, shot five years ago, surprisingly exhibited this very quality.

One student opened a project this way: "Chaung-Tzu once said, 'Flow with whatever may happen and let your mind be free. Stay centered by accepting whatever you are doing. This is the ultimate.' To me, this is the essence of Zen and the art of photography. When one can concentrate on the pictures they are taking and be free from all the surrounding distractions, not only will they be happy with the results, but they have captured the Zen way. Although there are multiple ways to do this, I think the three most important are being flexible and spontaneous, being 'in the moment' of where you are, and being personal with your work instead of detaching yourself from it."

This student not only assumes Zen art has an essence and cites a Taoist to illustrate a Zen Buddhist attitude but talks as if happiness with results is the obvious aim of Zen. In this view, the proper Zen way to achieve that goal is to tune out the surroundings (even though course readings and lectures repeatedly emphasized that Zen meditation was not about tuning out distractions or quelling thoughts). The writer, by no means a poor or even mediocre one, emphasizes flexibility and spontaneity despite the fact that zazen, the most basic of Zen Buddhist practices, is so heavily structured that expressions of spontaneity usually violate its decorum. The student's paper identifies "the Zen of" an art with its expression of the personal, despite the fact that Zen monks shave their heads, dress alike, obey their teachers, and otherwise comport themselves in ways designed to quell the ego rather than enhance the personality. In short, the writer of this paper sees only *similarities* between the style of her photography and the style of Zen. To me, the *differences* were blatant. When the Western way of photographing is laid alongside either Zen practice or Zen-influenced Asian arts, I have to work to find continuities. We had repeatedly talked about the ritual grounding of Zen, about learning by imitation, about formality, and about structure. Never mind, Zen is spontaneity, presence to the moment.

The student told about having been forced in a high school photography class to shoot a roll of film a week for twenty weeks. The subject matter was the schoolyard itself. She experienced the assignment as boring but nevertheless included some stunning old photographs along with this comment, "All of these pictures are pictures that I may not have taken had I not been forced to adapt to my surroundings; however I was pleased with the results." So even though she knew that there had been a rigid structure to the assignment, and that it, in part, was responsible for her photographic success, Zen was still about flexibility, spontaneity, and self-expression. What did the assignment teach her? She quotes Lao tzu, not a Buddhist: "Softness triumphs over hardness."

I wrote in her margin: "Zen photography is not merely about spontaneity. If you hadn't had the rule that forced you to photograph, you wouldn't have discovered the scenes you shot. The story you tell here is *not only* about adaptability and flexibility, as you seem to believe, *but also* about a strict form: Shoot a roll a week on and off the school grounds. The story is not about the triumph of softness over hardness, but about the integration of softness (be flexible) and hardness (follow the rules). Right?"

This student was one of the better ones in the course. I cite her paper as an example not because it was among the worst but because it was among the most articulate. Like the others in class, she had heard me say that Zen is not identical with spontaneity, or even with presence, and certainly not with personality enhancement—that's what North Americans *want to find* in Zen.

But saying is not teaching.

I was struck by how doggedly and systematically students were able to tune out what they had learned—rather, what I *imagined* they had learned. Regardless of how I squeezed the balloon of their brains, they returned stubbornly to the shape they originally had. Some force greater than I, "the culture," was responsible. Even though many students equated "the Zen" or "the art" of something with spontaneity, they neither noticed nor articulated the contradiction involved in submitting paintings or photographs done several years ago. Old photos and high school artwork were pulled out of drawers. Many of the projects implied the title: "Zen and the art of *retrospective* interpretation of *old* works of art *as if* they were executed under the influence of Zen practice." It had not occurred to me that an "art of" project would elicit such desperate or lackadaisical methods, so I had not written into the course requirements, "You cannot hand in old artwork" any more than I had specified, "You may not hand in papers from last year's courses." I had assumed that a new course meant new work. I had assumed too that the heavy Zen emphasis on attending to the present would elicit present-oriented experimentation and research. I expected students to pay concentrated attention to the details, fluctuations, and foibles of the creative process. I was dead wrong.

I had hoped that students would raise and explore difficult questions and struggle out loud with some of the perpetual quotation marks that plague courses on contemporary North American Zen:

- Would a "Zen photographer" sensibility search out "natural" rather than industrial content?
- Is a black-and-white photograph "more Zen" than a color photo?
- Does "the Zen of" something consist of its content? Its style? The attitude with which it is done? The manner of its performance?
- Should a "Zen photo" look more "Japanese" than "American"?
- Does photography become a "Zen art" when preceded or followed by meditation?
- Is "the Zen" of an art dependent upon how it is interpreted (rather than how it is executed)?
- Is an edited or touched-up photo by definition a "non-Zen" photo? (After all, you can't erase or edit the tracks of an ink brush.)

Wrestling with such questions in lectures did not guarantee that they would be considered in projects. Why not? Why was I so unsuccessful at eliciting paradox, play, irony, iconoclasm, and the other processes that had made the course work so well in years past? I've considered obvious ways of accounting for the failure of the 1999–2000 version of RE298, "Zen Mediation, Zen Art:" I am getting old and stale; this was a remarkably stupid bunch; the failure was a mere fluke and things will improve next time around; Tibetan Buddhism is now in and Zen, out. But in the end I have concluded that the most decisive factor is the cultural milieu, the culture of learning at university and in the larger culture surrounding and permeating it. The problem was not merely that Zen no longer has the exotic appeal that, say, Tibetan Buddhism has; it was that students resist rather than long for creativity and experimentation in the classroom. They are desperate to be given explicit rules and directions, preferably coupled with marks that can be achieved by following them. They are disoriented, even threatened, by paradox, silence, simplicity, playfulness, and the other "virtues" that made Zen and student life seem so obviously connected in the 1970s and 1980s. In short, the milieu makes "audience reception" of this course content much more difficult than it was a quarter of a century ago.

The social stream in which we all swim is not the stream that once was. We professors talk about religious traditions and religious studies topics as if they are eternal verities, which a good teacher can teach anytime, anywhere. In actuality, certain traditions and practices make better, or at least easier, sense in one time or place than in another. Teaching about Zen now is different and, for me, more difficult, than it was two decades ago because the motivating predispositions have evaporated. Even though it may well be deluded to enter a Buddhism course looking for enlightenment or for a master, that is at least a motivation. It is easier by far to redirect a motivation than to create one.

But the story I tell is not entirely dreary. Near the end of the course, two students working jointly on Zen and the art of tea asked if they might supplement their paper on traditional tea ceremonies with one performed for, and with, the class. Of course, I said. In years past I had been flooded with initiatives like this, so I was grateful for this single glimmer of hope.

On the evening of the class, the two young women came by my office at 6:15 to set up for a 7:00 class. I took the lateness of arrival, the harried looks on their faces, and the presence of a boom box as bad signs. Barry accompanied them to the room they were preparing as their tea hut. At a quarter to seven, when I arrived and figured out they were using beer cups, plastic flowers, and paper cut-out stepping-stones leading down the hall to their tea-hut classroom, I wanted to go home and pull weeds in the back yard. If I had sensed even the slightest tinge of irony in their demeanor, I'd have danced a jig.

Would I be the chief guest? they queried. Yes, of course, but what is my job? I asked, ever the educator. I should enter first, they said, and wash my hands so the other guests could see how it was supposed to be done. And I should leave last.

What music is on your CD player? I queried. It was some soupy, dreamy, astonishingly inappropriate piece. I suggested: Silence would be quite fine. No, they said, we want music. Well, okay, if you want music, I said, how about something a bit more in keeping with the spirit of the ceremony? Sure, they said. I hurried away and returned with Tony Scott's "Music for Zen Meditation," only slightly more appropriate. When improvising, improvise.

I didn't know whether to laugh or cry during the demonstration/ceremony. So I did neither. The ethos was that of a grade four Shakespeare play or a Christmas pageant. We were awkward and self-conscious, and none of the actions showed much sensitivity to the tea ceremony or suggested that educated choices had been made on the basis of serious reading. I was not expecting a replication, only something "in the spirit of" Zen. We sat uncomfortably on the hard tile floor, having tiptoed across the treacherous white cardboard stepping-stones, which, not having been taped down, slipped this way and that across the hall floor.

Not until the hot tea began to burn my hand through the plastic beer cup did I settle down into my belly and notice that several other participants were doing likewise. For ten minutes perhaps we sat sipping hot tea and watching our self-consciousness fade. For a few moments even the spilling of tea and the shifting of untrained, weary bones became part of the event. A few "guests" drifted off into boredom; a few were embarrassed; but most began to inhabit the cluttered, sterile place and actually taste the tea.

Ceremony over, we returned back across the bridge of cardboard stones to our regular classroom. Expecting criticism or indifference, I opened with a preface calculated to protect the two students, whom I addressed publicly: "I appreciate your courage in taking on such a difficult topic. I am also delighted to have had time in the midst of end-of-term madness to sit and sip tea that warms the hands and belly. So let me ask your classmates: 'If you were to perform a Canadianized tea ceremony, what would you do that is the same or different from what your two classmates have just done?'" I was hoping to elicit gentle critique and some comparison of Japanese tea and Canadian tea (or even Canadian beer).

The first response came quickly and energetically from a student who had regularly been critical of the class. "This is the highlight of the course," she exclaimed. "Now, for the first time, I get it," she said.

I believed her. The outpouring from other students echoed her sentiment. The enthusiasm and sense of recognition were so pervasive that I felt free to joke about the beer cups, the music that *almost* got played, the slipping cardboard stones, the plastic flowers, and the jammed-up desks that had surrounded us like a stack of ghostly bones in an elephants' graveyard.

The truth is that I would have been embarrassed had the ceremony been witnessed by any of my finely tuned, linguistically well-educated colleagues who teach university courses in Buddhism. It would not have measured up to their expectations or mine, and it would have been loud testimony that I had failed to teach Zen or the art of anything. The ceremony lacked simplicity. It lacked precision. It lacked silence. And it lacked attentiveness. Never mind the fine points of gesture and posture, its tone and tenor were off.

But something worked despite all that. The beer-cup tea ceremony became the high point of the course. I reminded myself that the rite was not of my doing and that it transpired despite my resistance and self-consciousness. It succeeded despite me, despite the course, despite the two students, even despite itself. Ritualizing, it seems, can work even when it fails.

Writing Religion

This story is not quite over. Running simultaneously with RE298 was RE400, "Writing Religion," a required course for religious studies honors students in their last year. As fate would have it, the course had only a dozen students, which meant it could be held in the Ritual Studies Lab, which, as karma would have it, is outfitted with just that many zafus and zabutons. "Ah," I said to someone, "writing close to the floor: good for the ass, the bones, and the soul."

The course is partly a reward and partly remedial. It is a reward for those who, in their last days at university, have finally learned enough to wish they could write well. It is remedial for those who not only don't, but also don't care that they don't. Half the class consists of creative or personal writing on religious themes; the other half is analytical. The first half is soft, nurturing, and vaguely Buddhist; it aims at producing a story or personal essay. The second half is hard-edged, secular, editorial, and critical; it aims to produce an article for a scholarly journal. Each student's writing goes through multiple drafts and multiple readers.

Except for having chosen Natalie Goldberg's *Writing down the Bones* as one of the books for the first half, everything else "Buddhist" about the course came about by accident or improvisation. One afternoon a student complained about writing trash (actually, she called it "shit"), so we did some deliberate trash writing and needed a god to whom we might offer such stuff. I remembered there was a sleepy-eyed, tilted-to-one-side Mexican Buddha in the closet; he would do. So out came a bowl, the Buddha, and a bell with which to mark the moment for feeding trash to the Hungry Buddha of Bad Writing. Had there been a Goddess of Bad Writing in the closet, we'd have used her too.

Then the obvious dawned: Why not offer Buddha some good writing too?

Then Christian and "other" students were invited to bring Christian and "other" "gods" for our improvised writing altar. We would not play favorites here. The advantage of Lord Buddha, I teased, is that he is indifferent to judgments of good and bad.

Isn't he?

Almost by accident "Writing Religion" became as much about religion as it was about writing. Why learn only about the craft of *writing* religion? Why not play along the edges of a *religion* too? Write Christian. Write Hindu. What does it mean to write not only using this or that technique but to write in, or at the edge, of this or that religious practice?

Education by indirection.

Indirectly, the writing course became more of a Zen course than the Zen course was. We sat. We drank tea. We wrote. We shared what we wrote. We trashed what we wrote. We treasured what we wrote. We offered Buddha the fruits of our writing. When celebrating, we blew bubbles over his dozing head. When disappointed, we burned or shredded writing trash.

The writing course was not a proper Buddhism course, but it kept becoming one by indirection and happenstance. Since this was a workshop, not a lecture course, aphorisms and teisho-like utterances popped out on their own accord. In addition, the space of the Ritual Studies Lab had its own mind about such matters, since it has been the scene of several decades of ritual experiment and critique. It, we noticed, seemed to be asking for aphorisms to be posted on the door, painted on the wall, and written in green ink on writers' hands so they would not be forgotten: "Show. Don't tell." This is the standard advice of creative writing teachers. Uttered repeatedly atop round cushions and punctuated by bell ringing and incense burning, the attitude is absorbed from underneath the writerly consciousness. While we debated the placement of commas and jerked misplaced modifiers into line, we also cultivated writing attitudes. Excerpted rightly, writing about writing can easily be made to echo sentiments that we North Americans have learned to associate with Zen:

> Writing is not . . . an art but breathing.
> —Anais Nin

> The ideal view for daily writing, hour on hour, is the blank brick wall of a cold storage warehouse. Failing this, a stretch of sky will do, cloudless if possible.
> —Edna Ferber

> Only the hand that erases can write the true thing.
> —Meister Eckhart

> Every time I sit at my desk, I look at my dictionary, a Webster's Second Unabridged with nine million words in it, and think: All the words I need are in there; they're just in the wrong order.
> –Fran Lebowitz

> We must write where we stand; wherever we do stand, there is life.
> –John Updike

> If you wish to be a writer, write.
> –Epictetus

One reason religions are so poorly understood is that they are so flatly and unevocatively described. One reason they are woodenly described is that we were never taught how to attend carefully and fully to words. Both as students and as teachers we spew them, rushing from term paper to term paper, then article to article. We don't sit with them. Writing in the Lab, we sat with words, sometimes even a word.

When I inquired how many people revised papers submitted for courses, one student raised her hand. For everyone else, revision, editing, and searching for just the right word were foreign activities. So "Writing Religion" became a course about attending, dwelling, pausing, and taking time with words. Words are treasures, we said, yet eminently deletable. Every word is special, even sacred, you could say. Even so, every word is subject to deletion. What we learned about writing in RE400 was not much different from what Zen teachers say about an inhalation or exhalation.

Natalie Goldberg's *Writing down the Bones* is not only a Zen book, it is a period piece and cultural artifact. The stench of popular psychology, Western aestheticism, and the American workshop circuit are all over it. It stinks not only of Zen but of American Zen. Americanized Zen writing is different, very different from Japanese calligraphy, not just in form or content but in fundamental sensibility. But Guatemalan Christianity differs radically from Roman Christianity, and African Caribbean religions differ remarkably from Ashanti religion. So how much does it matter whether the Buddhism taught is North American rather than Japanese or Korean, whether it arrives indirectly in a writing course or directly in a Zen course? They all reek, and they should; that is the nature of acculturation.

Is writing under Goldberg's tutelage "Zen" writing? Or merely American writing? Or turn-of-the-millennium writing? The answer to the question does not matter much. For the purposes of the course what mattered was that students learn to care about writing and then develop a writerly rhythm: attend, discard, treasure; attend, discard, treasure; attend fully, then discard. Have no attachment to a word, phrase, paragraph, or paper, yet write something you treasure passionately. Just remember: Treasuring has a life span. Today's treasure will become tomorrow's discard.

In the Ritual Studies Lab and with Goldberg's assistance we ritualized the act of writing. In other versions of the course, the aim had been the production of a work of verbal art or scholarship. In this version, the aim was to perform the act of writing in a ritualized manner. It just so happened that the ritual idiom was indebted to Zen Buddhism.

At the beginning of the course, I hung a blank scroll on the wall. This is how Ritual Studies Lab courses always begin. I invited students to sign it using traditional Japanese ink and brush. I gave no mini-lecture on calligraphy. "In your own good time," I said, "please sign the scroll, thereby formally entering the course. Write: 'I am a writer,' then sign your name below that."

Most participants sat still. I had made the task of signing in too heavy. After a while, I made the task less onerous: "You may mean whatever you wish by those words: 'I aspire to be a writer. I am hot stuff because I am published. I am a student, therefore I write papers, therefore I am, by definition, a writer.'"

Whatever students meant, they had to discover or invent it in the act of putting brush to scroll. Their first act required them to attend to a signature and to do so with an uncharacteristic intensity. The advice, "Every word in a story or article is like your name signed at the bottom of a cheque," is not much different from the advice, "Let every breath be your last" or "To sit is to die."

When the writing course was over, I felt it a success. When the Zen course ended the same week, I felt it a failure. Where I had intended to teach Zen I had not. Where I had not intended to teach Zen I had. In authoring this autopsy it occurs to me that perhaps I taught neither Zen nor writing but only Pauline theology: That which I would do, I have not done, and that which I would not do, I have done.

I teach Buddhism and I teach writing in unorthodox ways, but not because I think either is special. The arguments for "experiencing" Zen are no stronger than those for experiencing, say, Anishnabe or Muslim religion. The line between teaching and practice is fine, never easy to walk, but it is always worth trying. If I were teaching Christianity, I'd likely have students singing hymns in class. Pressed to defend the practice, I say something like: "Such subjunctive experiences, however complex and dangerous, are a necessary part of teaching and even research."

I do not claim that everyone should teach every course on Buddhism or on writing in this way, only that an embodied, "participatory" pedagogy is a valid form of teaching and learning and that it is not a propagandistic move aimed at making converts.

The quotation marks around "experiencing" and "participatory" are necessary. They signal the crucial subjunctive. An "as-if" marker does not render experience and participation unreal, but it does flag them, suggesting that the reality of the Zen and the writing that I teach is peculiar, even fictive. But fiction, like ritual, has real consequences.

6

Ritualizing September 11

This chapter began as two separate responses to the events of September 11, 2001. The first was written to be delivered publicly at a town hall–style meeting of the university community. The second, an account of a post-9/11 meeting of my "Rites of Passage" course, was written as a private journal entry. I had no intention of publishing either, but versions and fragments of both were borrowed and dispersed by others to peace centers, then, later, to scholars interested in ritual and the media. Eventually, the fragments became a whole and were coupled with a visual presentation. Rapidly, the verbal became visual, and the personal became interpersonal, political, and international.[103]

I hold two passports, one American, one Canadian. Who I am on a given day depends on who is bombing whom and for what reason, good or ill.

On the morning of September 11, my eleven-year-old son got up, put on his stars-and-stripes shirt (a hand-me-down from a Texas cousin), and went off to Empire School, a monument to a political realm once so far-flung that the sun could never quite escape sight of its flag. My wife and I had not turned on the news yet, and our son had not worn the ragged shirt for months.

Then came the news.

Later, in the afternoon, unsure how a stars-and-stripes shirt would play out on a Canadian school ground, I met my son to walk him home from school. He knew already. The kids and teachers had observed a minute of silence. Ritually speaking, they were ahead of me. No, he wasn't upset. He wanted to skateboard. So my parental worry shifted. No longer was it about how to play down the collapse of the towers so he would be less afraid. Rather, it was how to play up the event so it might become real rather than fictional for him and his sister. So we parents sat with the children. We watched and talked and lit candles and invited people over. We put out some special objects, hoping to bridge the gap between a televised September 11 and disastrous reality. We ritualized in order to render the event real.

Ritualizing Us and Them

After September 11, 2001, reporters surmised that disasters remind people of fundamentals, bringing out the best in all of us. The roles assigned to ritual were that of wrapping victims in a blanket of comfort and of replacing factionalism with solidarity. In the wake of 9/11, friends and relatives of victims found comfort in encountering other bereaved people at the site of the demolished World Trade Center and in joining mourners at memorials, both on and off the World Wide Web. Even the French were reported as saying publicly, "We are Americans too." The Democrats, who, the day before 9/11, doubted whether Bush was really the president at all, stopped bemoaning their sorry fate and joined the Republicans in "getting behind the president."

But there is more to disaster ritual than comfort and solidarity. For one thing, ritualizing continues long after rites end. September 11 has become a sacred time, a ritual date. If you don't think so, listen to the incessant incantation: 9/11, 9/11. Everyone repeats it, gets the allusion, feels its weight. The date, utterly symbolic in force, binds "us" together and, in so doing, defines "them." The date symbolizes who "we" are and who "they" are. It created, and continues to create, a shared memory, a holiday. 9/11 was born at breakfast time without the gods or ancestors having revealed this awe-ful holy day, without the holy books having prescribed it. Not quite a divine given, it is nevertheless difficult to speak of this sacred day as a social "construction," even though the event was planned to a T.

The terrorist attack was ritualized. In the newspaper we read translated excerpts from the preparation manual. It was a liturgical text prescribing the men's activities: Shave closely. Polish your shoes. Wear tight-fitting clothes. Chant verses. Visualize your goal. Anticipate your reward.

"They" ritualized the attack. "We" ritualized the counterattack by flying flags and lighting candles. A moment of silence here, a moment of silence there— several days running. Again. Then again and again. Suddenly, the higher powers were everywhere invoked: "God bless America" (even in Canada, where "his" grace is more thinly scattered).

Flags, flags, flags. Here a flag, there a flag, everywhere a flag. Prayer flags— not Tibetan, not Zuni, but pure, "good old" American flags. Wave them and you'll be a better one. Wave it and you'll know who you are. And aren't. Wave it and you'll know who's for you. And against you. There are only two choices. Those who are not our friends are our enemies. God is on our side. Through our homeland runs the axis mundi; through theirs, the axis of evil.

"They" wage holy war, jihad. A new word has gate-crashed the English language, likely other languages too. It has entered with such force and pervasiveness that we don't bother to italicize it. (Usually, foreign words have to pay homage, serve time in italics before being let out of jail to run freely off the tip of the tongue.)

"They" wage a particularly fanatical kind of war: holy war. When we utter the phrase, we put the "holy" in quotation marks. We don't really believe jihad is holy, no matter what "they" think or say. (The quotation marks are everywhere. Like the date, the quotes and the authorities are thick in the air. You can pluck, then fling or chant them.)

But think about it, have we North Americans ever fought a war that was *not* holy? God "gave" this land to "us." If our "boys" die over there, they are not on sacred ground. Here is sacred ground. So bring them home in bags and flags, so they may rest in peace.

Our wars are no less holy than theirs—just holy in a different way. Holy war: war for which no price is too high. Holy war—the kind that is waged when God is on our side.

Televised Commemorations of 9/II

In Canada, television fed viewers three national ways of post-9/II mourning: American, English, and Canadian. Viewers wondered aloud why they did not see other ceremonies—Japanese, German, or Dutch. The American ceremony, like the British rite, was held captive; it was indoors, in a church. It was "interfaith" American style, which is to say, the liturgical idiom was that of Christianized civil religion. Buddhists, Sikhs, Jews, and Hindus in attendance were required to pay homage to the one particular American-Christian God. Buddhists, Sikhs, Jews, and Hindus were dragooned into singing "The Battle Hymn of the Republic." The prayers, like the hymns, were generic civil-Christian ones.

In Britain, they sang more and talked less. Instead of a naval choir, there was a boys' choir. The singers' prepubescent innocence was as clear as a crystal goblet struck with a golden spoon. (In due time they will change; no longer choir material, they will be eligible to fight against evil, the way real men do.) The British rite, like the American one, was sacralized by the use of ecclesiastical space and clerical garb. The British, like the Americans, know evil when they see it, so they too sang "The Battle Hymn of the Republic." Its stridency echoed across the Atlantic. The British sang "The Star-Spangled Banner," even though it had been, historically speaking, the war cry of their rebellious offspring.

In stark contrast to the American and British rites, the Canadian rite, hardly seen or mentioned in U.S. media, was held outdoors in front of Parliament. Sixty-five thousand people participated directly in the ceremony, a high proportion of the population and therefore surprising in comparison with the American or British liturgies. In Canada no privileged indoor crowd displaced a liturgically disenfranchised outdoor crowd. There were no hymns and no prayers. After all, whose god stands so clearly above the others that all of us should pray to "him"? The crowd stood for three full minutes of silence. For three minutes CBC television sat silent, its cameras nervously cutting here and there. Silence, though ritually venerable, does not air well; it worries directors who fret over attention spans.

Not in My Back Yard

At the university where I teach, a town hall meeting was called. In preparing for it, I queried my colleagues in religious studies about what perspectives our discipline might contribute. There was a testy internal debate. Some thought it obscene even to consider a public discussion replete with scholarly perspectives and technical terms. Such a meeting would become a pool of empty words; we should wait a year. Now was not the time.

With my departmental colleagues' warnings in my ears, I proposed to the university's organizing committee that we ritualize the event, frame the words with elemental acts capable of grounding the talk, reminding participants of the gravity and complexity of the situation. The proposal was rejected: We don't do that kind of thing here. Here, ritual is out of place; we have no ritual tradition, no ceremonial vocabulary, on which to draw. We are a university, a place of higher learning.

Ignoring the outlay of time and money spent on orientation and commencement ceremonies, the committee's chair declared that constructing and enacting ceremonies should be left to religious communities. So instead of responding ritually, the organizers invited a music group to perform and professors to speak.

That, of course, was not ritual.

I seem constantly to rediscover what I already know about my community, my workplace, and the culture: Ritually speaking, we are profoundly disabled. Our gestural, postural, and symbolic vocabulary is pinched, poverty-stricken. We reach for candles or flowers and then dead-end; that's it. We've exhausted our ritual resources. So we turn over the problem to professionals—to clergy and undertakers. But they were no better prepared for September 11 than us ordinary lay folk. They reached for what was nearby: flags, national anthems, military garb, and military cadences.

Unable to construct a community rite, and unwilling to join the nationalistic one, my only choice was to ritualize the talk I was asked to deliver at the town hall meeting. I am a ritual studies scholar. What should a ritual studies scholar say on the occasion of a disaster? Longing for a richer, more layered, more critical vocabulary, one that is not only political but also incantatory, I uttered these words:

Eleven Words for September: An Incantatory Glossary

Symbol:
an object fraught, pregnant, laden,
and capable of acting.
Symbol: a thing, action, or word
bearing many,
often contradictory, meanings.
Symbol: a multivocal device
speaking in many voices.
Symbol:
    Tower of World Trade,
    Tower of Babel.
    They all fall down.
    Tower of too much talk,
    Towers of too much money,
    Tower of arrogance.
The tower is always *over there.*
It could not possibly be *here.*
    Could it?

Myth:
a symbol dressed up in an image or a narrative
Myth: "Wanted, Dead or Alive."
Myth: "Axis of Evil"
    We are cowboys, grade B; they are Indians, grade F.
    We are Christians; they are Moors . . .
Myth: the stories we tell ourselves during the dark nights of the
    global soul
Myth: the values and images and tales we are unable, or unwilling,
    to question
Myth: the set of assumptions that underwrite us,
    on which we stand, like the ground:
    We, the free world, stand on guard for thee.

Sacred text:
    a myth in a book,
    a myth of a book:
the Koran says, the Gita says, the Bible says . . .
The king says, the pope says, the scholar says, CNN says . . .
Sacred text: A document that does not welcome editors.

Sacred text:
    A text that does not go out of print.
    An utterance to live for,
    a document to die for,
    die with,
        die from.

Ritual: a symbol embodied and enacted.
Ritual: a red, white, and blue ribbon on a custodian's lapel
Ritual: the Stars and Stripes torn between the teeth and set aflame
Ritual: the color guard, guarding the president standing by the priest
Ritual: the turbaned gathering of the Taliban to debate the fate of the
    nation
Ritual: the un-turbaned gathering of scholars in ivory towers
    to debate and bemoan the fate of the world.

Performative utterance:
    using words to do things.
Performative utterance:
    words that not only describe
    but also effect,
    words that transform
Performative utterance: "I pronounce you husband and wife."
Performative utterance: "This is war."

Good & Evil:
the fate of the world
held in the balance
of two hands alone;
Good & Evil:
the ultimate divide
inscribed into the ideologies and ethics
of the several religions
and the multitude of nations.
Good & Evil:
The most gaping fundamental abyss
into which all the others fall,
chasm cascading into chasm:
us and them,
East and West,
Muslim and Christian,
men and women,
terrorists and
    nice people like us.

Religion:
> that which underwrites
> deep or elemental concerns.

Religion:
> All that is implied in the phrase,

"No price is too great."

Religion:
> All that drives people to war.

Religion:
> All that binds up people's wounds after war.

(Religions are not only that to which they aspire,
but also that which they evoke.)

Religion:
> What would we do without it?

Religion:
> How can we survive it?

Civil religion:
> that peculiar variant
> of public piety

not confined to religious institutions.

Civil religion:

Let the Americans stand and sing "The Battle Hymn of the Republic."
> "He is trampling out the vintage where the grapes of *wrath* are
> stored.
>
> He hath loosed the fateful lightning of his *terrible* swift sword."

Let the British stand and join the Americans in singing "The Battle
Hymn of the Republic."
> "He has sounded forth the trumpet that shall *never* call retreat."

Civil religion:

that form of public piety discreetly closeted in Canada.

Let us mourn,
out in the open air,
without hymn,
without prayer.
Three minutes of silence,
standing,
Please.

Passage:
A moment,
a transition slicing time in half,
creating a divide,
a distinct BEFORE and AFTER.

Passage:
Life before
and life after
the fall of the great towers.
Passage:
The moment
of the loss of innocence
and entry into experience.
Passage:
the moment
after which there is no return
except in symbol, myth, and ritual.

Scapegoat:
The kid offered up.
The scapegoat is a kid,
the bleating one
sent out to starvation
or slaughter
on our behalf.
Scapegoating:
He hit me first!
No, no, he did it!
He deserves it;
he's not one of us!
Scapegoat:
Thank god for that kid.
Thank god, I am not that kid.
The scapegoat will not escape;
it carries our complicity
into the wilderness.

Peace:
The state of being reconciled,
connected with all that pulses and breathes.
Peace: What used to be.
Peace: How things were yesterday
and might be tomorrow
but are not today.
Peace:
the time when
each of us says yes
to whatever and whoever is Other.

Peace:
Even those who do not pray,
    pray for it.

The house divided over these words. Some left the university's town hall meeting wishing that I had spoken more plainly and accessibly. Others left saying the words should be published. To my mind both responses missed the point.

Elemental Gestures

The next evening I baited the students in my "Rites of Passage" course. We were just starting the death section of the course, so I asked, "The time since September 11—has that been like an extended funeral rite for you? For the nation?" They weren't sure.

I continued to probe: "Did you 'do' Diana? Or 'get into' other televised funeral rites—Mother Teresa? Pierre Trudeau?" They were too young for me to ask about Martin Luther King or John F. Kennedy.

Some confessed they had been taken by the funerals of Diana and Trudeau, so I teased them out further: "Won't you be a peculiar generation, if your most formative ritual experiences are televised funerals and memorials? Compared with funerals that you attend bodily, are televised death rites less real? Or more real?"

At the end of the discussion I posed what turned out to be the most evocative question: "When there is a great imponderable (an event so profoundly questioning that anything remotely resembling an 'answer' sounds false), what is your impulse?"

A young man's hand shot up instantly. "To go home," he said. "I landed in San Francisco on September 11, and all I could think about was getting back home to Canada."

A woman replied, "I just wanted to drive to New York City. I felt removed and wanted to go there, to participate."

Another added, "I become quiet, very solitary."

Then another confessed, "I flipped. After September 11, I almost lost my faith. My family worried that I'd quit school. But then we talked. We just talked and talked and talked until I came back to normal. Talk, that's what I need when there is a disaster."

The actions reported by the students were not formal ceremonies like the ones we had been discussing in class or seeing on television, but they were ritualized responses. Or, if that way of putting it seems like stretching it, then let's say that these are the impulses (go home, go to the center, pull away, go nuts, get together) on the basis of which rites of dying and healing are often constructed.

9/11 was a teaching moment if there ever was one. The surrounding weeks were fraught with pedagogical possibilities. People on the street were telling the media: "Everything is different. After September 11, everything is different; the world has forever changed." These words sounded like a formal definition for a rite of passage: a deep transformation, a moment with a before and after so distinct that one can never return to the previous state.

So, even though the class was designed as a lecture and discussion course, we ritualized. I prepared a few volunteers and they performed.

Elemental Gestures: A Script for a Rite

Setting: On a draped or matted table in the center of the room:
a mound of sand, earth, or stones; a bowl or small sandbox to
contain them
a pitcher of water; a bowl to pour it in
a candle or lamp and matches
a piece of fruit or a flower; a knife
incense and matches or a wind instrument

Participant #1 introduces the actions with words calling attention to the purpose of the gathering or to one or more of the following themes: the emptiness as well as the importance of human speech and social gatherings; the preciousness of the moment and the importance of small things; the pervasiveness of trouble.

The choice of words should fit the occasion and reflect the constituency of those gathered. The words below are only examples.

[Alternatively, no words are said and no introduction is given, especially if the rite is enacted repeatedly by the same group, in which case the actions are sometimes preceded and accompanied by words; sometimes not.]

"Buddhists say that all suffering, and all release from suffering, is now—in this very moment and in this very place."
"The Gospels say that not even a sparrow can fall without divine notice and divine compassion."

[etc.]

Participant #2 approaches the table, scoops up a handful of earth in both hands, speaks the words, then sprinkles it slowly into the bowl, on the floor around the table, or onto a flat stone or board. This and each subsequent gesture is slowly paced, enacted simply and without pomp or deliberate stylization.

[Alternatively, each participant, repeating the words, pours sand into the hands of another participant until all hands are soiled.]

"This is earth.
May it ground our words and actions
and continue sustaining the multitude of life forms
around the world."

Participant #3 approaches the table, lifts the pitcher, and, speaking the words, pours the water into a bowl, slowly, so the splashing can be heard.

[*Alternatively, each participant, repeating the words, pours water into the hands of another participant until all hands are washed. This alternative requires a large towel.*]

"This is water.
May it cleanse us
and refresh flagging spirits everywhere."

Participant #4 approaches the table, strikes a match, lights the candle, and speaks the words.

[*Alternatively, each participant, repeating the words, lights a candle from the preceding candle. This alternative requires enough candles for everyone.*]

"This is light.
May it clarify decisions in high places
and enlighten choices everywhere."

Participant #5 approaches the table, picks up the flower or fruit (or other living thing), and says,

"This is living . . .
but not for long.
[*The fruit or flower is cut.*]
May its short life
and ours
fructify the planet."

[*If fruit is used, it and the knife are passed so the fruit can be cut and eaten.*
If a flower is used, it is merely passed along with the knife.]

Participant #6 approaches the table, takes the wind instrument, speaks the words, and begins to play:

[*Alternatively, incense is lit from the candle and blown into the air.*]

"This is air, human breath.
May it suffuse all that throbs,
　　permeate all who suffer,
　　　　surround all who breathe,
　　　　　　and all who have ceased to breathe."

Participant #1 says, "The rite is finished. We are ready to _____
[talk, work, eat, etc., whatever the main activity is.]

Ritual Criticism

The actions of this tiny rite are elemental, not the property of a particular religious or ethnic group, not the product of an explicit tradition. The words do not mention 9/11, even though 9/11 was their occasion. Of course, the actions were not perfectly generic, which is to say, universal. Nothing ever is. The aim was to create a pause in which attentiveness could deepen and a sense of connectedness could occur before discussion, debate, and other divisive moves happened. The rite was constructed as a frame inside of which different kinds of things could transpire.

After we enacted the brief gestures, I invited response and critique—in effect, transforming the meditative pause into a ritual demonstration. I explained that people need spaces in which it is possible to reflect on rituals; otherwise, we can abuse them or be abused by them.

After several minutes of appreciative but polite discussion, a mature student from Six Nations Reserve raised his hand, "Professor, I don't mean to insult you or anything, but could, maybe, that have been a little hokey?"

Other students gasped or held their breath, but I laughed, "Sure. Of course, it could. But why? Say more."

"Well," he said, "you made it up, right?"

"Right."

"Well, there was no tradition or anything. And you are not a medicine man or a priest. The whole thing was artificial."

I agreed. Rites whose constructedness is known or visible can be awkward or unconvincing. Hokey.

"How do traditions start? I asked him.

"I don't know; you're the professor," he said. More laughter.

I responded with a story and mini-lecture that went something like this:

When the Montreal Massacre occurred on December 6, 1989, at
l'École polytechnique de Montréal and fourteen women lay dead at
the hands of an antifeminist murderer, people at universities had
debates about ritually marking the occasion. Some said, We don't

have any ritual resources with which to handle traumatic public events. Others said, We should keep our mouths shut; words at such times are obscene or embarrassing. But in the end, many students and faculty ritualized their awkwardness and embarrassing silence. We did so because we felt we had to. After December 6 we invented a commemorative ceremonial tradition, and it continues to this day. The commemoration lives largely at universities, not in civil or ecclesiastical institutions, and we continue to reinvent it. Universities do have rites.

Ritual inventiveness around September 11 has been forced upon us. Your people too have been forced to invent ceremonies. I am thinking, for instance, of repatriation legislation, which returned Native burial remains to First Nations people, most of whom had no rites for reburying bones long held in museums. Ritual creativity became a necessity.

So, yes, when we first construct rites, invent a tradition, if you will, it seems silly, and we all become self-conscious. But rites start somewhere. And right now ceremonial innovations, borrowing from the past, are transpiring as Americans and British and Canadians, as well as students and faculty around the world struggle to transpose their emotions and politics into gestures, postures, and ritual texts. If you don't want to be drafted into someone else's politics and religiosity, then your only option is either to ensconce yourself in a tradition you trust or to use your imagination to choreograph what you are driven to enact.

Later in the year, the student who raised the question and dared to say what others were afraid to say presented his own account of a constructed rope-climbing rite used by Mohawks and other Six Nations people. He had grasped the point that even among the most traditional people, new situations require ritual invention.

9/11 began with a ritually driven attack. The event was followed up by a ritualized declaration of war on terrorism. Meanwhile, searching for bodies and sifting rubble at site of the World Trade Center was ritually conducted and ritually concluded on May 31, 2002. It became virtually impossible *not* to approach the site in a ritual manner—not so much in response to what *was* there but to what was *not* there. In the face of a looming, animated absence, ritualizing necessarily becomes liturgical, a way of negotiating ultimate things.

"Elemental Gestures," a rite that could not be enacted in public university space, but which hatched anyway in the more protected sanctity of the classroom, is now circulating in peace centers. It is being rewritten, adapted, dismantled, and reassembled. It's a small, paltry thing, but it is an alternative to waving flags. 9/11, Americans said, drove them back to the basics, by which they meant country, family, security, the Stars and Stripes, the American way of life. "Elemental Gestures" suggests that other things—air, water, soil—are even more basic, because they are more widely shared and more profoundly endangered by both terrorism and the war on terrorism.

Neither "Eleven Words for September" nor "Elemental Gestures" is representative of the ways Americans and Canadians responded to 9/11. Both pieces were performed acts of ritual criticism, and they precipitated as many questions as answers: In the face of terrorist disaster, who are "we," and who are "they"? In the face of a disaster, with whom is it most urgent to express solidarity—"fellow countrymen" or the planet? In the face of disaster, what subtexts seep from beneath pious declarations uttered in public?

There is not only acute danger in disasters (towers falling, planes dropping, floods rising, wars breaking out) but also the chronic danger of ritually sanctioned self-righteousness. The danger in disaster rituals is that they can underwrite a desperate obsession with declaratives and imperatives: The truth is . . . The truth shall be . . . The danger is that disaster rituals can buttress an impatience with questions and an unwillingness to abide with ambiguity or uncertainty.

No one can deny that ritualizing the disaster of September 11 provided consolation and created solidarity, but it also suppressed dissent, stoked the fires of nationalism, and consolidated a move to the political and religious right.

Unless they wish to embrace their own co-option, ritual studies scholars must become as adept at analyzing disastrous rituals as they are at analyzing disaster rituals. Assuming such a posture is risky, but so is severing ritual theory and analysis from ritual criticism. It is easy to engage in retrospective ritual criticism of the 1934 Nuremburg rallies or the 1936 Olympics in Berlin. The real challenge is to think critically and analytically in the midst of politicized ritualizing rather than after it.

7

Sequestering Sacred Space

Initially, I declined the invitation to present the plenary address that eventuated in this chapter. The invitation was extended by the steering committee of the Dumbarton Oaks Byzantine Symposium, Sacred Screens: The Origins, Development, and Diffusion of the Byzantine Sanctuary Barrier.[104] *The subject matter was beyond the range of my competence. In addition, the topic seemed arcane. However, as I explored the range of ritual screening devices, they became metaphors for fundamental ritual processes.*

My official job description charges me to cover a domain tagged "religion and the arts in contemporary North America." In dutiful obedience to this daunting commission, I have acted as a consultant for WordBridge and for the Sundance Institute.[105] These are labs where actors, directors, and dramaturgs incubate plays. Nontheatrical, or "wildcard," consultants are often brought in as well. As a consequence of such consultative research, my reflections on sacred screens were not rooted in the iconoclasm and iconophilia of the Byzantine world but rather in turn-of-the-millennium, North American theater labs.

In 2001, consulting on several WordBridge plays suffused with ritual motifs, I encountered Jeff Wirth, an improv artist. He and I met for the first time a few minutes before taking on our first play together.

"Have you read it?" Jeff whispered.

"Sure," I said. "Several times. Have you?"

"Nope," he replied, without a trace of shame.

The crowd of theater professionals began to move inside the studio. Jeff entered, hesitated, then turned on his heels.

"Where are you going?" I asked.

"Outside," he replied.

I assumed he was embarrassed about not having read the play manuscript.

Now seated at a table, ready to read it aloud for the first time, were the actors. Behind them was a large set of sliding glass doors partially obscured by a black curtain. As the actors began to read the play, *Polar Bears on U.S. 41*,[106] Jeff's thick glasses gradually became visible. From behind the sliding glass barrier, he was peering in at the play from outside. Occasionally, his antics would evoke audience laughter, leaving the actors puzzled, wondering what was funny in the lines they had just read.

Jeff watched, quietly and intently, shifting his position every now and then. A few of us audience members began to squirm as it dawned on us that, by gazing at our faces and postures, Jeff was turning us into actors. I envied him a little. Whereas scholars are expected to behave, improv artists get to play the ritual fool.

Later, after the play reading had concluded and the crowd was mingling, Jeff sauntered back into the studio.

"What on earth were you doing out there?" I asked him.

"Ahhhh . . . , well," he said, "preserving my theatrical virginity. If I learn too much, too fast, I miss what's essential."

There was a pause, then: "Hey, Grimes, where d'ya think the play's center of energy is?"

I hesitated. "I'd have to speculate," I said, a little wary.

"And?" he urged.

I said I supposed the center of energy was offstage—with the polar bears, who are wandering on the highway in a Wisconsin snowstorm. (Because of their color, they are in danger of being run over by cars.) No bear, I said, ever appears onstage. No character ever suggests that the bears are the "real" actors, since they loom over, rather than participate in, the play. Their presence is metaphysical. I thought he would wince at the word, but he did not.

Then, I hedged my bet by warning Jeff that the playwright may well think otherwise. I also suggested, a little testily, that if he had read the play, he could have answered his own question.

Polar Bear

Then it was time. The playwright was coffeed up, the director was ready, and it was our turn. What would these two wildcards do? We had no sooner reconvened than Jeff, not prone to wait for authoritative scripts, much less defer to scholars, snatched my backpack, put it on, covered it with a baggy sweatshirt, and began to lumber around the room. He *became* the polar bear. Without rubrics, plot, or direction, he roared and ate and slept and farted and swam and gobbled salmon, providing the actors and the rather overwhelmed young playwright with a truckload of fish for thought.

After an hour or so, the bear, now caged in a zoo, began responding aggressively to the bidding of a little girl up on the catwalk. She desperately wanted the beast to climb out of the pit and over the barbed wire fence. But suddenly, two actors-become-cops shot the beast dead at her feet.

The bear crashed heavily to the floor and expired.

The polar bear was about to pull off his improvised mask and hump in order to re-become Jeff Wirth, when, under the force of divine inspiration, I pressed his head back to the floor and whispered in his ear, "Your life is not finished yet; stay put."

I, after all, was the appointed court ritualist, and I had not yet earned my keep. So we conducted a funeral, which not only laid the polar bear to rest—may he forever roar in peace—but also ensured his spiritual and artistic continuation forever and ever, amen.

The made-up words and gestures left some actors crying—not actor tears but real tears. As the shift from acting to ritualizing deepened, the salty drops sprang up in surprising quantities. No one was entirely sure how to respond to this intrusion of hyperreality into fictionality.[107] By the end of that year's lab, though, some were paying proper homage to education-by-unlearning, to going forward with sideways moves, to seeing through glass doors, darkly.

Doors, Curtains, and Screens

For most scholars the gods lurk in details; for ritual studies scholars, sometimes in quite ordinary details. So I return to a tiny detail of the scene I have painted, namely, the sliding glass door. During an actual play, a door transparent to exotic Florida birds strutting and preening outside, a glaring piece of glass through which an intruder might gawk at the action in this theatrical incubation chamber, would not have escaped notice. An alert stage manager would have pulled the black curtain over the door, rendering it invisible.

However, during this particular script-focused lab, the door had been ignored. Audience members, almost all of them theater people, would surely exercise good sense and ignore the door. They would pay attention to the actors, just as ordinary worshipers, also graced with good sense, would know to focus attention on icons rather than on icon screens.

What difference does this apparent oversight make—namely, that the backstage curtain was not pulled, revealing a set of sliding glass doors? One of the great difficulties in studying ritual is that participants, as well as scholars, miss the utter ordinariness that suffuses rites, even those that are formal and elevated.

So a typical ritual studies tactic, especially when investigating things sacred, is to search out the ordinary beneath the special and sacred.[108]

However true it is that altar screens embody deities and saints, mediate between heaven and earth, and visually constellate cosmic mysteries, it is also true that they are merely wood, stone, and plaster. They are ordinary items of material culture, not altogether different from sliding glass doors through which breeze blows or freight enters.[109] Even ordinary doors, like gilded gods' gates, simultaneously barricade and invite passage. Even ordinary doors can mystify things by framing—which is to say, by revealing, concealing, and focusing the actions of performers.[110]

Even theologians insist on *dis*identifying (as well as identifying) sacralized objects with *the* sacred, so one is not being iconoclastic, or even disrespectful, by teasing out a comparison that reminds us of the ordinariness of screens and doors.[111] Comparison is inevitable, and when working with religious phenomena, strategic comparison requires ordinary examples alongside exalted ones.

Popular conceptions often construe ritual as, by definition, religious, thereby putting it in a cultural domain different from that of theater and the arts. In ritual studies, however, liturgical enactment and theatrical performance are construed not only as different but also as akin.[112]

Ritual studies is not wed to a particular theory, but since its inception in 1977, it has been closely allied with religious studies, anthropology, and performance studies. As a result, much ritual studies research is ethnographic, drawing heavily on participant observation and interview. It is also doggedly comparative, committed to charting cross-cultural similarities and differences.

In field research on ritual, observation and interview are the usual correctives against stereotyping, projecting, and other ways of misunderstanding data. However, before arriving at a field site, it is crucial to know what one knows, to disgorge what one takes for granted. In short, self-knowledge, not just knowledge of the other, is essential to ethnographic research. As a classroom teacher, I encourage students bound for the field to imagine, or better, act out, what they expect to encounter. They record these imaginings and later, check them against what they actually find.

So let us imagine. Pretend that you are as ignorant as I am about screening devices. Let us say you hardly know what the terms "iconostasis" and "tramezzo" refer to. Suppose you do not know what such things are for, and you cannot imagine why scholars of things Byzantine or liturgical spend their time writing entire books about mere backdrop. What would be your ignorant-outsider answers to this question: What *might* a screening device do?

These are among my guesses:

Aesthetic answers:
- provide something pleasing to look at
- provide a frame to look through

- cordon off actions, hiding, half-hiding, revealing, or focusing them
- change the quality of sound and light
- select for certain kinds of action and not other kinds
- create distance, a here-space and a there-space

Practical answers:

- serve as a support, for example, for pictures and statues
- divide a big space into smaller sections
- provide carpenters with work
- provide painters with a task
- keep "the ladies" busy with holy cleaning
- reduce the visibility of unsightly things

Social-political answers:

- grant certain classes of people access[113]
- keep other classes out
- protect those behind the barrier
- engender or enforce a hierarchy
- offer a substitute ("Since you are not permitted to see that, watch this instead")[114]

Religious answers:

- make hierophanies possible, actual, or apprehensible
- incarnate powers that would otherwise seem absent or ineffectual
- concretize a topocosm (a "this place" that functions as a prism for "everyplace")

Ritual answers:

- back up, evoke, or continue liturgical actions
- constellate a gestalt with a center and periphery, rendering some liturgical actions more important than others
- make one performance locale more valuable or important than some other
- provide a contemplative focus for wandering attention

What would you add? Or subtract? Or edit? The particulars of the list are less important than disrupting the impression that altar screens have only a couple of functions, that of rendering mystery apprehensible and that of mystifying sources of authority (thereby keeping a priestly class of men in power).

This list of possibilities would likely have to be recast if one were to carry it into an encounter with the particulars of a specific liturgical era and site. Even so, the act of imagining helps form a ritual studies attitude, which likely differs from that of a liturgical theologian, art historian, or archaeologist.

A ritual studies approach:

- avoids either/or alternatives, for example, either mystery or politics
- makes space for multiple points of view, for the perspectives of several classes of participants. It is not content with only theological or solely official voices; it inquires into ordinary, folk meanings

- attends to all kinds of ritualizing and performative activity, not just to canonical actions in liturgies
- treats objects and spaces as animators of the behavior that transpires around them; objects and spaces are not rendered as inert backgrounds for human activity[115]
- implies methods and values that may evoke dissonance when brought into contact with "the native point of view"

I am no historian of Byzantine art, nor am I a theologian of Orthodox persuasion. But ethnographically inclined religious studies scholar that I am, I ransacked such writings, trying to figure out how to speak the language. I began asking ignorant, outside-observer questions: What do the "natives" (scholars in fields other than my own) call these barrier-things? Are there clear definitions and compelling examples?

As I read major works in these "other" fields, I did what one does in field research: compile a glossary. I was delighted with the sonorous, chantable terms: balustrade, rood screen, monumental gateway, god's gate, firmament. There were ordinary labels too: parapet, grille, screening apparatus, screening paraphernalia, portal barrier, gate, veil, screen, chancel, perimeter fence. And then there were the imported exotic foreign words, laden with etymological milk: *soreg, mechitzah, devir, paroket, katapetasma, templon, temenos,* iconostasis, *fastigium, tramezzo.* Finally, I happened upon some wonderfully au courant jargon, words one could drop at wine and cheese parties: substitutive spectacle, interposed visual spectacle, architectonic membrane.

The "foreign" language of art history and allied disciplines was so enthralling that I became disoriented. Which words, I wondered, were synonyms, and which actually referred to different things? Which things, I wondered, are at the center, and which are on the periphery of scholarly discourse about screening paraphernalia?

The "indigenous" term that most fueled my reflections was one of the simpler ones: veil. The altar screen is a kind of veil? Perhaps the image struck me so forcefuly because hijabs were much in the media then. The altar screen *is* a veil? Or just historically derived from the temple veil? Or merely *like* a veil?

Soon I could not distinguish pairs that were synonyms from pairs that were the result of metaphoric equations. If an altar screen is a veil, shielding and shrouding, can a veil be an altar screen? And if a screen is a veil, does that mean it functions like a mask? And if even a poor Protestant chancel functions something like a mask, is not looking *through* a mask (from the back) a different experience from looking *at* the mask (from the front)? A comparativist must surely recall how Apache and Hopi kids who, after being thoroughly *en*chanted by watching masked spirts dance, are soundly *dis*enchanted by being forced to look through the eye holes of sacred masks.[116]

To gain comparative perspective I began to pose crude questions: "What are other things non-Byzantine that define a sacred space, have doors in them, and that people paint sacred pictures on?" One answer: a plains tepee, of course. Made of skin, it becomes a canvas for icons, pictures that not only depict but also embody.

Once I grasped the connection between a veil and an iconostasis, then between an iconostasis and a teepee, other examples began to cascade. In Calgary's Glenbow Museum, as well as in the Canadian Museum of Civilization, sacred pipes of First Nations people are put on display in glass cases. Native people sometimes find the curatorial ritual of enclosure disconcerting. Whereas white people say they are protecting pipes from deterioration induced by oily, greedy human hands, Native people say sacred pipes are alive and that glass cases are not good for living—therefore dying and deteriorating—beings. The paradox of enclosing sacra in glass cases is that holiness is trapped in, while observers are trapped out, reduced to voyeurs.[117]

The paradox of a sanctuary is that it not only keeps the uninitiated out, it also traps the initiated in. In Miguel de Unamuno's story "St. Immanuel the Good, Martyr," the priest masturbates behind closed doors, then goes, hands unwashed, to serve communion.[118] As he hands people bread, they have no idea what else they are receiving.

Closed doors and less-than-transparent screening incubate mystery, for sure, but they also closet away sin and cover up abuse. There is no way that a room divider can divide a room into only one space. Whatever shuts out necessarily shuts in.

Once the notion of ritual screening is softened under the impact of repeated comparative moves, one begins to notice how ritual authorities, even when they stroll outside sanctuaries, still carry portable curtains with them in the form of collars, rings, or gowns.

Gestural Screening

Students of artistic and ritual framing devices could benefit from expanding the repertoire of objects classified in the same bin as altar screens. In addition, they should attend to acts of screening as well.

Most of my colleagues, kindly folk, sit behind their desks and face the door. They can see people pass, greet them, and earn teaching awards in recognition of their open-door policy. When a student enters a faculty office staged in this manner, the desk is between the teacher and the student. The faculty member rocks back, while the student leans in, elbows on desk.[119]

Being of the cantankerous school, and deeply desirous of writing time, I inhabit my office a little differently. I face the window, turning my back on people outside the door, rendering it, perversely, a kind of sanctuary barrier. But when a student enters, I swivel around. Even without a room divider, the gesture of swiveling divides the room—first this way, then that. Once I swivel, however, there is no desk between the student and me.

Divergent messages are encoded in these two different ways of setting the professorial office scene. They are distinctly different ways of performing one's accessibility and authority. They dictate different rhythms of screening oneself from the world and then reconnecting with it.

Perhaps you see where I am headed now. One can divide a space with a mere gesture; you do not need walls or room dividers or rails. Because of the nature of the human body, sectoring happens, even when there is no altar screen, glass case, or desk between an actor and audience. The human body is quite enough; and clothed, it is doubly enough.[120]

A piece of clothing, a thin layer of skin, or a mere swiveling gesture can act as a screening device that blocks or filters entry. Like an earlobe or a T-shirt, a gesture flung into the air or inscribed reverently above a dying person enacts a screen on which it is possible to post a portrait of oneself or an icon of some sacred other.[121] If the likeness has been ritually executed, duly honoring the conventions, observers may even be inspired to pay homage to the image flashed upon a gestural screen. The image will have become a metaphoric embodiment—a tangible positing of identity and difference.[122] In such a drastic state, there is no difference, at least in the moment of the devotional act, no difference between the icon and the iconized.

Conceptual Dividers

Ritual partitions, then, may be architectural, but they may be sartorial or gestural as well. In fact, screens may be completely immaterial; they may be purely conceptual. To define something—a space, a word, a field of study—is a way of dividing up territory. Classificatory boundaries, like shared New England fences or Orthodox iconostases, both connect and divide up the shards of a culture.[123] The resulting whole, variously imagined as a grid, a system, or a tapestry, maps out a cosmology that can be strikingly consistent or powerfully dissonant.

Any means of ordering or classifying, whether explicit or implicit, creates a set of conceptual screens. Although less tangible than altar rails and room dividers, epistemological screens—whether constructed of abstract ideas or mental images—are no less determinative of action than physical barriers are. Consider the slashes between these pairs: black/white, east/west, good/evil. Each pair creates two conceptual zones with a slash, a strip of nobody's land, down the middle. The slash dividing these two *conceptual* zones operates like a sacredly guarded barrier. Such a boundary divides and is divisive. People kill each other over partitions they cannot see: Northern Ireland/the Republic of Ireland; the West Bank/the East Bank.

Sets of polar distinctions organized into cultural cosmologies or religious traditions can be diagrammatically represented. As anthropologist Mary Douglas characterizes the grid of Leviticus, creatures, such as pigs, falling upon a taxonomic boundary (that is, across adjacent classificatory spaces), are treated as ritually impure, inedible, even evil.[124]

As I am playing it out, then, the Byzantine icon screen is but an example of a more widespread, utterly ordinary, quite political, necessarily theatrical human activity, that of partitioning and enclosing. Of course, one could define "iconostasis" in such a way as to deny the connections and similarities between it and other kinds of screens. One could insist on its distinctiveness, therefore upon the need to attend exclusively to its historical and cultural specificity. But if we did only that, we would be hedging and cordoning our subject matter like academic priests, would we not?

Please forgive me for playing the fool, the jeff, the globetrotter, who entertains the crowd by shooting baskets while breaking all the rules of basketball. I am playing at achieving a global perspective by spouting a grand narrative that links a sliding glass door in St. Petersburg, Florida, with iconostases in St. Petersburg, Russia, with human skin, with gestures of turning this way and that in a swivel chair, with the epistemology of cultural taxonomies. Such is the struggle for a perspective that aspires to the status of a theory.

My rendering the icon screen as an example of a larger phenomenon makes the terrain slippery, so a good historian of anything, art included, would surely insist on interpretive moves that protect the historical and cultural specificity of the data.

Fear not. In the end, I too revere the minute particulars of the times and places I study. Sound scholarly methods, whether historical or ethnographic, are doggedly local and ultimately modest. But I am making a pitch—you recognize it as that—for supplementing micro-focused, historical research with macro-driven methods and metaphoric moves that are playful, imaginative, and challenging to the data rather than merely reflective of it. This position, of course, reflects a sensibility steeped in the arts and humanities rather than in the sciences, physical or social.

Metaphoric Moves

Why make metaphoric moves? To answer that question, I return to Jeff. I confess that I have been distracting you with a little side show by calling attention to the sliding glass door (and its holy analogues). If you reflect on the parable of Jeff the Improv Man, you will recognize that the most dangerously disruptive act was not really his peering through the door. Rather, it was his becoming the polar bear and, worse, playing the bear *before* reading the play.

In the WordBridge playwrighting process, there are four centers of dramaturgical authority: playwright, script, actors, and audience. The playwright authors (and thereby authorizes) the script, which in turn is performed by the actors who present the play to an audience of other theater people, which provides feedback for use by authors who are revising their plays.[125] By attending to the fourth center (audience) rather than the first (author), Jeff was not only subverting the usual hierarchy, he was putting himself in the position of having to depend on a circumspect, mediated version of the playwright's vision.

Why would anyone take such a risk when standard communication theories would require us to treat Jeff's understanding of the play as suspect? Surely, his view of it would be clouded by all his indirection, filtering, and calculated ignorance. Jeff's knowledge was "screened" even though the screen was transparent. Jeff had positioned himself where he could see but not hear, deliberately cultivating auditory ignorance.

My own ethnographic predisposition required that I ask Jeff *directly* what he thought viewing dramatic reality through a sliding glass door had accomplished.

Such a posture, he explained, provides a peculiar kind of knowledge unlike the lofty kind I was touting, namely, intellectual knowledge derived from multiple readings, careful exegesis, and focalized listening from the front row. He was tuning in, he said, not to the script, the playwright, or the actors but rather to the entire social-gestural interaction. He first came to know the play not as a script or dramatic reading but as reflected in the faces and postures of an audience responding to actors. He was, in effect, watching the play as a reception, or consumer, critic might have done.[126]

If you had not read the script, interviewed the playwright, or listened to the first reading, you would think the chances were high that your contribution to the play's development would be either disruptive or just plain silly. So what is the test of success in a metaphoric intervention? What determines whether Jeff gets it right when he makes his powerful metaphoric move of becoming a polar bear and consuming an hour of fifteen professionals' time? The test in a playwright's lab is whether the lightbulb goes on for the playwright, whether, in the end, the script is improved, rendered more effectively engaging. Getting a metaphoric improvisation wrong is obvious: It skews the playwrighting process by confusing the actors or sidetracking the playwright.

When the director asked the playwright what the play was about, she did not mention bears at all. She talked instead about the waitress in the diner, with whom she clearly identified, and about the boss and a strange customer. Asked why she named the play after the bears, the playwright sounded like many participants interviewed after rites. She said she did not know.[127]

By making such an oblique move and playing the bear, Jeff took the risk of derailing the process. But the outcome of the improvisational strategy was, in fact, enormously fruitful. In religious language, we would say that the playwright and actors experienced a "revelation." By the end, the playwright had begun to discover what her play was about and what polar bears have to do with waitresses who talk to their alphabet soup, but that is another story.

Theories as Metaphoric Screens

Like theater, ritual depends on symbols. When symbols do more than point, when they embody that to which they point, they become metaphoric.[128] A ritual metaphor is a drastically embodied symbol, one in which symbol and symbolized are simultaneously identified and differentiated. This bread *is* my body; this bread is *only* bread. That icon *is* sacred; that icon is *only* wood and paint.

Scholars usually recognize the metaphoric dimension of ritual.[129] Sometimes, however, they do not recognize their own metaphoric moves. Theories in the humanities, social sciences, and theology are predicated, sometimes tacitly, sometimes explicitly, on generative metaphors, for example, the threshold, or *limen*, that underlies the rites-of-passage theories of Victor Turner and Arnold van Gennep.[130] Applying a theory, like performing a play or enacting a liturgy, amounts to a metaphoric move. To apply a theory is to interpose a sliding glass door (clean, hopefully) between onself and the data. To query data with theoretically driven questions is to play the polar bear, because to theorize is to know what to expect before one has read the script.

The dedicated comparativist tries to gain perspective on things doggedly local by setting up parallel columns and then mapping out similarities and differences: An Orthodox iconostasis is to a temple veil as a sliding glass door is to a Plains tepee as human skin is to a museum display case as swiveling this way and that in a chair is to a conceptual grid.

When studying comparatively, the items set up for comparison are discrete and stubbornly local. To be most effective, researchers ought to choose their items from *differing* cultural domains in order to challenge the interpretive scope of their models. Then, sometimes, an electric, metaphoric arc occurs: The icon screen *is* a veil, *is* skin, *is* . . .

Seeing such equations on the conceptual screen, historians and ethnographers may be tempted to shut down their computers, lest the big bear of imagination eat up their data and them along with it. But I suggest otherwise. We should stay the course and make the metaphoric move. Play the jeff. If all goes wrong, we will at least have had fun, and you can blame the mess on me (or him).

Suppose we play out the metaphor: altar screen as altar skin. What does skin do that an altar screen might do? Skin contains. It is a stretchable, flexible bag. Skin protects. It is a boundary, keeping out rain, sun, and foreign organisms. Skin regulates. It maintains consistent body temperature. Cold, it tightens into goose bumps. Hot, it sweats. Skin conducts, takes in. It is a sensor, a conductor. It grabs vitamin D from the sun, conducts the vibration of a lover's touch. Embarrassed, it turns red. Skin communicates ("See my pimples; I eat too much chocolate and too many greasy fries." "Look at my skin: I am a Black person." "I am dead." "I am very hot. I am alive.") Skin advertises who we are.

So much for skin. Now let us make the metaphoric leap by asking: Understood on the model of skin, what might altar screens do that skin does? The answer is already obvious. Screens contain, protect, regulate, conduct, and communicate.

Of what use is the metaphoric move, altar screen as altar skin? When one sets an icon screen in a comparative, cross-cultural context, the larger, almost universal, question that arises is this: How permeable or impermeable are thresholds of sanctity? Is this screen, or act of screening, like a solid wall, or is it like a membrane? Every boundary creates an inside and out, a here and a there. And the most fundamental question about ritually maintained borders concerns their permeability—not only to bodily passage but also to sound, light, smell, and sight. Again and again, we humans try to understand screens and boundary markers by inferring the rules for passage through them: This can pass through, that cannot. This can pass, but only in the presence of such-and-such an agent. If we cannot discover the rules of passage either by direct inquiry or by inference, then we will likely discover them the hard way: by violating them accidentally.

What makes a screen work is what makes a veil work is what makes a mask or a beard work: Something is back there, over there, in there. We out here wonder what is up. From outside, it may seem that the power behind the screen knows me intimately, better than I know myself. The screen does not merely point to this felt sense; it creates it by setting the stage for it.

Even though magic men behind curtains can generate blazing auras and stunning light shows, reality backstage can seem pretty flat for a stage manager. But for the profane, the great unwashed who are kept out, screening heightens interest and focuses attention.

Lest you go away complaining that I *only* played with you and did not earn my keep by tendering a scholarly argument, I will summarize it, making it an easy (though moving) target:

- Screening is an act of stage managing. It constructs inside spaces in ways that cast others as outsiders; or, alternatively, outside spaces in ways that trap others inside.
- Screening is a calculated act of unknowing. It is simultaneously conducive of conceptual humility but also expressive of epistemological arrogance.
- Metaphoric moves are hyperreal, acts of theatrical supererogation, risky but potentially revelatory sorts of stage magic.
- Metaphoric moves are explicit in both ritual and the arts, although they are more constitutive in liturgical rites, in which predications of identity are guarded as sacred rather critiqued as fictional.
- Metaphoric moves also determine scholarly research. Metaphors suffuse the theories that frame and drive research. Like the metaphoric

moves of priests and actors, those of scholars consume as well as reveal their subject matter.

In ethnographic field research on ritual one may try to enter an arena of action free of presuppositions. But, at best, we are jeffs, playing at unknowing. Try as we might, one never enters a field, faces a text, or contemplates an artifact in a state of epistemological innocence. Becoming a blank slate, empty cup, or transparent window is a spiritual aspiration, not an academic achievement. (Even Jeff Wirth has to practice the spontaneity that underlies his improv artistry.)

Arts theories are less important for outcomes they predict than for perspectives they provoke. At the heart of every arts theory and method are metaphors so pervasive and tenaciously guarded that they function as ultimate, or sacred, postulates. Pregnant with fructifying metaphors lying curled deep in their bellies, theories facilitate interpretations that are at once stronger and deadlier than untheorized approaches. Scholars, like celebrating priests and enterprising stage managers, screen their performances (and not just when they return home to show Powerpoint presentations on dances that native do). Interpretive screens are knitted not only of theories and methods, but also of images, preconceptions, definitions, values, hunches, and stereotypes interposed between ourselves and what we study.

Like Jeff, seizing upon a sliding glass door to provide him with a less captive, more creative, more critical perspective, we scholars use theories to gain perspective, to tune in to undertones. But whatever tunes in also tunes out. Whatever reveals also conceals. Whatever selects for this, selects against that. Theory-using is a form of screening, and, like it or not, it is, in this respect, both priestly and performative.

Whether artistically inspired, religiously prescribed, or theoretically driven, making metaphoric moves is risky. When one improvises the bear in order to play the data, dormant values and meanings may awaken, emerging into daylight, hungry for recognition. But the other possibility is that the bear escapes the zoo. And having escaped, he gobbles up the little girl who wants to take him home as a playmate.

By jeffing, by posing as outsiders who ask disturbing questions to ritual insiders, scholars can perform a valuable intellectual and social service. But the blessings of scholarly arrival upon scenes ceremonial and sacred are mixed. Scholarly research is a form of hunting, predatory, even parasitic, upon whatever it studies.[131] Things studied are soon deadened, rendered corpselike. Scholarship necessarily, not accidentally, consumes what it studies. For having transposed persons, gods, spirits, and the departed into data, we scholars repeatedly incur social and ecological guilt. And the only acceptable form of paying off the debt is a good sideshow fearlessly imagined and disarmingly improvised.

8

Putting Space in Its Place

Jonathan Z. Smith is one of the most influential essayists currently writing in North American religious studies. Not only are his wit and insight evident in everything he writes, his essays usually make simultaneous theoretical and historical contributions. By requiring students to read him, by quoting and rereading him, I count myself among those instructed by his work. In fact, this book's title, Rite Out of Place, *invites readers to play it off his crucial collection of essays* To Take Place. *Whether theorizing or working experimentally with ritual, I find it easy to begin where he does, with places and emplacement. When I am invited to lecture, the first question I ask is, "What's the room like?" When I arrive, the first thing I do is move things around, reorganizing the space. I am tempted, therefore, to agree with Smith by making place central to the study of ritual. However, in the final analysis, I resist the temptation. My theoretical premises differ from his, so this is an admiringly argumentative engagement with Smith.[132]*

When scholars want to connect a conception of sacred space with that of ritual, they naturally invoke Smith's writing.[133] This choice is an obvious one, since Smith grants space a privileged position in ritual theory, and since he offers an alternative to Mircea Eliade, whose views of sacred space long dominated the field of religious studies.[134] My disagreement is not with attempts to forge a theoretical link between sacred space and ritual or with critiques of Eliade. It is with some of Smith's assumptions and with the uncritical way that his arguments are appropriated by others. Astute theorists, after all, deserve astute critique.

To me, it seems obvious that ritual is a kind of action, that it inevitably tran- spires in a specific place, and that such places vary in their importance to the rites they ground. To Smith, however, it is obvious that ritual is a kind of em- placement and that emplacement constitutes ritual. Both Smith and I theorize about ritual, but he privileges space, and I do not. If I privilege anything, it is action. Accordingly, my aim is to engage in a critical reading of Smith's spatial theory of ritual from the point of view of a more action-oriented theory.

The Bare Facts of Ritual

Smith's most sustained theorizing about ritual occurs in two chapters, "The Bare Facts of Ritual," originally published in 1980, and "To Take Place," published in 1987. Although the earlier piece treats the issue of sacred place, this notion is not as central as it becomes in the later one. In "Bare Facts" Smith speaks of sacred places as "focusing lenses,"[135] implying, it seems, that in ritual, humans and gods are "transparent" to one another. By use of the lens metaphor, he implicitly locates sacred space in a middle zone with human beings on one side and the divine on the other. Smith does not claim that such places are the *only* lenses, just that they are lenses—by implication, conditioning how humans and gods gaze at one another.

The emphasis in "Bare Facts" is not only on space but on the work of ritual, that is, on what a rite does and how it does it. Smith says that ritual, by means of its repetition and routinization, displaces the accidental features of ordinary, nonritualistic existence. The definition that results from his argument is this: "Ritual is a means of performing the way things ought to be in conscious ten- sion to the way things are in such a way that this ritualized perfection is recol- lected in the ordinary, uncontrolled, course of things."[136] Smith characterizes ritual as an idealized, or "perfected," domain in which nothing accidental hap- pens and in which everything is potentially meaningful. Insofar as ritual is a kind of space, it exhibits a dialectical relationship with that less focused domain: uncontrolled, quotidian life. One could diagram Smith's argument this way:

TABLE 8.1. Ritualized and Nonritualized Domains

Ritualized Domains conscious tension →	Nonritualized Domains ← conscious tension
Idealized:	Ordinary:
the way things ought to be	the way things are
Ritualized perfection	The ordinary, uncontrolled course of things
Nothing accidental	Much that is accidental
Everything is meaningful—at least potentially	Potentially meaningless; partial meaningfulness

Smith displays two tendencies. The dominant one is to conceive ritual as half a bipolar set, ritual versus nonritual, and to emphasize the lack of mediation between the two sides. In both "Bare Facts" and "To Take Place" he emphasizes the dissonance between the two domains, making their incongruity the definitive feature of ritual. Smith does not say why incongruity is so important to ritual, but one might infer from his other writings that it is because he thinks incongruity is a source of cultural creativity.

The other tendency one finds in Smith's theorizing about ritual is less pronounced. He either implies or posits some third domain or activity that mediates between the ritualistic and nonritualistic. His definition-like statement about ritual casts recollection in the role of mediator. Memory connects the ritualized with the nonritualized domain. Ritual actors *remember* their ritual actions in nonritualized space (or, vice versa: they recall the chaos of nonritualized life in the midst of ritual performance). These acts of recollection are a source of both tension and interconnection, but Smith emphasizes the former. In "To Take Place" the role of mediator is played not so much by memory as by thought. In the first two rows below, ritual is one of the parties in need of mediating:

However in the third row, ritual appears as mediator rather than party-in-need-of-mediation. The reasoning seems to be this: In "Bare Facts" Smith introduces an important bipolar distinction: word versus deed. The split arises from a set of examples: What hunters *say* a bear hunt is like differs from what one is *actually* like. Words about hunts are idealized, whereas actual hunting deeds are messy.[137] However, the hunter, Smith says, "has some means of overcoming this contradiction between word and deed. This, I believe, is one of the major functions of ritual."[138] Thus, the ritualized/nonritualized distinction is parallel to, or overlaid with, a word/deed distinction, implying the following analogy of proportion: Ritual is to word as nonritual is to deed. Thus, word belongs on the left side of the chart, since, like ritual, it is "perfected." Deed, since it is messy, belongs on the right, nonritualistic side. But this distinction casts ritual in a mediating position. So we are left with the contradiction created by casting ritual as both mediator and party-in-need-of-mediation.[139]

Another difficulty with Smith's definition is that it, like ritual, is idealized. Ritualists do not always enact fully controlled or idealized scenarios in their

TABLE 8.2. Mediating Opposites

Polarized Opposite	Mediator	Polarized Opposite
Ritual	Memory	Nonritual
Ritual	Thought	Nonritual
Word	Ritual	Deed

ceremonies. There are spontaneous, uncontrolled elements in divination rites, and performances of failure appear in rites of confession. Rites employ both good and bad examples, and neither the actions nor the structures that contain them are necessarily perfect or fully controlled. Some brief examples illustrate the point. In Madagascar, Bara funerals are not islands of orderliness, reflecting the ideal of everyday life. The Bara interpret death not as an eruption of chaos into orderliness but as an overdose of order.[140] In a funeral an increase in symbolic vitality counteracts an excess of order. So Bara funerals, by becoming bawdy and drunken, enact *the opposite* of the social ideal of orderliness.

Also in Madagascar, Betsileo funerals include a phase in which people copulate incognitio with complete disregard for incest regulations.[141] In essence, a violation of the ritual paradigm is structured into the rite itself.

In the Gisaro rite enacted by the Kaluli of New Guinea, dancers are burned; grief and crying follow.[142] How one *should* act is depicted alongside how one *should not* act.

Smith's definition is idealized not only in claiming that rites depict "perfection" but in its assumptions about the recollection of that perfection. People are not always able to recall idealized ritual action outside the ritual context. Sometimes they forget the ritual paradigms that they have practiced, or they are not conscious of the dissonance between the ritual ideal and the ordinary real.[143] For example, when American Catholic liturgy centers conducted a study of the effectiveness of Vatican II liturgical reforms, they found that worshipers interviewed immediately after worship could recall little of the ceremony they had just undergone.[144] Rites, then, may be ineffective in inscribing images of sufficient strength to persist in imagination and memory. So perhaps the latter part of Smith's definition should read this way: "Ritualized perfection *ought to be* recollected in the ordinary, uncontrolled, course of things." This way of putting the matter would make it clear that he is defining ritual ideally.

There is another difficulty with Smith's formulation. By the end of "Bare Facts," he has shifted from speaking of sacred place as the focusing lens to speaking of ritual as the focusing lens. What warrants this shift in the subject of the argument? How is it that in speaking about the one, we are drawing necessary conclusions about the other? He seems to assume an equation between ritual with one kind of ritual: religious, or sacred, ritual.

"Bare Facts" seems fairly congenial to action theory, because it shifts from a spatially grounded position ("The *sacra* are sacred solely because they are used in a sacred place")[145] to implying that sacrality has less to do with *where* something is performed and more to do *how* it is performed—that is, in dialectical tension with ordinary behavior. But this balance between a spatial and "actional" view of ritual becomes less apparent in "To Take Place."

To Take Place

If in "Bare Facts" Smith is clearing away an established theory of ritual space and tentatively proposing the germ of a new one, in "To Take Place" he is conceiving what we might call a spatialized theory of ritual. Although both spatial and "actional" rhetoric appear in "To Take Place," spatial metaphors assume a pronounced theoretical ascendancy. Smith makes statements that sound like they could support an action theory of ritual, for example, "Ritual is, first and foremost, a mode of paying attention." However, such statements are regularly displaced by a spatial reductionism evident, for instance, in the chapter's epigraph, "Nothing shall have taken place but place,"[146] and in repeated assertions such as, "Sacrality is, above all, a category of emplacement."[147] The "where" of ritual becomes theoretically more important than the "how" of it, sometimes occluding the latter entirely—a move that is the source of my most fundamental disagreement with Smith.

Making place so radically central locates Smith, despite his critiques of Eliade, in Eliade's enormous wake. He too granted a primacy to space in his understanding of religion. In the first chapter of *To Take Place*, Smith criticizes Eliade's treatment of sacred space by showing that the notion of the center is not supported by the Australian or ancient Near Eastern sources that Eliade used as primary examples. Smith speaks of "place" rather than "sacred space" to differentiate himself rhetorically from phenomenologists like Eliade and to evoke the more specifically social meanings of "place." Nevertheless, spatiality and placement remain determinative of Smith's conception of ritual. It is treated not simply as *one dimension* of ritual but as *the fundamental* one. Ritual action does not make space sacred; rather, placement renders actions sacred. Whereas Eliade construes the center as sacred to religion, thus to his theory of religion, Smith renders placement central, thus privileged, to his theory of ritual.

Smith talks as if his spatializing strategy regarding ritual is warranted by ritualists themselves. He quotes Claude Lévi-Strauss approvingly:

> A native thinker makes the penetrating comment that "All sacred things must have their place." It could even be said that being in their place is what makes them sacred for if they were taken out of their place, even in thought, the entire order of the universe would be destroyed. Sacred objects therefore contribute to the maintenance of order in the universe by occupying the places allocated to them. Examined superficially and from the outside, the refinements of ritual can appear pointless. They are explicable by a concern for what one might call "micro-adjustment"—the concern to assign every single creature, object or feature to a place within a class.[148]

The emphasis on ritual placement, that is, on ritual's role in maintaining intellectual and social order, locates Smith in the lineage that connects Émile Durkheim and Mary Douglas. They too believe that ritual's primary function is that of social, therefore intellectual, placement. Smith's emphasis on the sacrality of placement is so strong that one is tempted to infer that placement is sacred to him, not just to Eliade or the native thinker quoted by Lévi-Strauss.

Essential to maintaining the primacy of place in Smith's theory of ritual is his deployment of the notion in both a literal and a metaphoric fashion. Sometimes his topic is an actual geographical place, Jerusalem, for instance, but often it is placement, that is, mental schemes and social classifications. Too often, he slips between one usage and the other, making the shift without calling attention to it.[149]

In "To Take Place," temple rites ground Smith's generalizations about ritual. He construes temple ritual as exemplary of ritual itself.[150] He argues that within the temple, "All was system from which nothing could distract."[151] For Smith, the temple was, metaphorically speaking, a map. In effect, he implies that there is a process whereby geographical sacred places give rise to nonspatialized modes of emplacement, that is, to intellectual systems. He argues that places facilitate a "prescission," an abstraction, from place while at the same time maintaining the centrality of place. Her goes even further to claim that there is no rift between the literal or geographical level and the conceptual or metaphoric one: "There is no break with the dynamics of ritual itself."[152]

My view is that there *is* a break and that interpreters, not places, make the move from geography to mental classification. Smith implies the existence of a smooth and necessary connection between intellectual and social order, on the one hand, and ritual, on the other. However true such a claim may be of temple ritual, I see no reason to conclude that this move is definitive of ritual everywhere or ritual in general. Smith, I believe, is right in maintaining that ritual relies on ordinary activities, and intellectual activity must certainly be on the list of ordinary activities. So I do not claim that ritual action and intellectual activity are fundamentally or necessarily opposed.[153] I do maintain, however, that they *may* be, in other words, that there is often a seam, a difference, between them. Intellectual systems are not necessarily coextensive with ritual systems, no matter how much they may overlap. Smith says that "ritual . . . provides an occasion for reflection."[154] I would say "*may* provide," because it is also true that some ritualists and some ritual traditions discourage reflection. It would, for instance, be unseemly for anyone, even Navajos, to sit around a table describing, discussing, and analyzing Navajo chantways. Some are authorized to reflect on rites; some are not. Certain kinds of reflection are acceptable; others, not.

Even when reflection is encouraged to the point of generating a class of specialists—"liturgical theologians," let us call them—whose job it is to think and write about religious ritual, such reflection is perhaps better understood as an extension of the rite rather than as an explanation of it.[155] The degree of separation or integration between ritual action and intellectual-social categories varies from one historical period to another and from one culture or religion to another.

Smith's view of the relation of ritual to thought is epitomized in this passage:

> Ritual is a relationship of difference between "nows"—the now of everyday life and the now of ritual place; the simultaneity, but not the coexistence, of "here" and "there." Here (in the world) blood is a major source of impurity; there (in ritual space) blood removes impurity. Here (in the world) water is the central agent by which impurity is transmitted; there (in ritual) washing with water carries away impurity. Neither the blood nor the water has changed; what has changed is their location. This absolute discrepancy invites thought, but cannot be thought away. One is invited to think of the potentialities of the one "now" in terms of the other; but the one cannot become the other. Ritual precises ambiguities; it neither overcomes nor relaxes them.
>
> Ritual, concerned primarily with difference, is necessarily an affair of the relative.[156]

Here, Smith makes himself unnecessarily opaque by mixing temporal and spatial metaphors. In doing so, he exposes his tendency to render things nonspatial in spatial terms. He shifts rapidly from "now's" to "here's" and "there's." But the more important point is not Smith's mixture of metaphors. It is his insight into the way ritual holds ambiguities in tension with one another without dissolving that tension. I agree with him in his characterization of ritual ambiguity, but his next move in this passage is one I resist. Ritual, claims Smith (echoing, I suspect, Ricoeur on myth), gives rise to thought. He claims that the incongruence between (nonritualistic) blood that pollutes and (ritualistic) blood that purifies drives one to thinking. Such a move is possible, I agree, but is it necessary? The move from ritual enactment to thought is an option. We might ask, *Whom* does ritual drive to thinking? Scholars, probably all the time. Ritualists? Perhaps some of the time. The logic of this passage is characteristic of Smith's writing on ritual. It shifts rapidly from performances (which are specific and located in space and time) to systems (which are abstract). The logic takes us from literal, geographical places to metaphoric conceptual space. The connection is seamless only if we do not notice the shift he makes from the geographical to the metaphoric.

For Smith, place is not only central, it is active. As he imagines it, a place is not a mere empty or passive receptacle.[157] It is not just the context or backdrop of action but rather a force that forms actions and actors. As Kenneth Burke might have put it, "Scene acts."[158] Smith rejects so-called performance theory in favor of a spatial theory, but he does so by casting place as lead actor.

For Smith, placement is not only active, it is hierarchical: "Place," he says, "is not best conceived as a particular location . . . but rather as a social position within a hierarchical system."[159] "As such, ritual is systemic hierarchy par excellence."[160] So, in Smith's view, metaphorically speaking, place is not only an actor but an actor in search of power, of a superior position. Is this characterization what leads him to mythologize place as masculine ("Father Place" is one of his chapter titles)? He does not say.

To summarize the key premises and claims of Smith's theory of ritual:

- Ritual is by definition sacral, or religious. (Smith implies rather than argues this identification of ritual with sacred ritual.)
- The domain of ritual is incongruous with that of nonritual activity.
- The where (place, location) of ritual is more definitive than its what or how, for the same reason that system is more determinative than performance.
- Place acts; it is not a mere, passive, empty receptacle.
- Place is both geographical (literal) and metaphoric (conceptual and social).
- Metaphoric emplacement is more determinative than geographical place. (He implies but never quite says this.)
- Emplacement implies social hierarchy.

Putting Space in Its Place

I agree that place is important to ritual. In 1977, when Lonnie Kliever issued a call for religion scholars to attend to space and stop privileging time and narrative, he was right to do so.[161] Despite Eliade's influence, space had been a neglected category in religious studies, and religious studies scholars needed to attend to it more fully.

I have no objection to extending the notion of place (as Smith does) until it becomes a metaphor for intellectual categories. But to suggest that either sacrality or ritual is a function of place, or that there is a compelling reason for privileging space, is not at all evident to me. Smith writes, "The *sacra* are sacred solely because they are used in a sacred place; there is no inherent difference between a sacred vessel and an ordinary one." One can decide whether his emphasis is on "used" or on "sacred place." In my view sacralization is, more typically, a function of use. One possible use of sacra is to demarcate place, but it is quite possible to deploy sacra ritually outside of sacred places. For example, Western museums are full of Native burial remains, including human bones. Treated profanely by scientists working in profane places, they are nevertheless regarded by many Native people as sacred *despite* their residence in nonsacred places. So in my view, we know which places are sacred and which are not by observing what is enacted (or not enacted) in them. Sacrality becomes evident in *how* people act. To be sure, ritualists cannot escape place—they act somewhere, not everywhere—but this fact alone does not imply that space is *the* constitutive ritual component.

I agree with Smith that ritual is a means of marking and thus introducing difference, and I agree that ritual's presence often heralds discontinuity.[162] But the question is, What does ritual mark? Does it necessarily mark a place? Even when Smith is using as his example Australian *tjurunga*, wooden *objects* bearing marks that make them sacred, he transposes object into place much in the same way that he transforms time into space.[163] Even when he is discussing sacred *acts* such as speaking or washing feet, he renders gestures in terms of their place. I reject this reduction of a multidimensional phenomenon to a single, key dimension that presumably explains the whole. Against this reduction to a single dimension, I suggest that ritual is multidimensional, consisting of several kinds of components:

TABLE 8.3. Components of Ritual

Component	Example
Actions	dancing, walking, kneeling
Places	shrines, sanctuaries
Times	holidays, seasons, eras
Objects	fetishes, masks, icons, costumes
Groups	congregations, sects, moieties, nations
Figures and roles	gods, ancestors, priests, shamans
Qualities, quantities	circularity, seven, red
Language	myths, stories, texts, orations
Sounds	music, songs, chants
Attitudes, beliefs, intentions, emotions	belief in ritual efficacy, thankfulness, ecstasy

Even if there are more, fewer, or other components of ritual, why should we consent to ritual's implicit reduction to place—whether literally or metaphorically conceived?

Another objection to Smith's view is that he not only renders ritual one-dimensional, he also seems to prefer the metaphoric social and intellectual aspect of this dimension to the literal and geographical aspects of it. There is an implicit hierarchy not just in ritual but in his theory of it: Performances in specific places are superseded by systems of classification in minds and in societies. In effect, Smith's theory disembodies ritual. Surely, it is true that space *can* direct attention, but just as surely it may not; it may serve as mere backdrop or practical necessity. Low-church Protestant rites, for instance, de-emphasize space; worship can happen anywhere: a home, a school, a restaurant.

Alternatively, other components of ritual may also direct attention. The component of ritual that is emphasized varies from rite to rite, tradition to tradition. In one, space may indeed come to the fore and determine the nature of actions occurring in them. Pueblo rites, for example, are strongly determined by spatial considerations. In another tradition, a particular object, for instance, a holy book, may be determinative. In yet another, a specific gesture or posture (such as sitting in full lotus position) may be foundational.

One can read Smith's book *To Take Place* in two ways—broadly as a work aimed at laying the foundation for a general ritual theory, or narrowly as a treatment of one aspect of ritual, namely, space or place. As I read Smith, the dominant intention implied by his writing is the former, a general theory of ritual that construes placement as its key. So we have to ask what might warrant giving such prominence to place? Among the answers Smith actually gives or seems to imply are these: The ritual/space connection could be

1. purely coincidental.

   In his acknowledgments for *To Take Place*, Smith links the two topics merely on the basis of invitations received to deliver lectures on the two topics. But coincidental association hardly constitutes grounds for a spatialized theory of ritual.

2. a given.

   Like a Kantian category, it cannot be escaped. Just as one cannot perceive the world except through space, so one cannot conceive ritual except as essentially spatial. Smith never quite makes such a claim, but he occasionally edges up on it.This argument would fall as soon as we asked, "Why not privilege time (another Kantian category) instead?"

3. due to conscious or unconscious influence by another writer, practitioner, or theorist.

   For example, Ezekiel, also has an ideology of place and maps an ideal cultic space,[164] and Smith's argument mirrors some aspects of Ezekiel just as it does of Eliade. But an influence or example does not constitute a convincing argument.

4. the generalization of a specific case into a theory.

   Smith explicitly employs arguments built on this kind of logic: "If the Temple ritual may be taken as exemplary of ritual itself . . . ,"[165] But why should we grant the "if" clause? Many scholars engage in this kind of argumentation. Their doing so is the reason we need critiques from other scholars using different data.

5. based on a similarity of function.

   Smith writes, "Ritual is, first and foremost, a mode of paying attention," and "It is this characteristic, as well, that explains the role of place as a fundamental component of ritual: place directs attention."[166] The logic seems to be something like this: Ritual and place *do* the same thing; therefore, they *are* same thing. If this is, in fact, the logic of Smith's claim, his conclusions seem to me unwarranted.

If the first way of accounting for the necessary connection between space and ritual is correct, its arbitrariness would invite others to posit other arbitrary connections.

If the second were the case, Smith's claim would be in principle unfalsifiable: How would we know if ritual were *not* essentially spatial? If the third were true and we were influenced by, say, Heraclitus and Victor Turner rather than, say, Ezekiel and Eliade, we would arrive at a different conclusion. If the fourth were so, and we were to choose other case studies, we would arrive at different conclusions. If the fifth kind of reasoning were employed, one could counter by showing that there are other aspects of ritual—objects, for instance—that direct attention. So I do not find any of the reasons quite convincing.

Ritual studies scholars are probably less interested in what gave rise to Smith's theory than in imagining some of the consequences if they were to accept his view of ritual. Smith quotes Maurice Halbachs to the effect that "it is the spatial image alone that, by reason of its stability, gives us an illusion of not having changed."[167] A spatialized theory of ritual would make ritual appear stable, but is this a virtue in a theory? Lakoff and Johnson reach a similar conclusion regarding the stabilizing effect of spatial metaphors.[168] They show how such metaphors, especially those embedded in prepositions and reified nouns, lead English speakers to construe the world as static and as having an inside and outside, like a container. It is understandable that using spatialized imagery to make the world seem static might be desired by ritualists who want their rites to appear sturdy, if not eternal. The book of Hebrews in the New Testament, for instance, paints an image in which Christ celebrates a rite above, while a mortal celebrates the same rite below. However, this or any other static, spatial image does not serve ritual theorists as well as it does ritualists. Ritual theory should be historically and socially grounded, and it can only do so if theories and theorists call attention to change and lack of stability. Smith needs no lecture on change and incongruity; he is a master of the topics. However, hyperspatializing ritual theory has, I believe, the unwanted consequence of making ritual seem more static than it really is.[169]

Smith subordinates actual places to emplacement and, implicitly, renders place nongeographical. One consequence of this strategy is a kind of gnosticizing of ritual. In criticizing the a-topia of the Gospel of John and of Christianity generally, Tod Swanson argues, "Rituals are irreplaceable responses to . . . irreplaceable places."[170] He sounds almost like Smith, but the difference between them is important. Ultimately, Smith volatilizes places into emplacement: Place is best conceived not as a particular location but as a position in a hierarchy. Swanson, however, shows that Johannine Christianity's spacelessness, its lack of rootedness in local places, helped authorize the "Christian claim to all the territories of this world."[171] I worry that the theoretical minimization of particular places (the utopian tendency) may have a similar effect, even though Smith would not likely intend it.

My aim here has been less to construct an alternative theory than to mount a critique, but I conclude with a summary of Smith's position compared with a summary of the theoretical alternative I have been implying:

Table 8.4. Comparing a Spatialized Theory with a Multidimensional Theory

Jonathan Z. Smith's Spatialized Theory of Ritual	An Alternative, Multidimensional Theory of Ritual
Ritual is by definition sacral, or religious.	Not all ritual is religious. Sacred enactment is a subcategory of ritual, not the whole of it; let us call religious ritual "liturgy."
The domain of ritual is incongruous with that of nonritual activity.	Between ritual and nonritualistic domains there is congruity as well as incongruity. Ritual studies scholars, like ritualists, should attend to both, inferring their proportions from actual practice.
The "where" (place, location) of ritual is more definitive than its "what" or "how," for the same reason that system is more determinative than performance.	Space is no more determinative than any other component of ritual, for instance, actions, objects, or times. In interpreting a rite, scholars should attend to the relations among components, not assume that one is definitive.
Place acts; it is not a mere, passive, empty receptacle.	In some ritual traditions, space acts. In others, space is ignored or allegedly transcended. The relative activity or passivity of space is culture- and religion-specific.
The term "place" designates something both geographical (literal) and metaphoric (conceptual and social).	The term "place" refers to a specific geographical location. "Space" connotes that which is empty like a receptacle. "Emplacement" refers to location on a conceptual map, classificatory grid, or social hierarchy.
Metaphoric emplacement is more determinative than geographical place.	Emplacement may metaphorically extend the "reach" of a place, but it does not transcend that place, nor is it superior to it.
Emplacement implies social hierarchy.	Places and schemes of emplacement may either consolidate or critique hierarchy. They do not *necessarily* reinforce or reflect it.

My aim is not to constellate two camps, the "spatialists" and "multidimensionalists." Smith would likely disaffiliate from the former and I, from the latter. The differences between us are, perhaps, partly attributable to intellectual lineage. Smith is indebted more to Durkheim and Eliade; I, to Turner and van Gennep. But if one examines the writings of the latter pair, it is clear that the key notion of the "liminal" is played out in two quite different ways. One way construes it as a kind of privileged "space," an in-between "place" that is both geographical and metaphoric, and in which things ritualistic and cultural are incubated. But another, equally valid reading makes of liminality a "moment" in a temporary process. In other words, the tension between the rhetoric of structure and the rhetoric of process does not separate only theorists into camps, Durkheimian and van Gennepian, it also appears *within* theories and theorists' writings. The study and construction of theories requires careful attention to the metaphors that ground those theories. The fundamental metaphor of rites-of-passage theory (largely the legacy of van Gennep and Turner) is that of crossing a threshold or national frontier. If one attends to the boundary itself, the emphasis becomes spatial, but if one attends to the person making the crossing, the emphasis becomes temporal and processual. Accordingly, I suspect that the difference *between* Smith's position and mine can probably be rediscovered *within* each of our respective theories. Incongruities, after all, are as typical of theories as they are of rites.

As part of his larger project of theorizing about religion, Smith emphasizes what he calls the "utopian" rather than the "locative" vision. Whereas the locative is centered, structured, and integrated, the utopian is decentered, "wobbling," and incongruous. It seems to me that his larger project is compromised by excessive reliance on spatial metaphors, which have historically served locative interests, and by his choice of locative examples such as long-standing temple rites rather than more utopian examples, which is to say, more recent, "invented" rites. If it is true, as Smith claims, that the category "religion" is really a scholarly invention, then scholars bear the ultimate responsibility for selecting the examples and metaphors that form the basis of theories. Smith typically selects locative metaphors and locative examples. Why not utopian rites as well? One reason is perhaps that he is a historian with little interest in, or access to, rites in the process of being invented. But there is perhaps another: Smith prefers introducing the free-wheeling utopian elements himself. He typically likes pulling the rug out from under a tradition (for instance, by exposing the contradiction between Ainu bear hunting rites and Ainu talk about those rites) or a theorist (by, for example, pointing out interpretive errors made by James Frazer or Mircea Eliade).

My intention in critically engaging Smith's writings is motivated by a larger aim. I would like to counteract the tendency in ritual studies for theorists to talk past each other, or worse, never to engage each other's ideas either in public or in print. Anthropologists who write about ritual read and argue with each other (and, with astonishing consistency, ignore religious studies writings about ritual). In religious studies we read anthropologists on ritual but seldom take each another's theorizing with sufficient seriousness to write about its nuances. As a result, religious studies is interdisciplinary without bothering to be disciplinary. We will overcome this deficiency only when we press our own theories hard against texts, performances, or other theories of ritual.

PART III

Ritual in Environmental Space

9

The Barn and the Lab

with Susan L. Scott

The following is a conversation with Susan Scott, coordinator of the Water Stories Project.[172] She and I contemplate the possibilities for ritual and performance in starkly contrasting spaces: a barn near Walkerton, Ontario, site of a devastating, tainted-water scandal in 2000, and the Ritual Studies Lab, a workshop housed in a university town. The timber-frame barn on a 150-year-old farm called Stonyground is used on occasion as a performance site and gallery, as it was during the Walkerton Water Stories Project, an arts-based, community restoration project that sprang up in response to the water tragedy. For thirty years, the Ritual Studies Lab was a site of experimentation and research on ritual. The Lab was tucked away discreetly in a series of bungalows in Waterloo, Ontario, earmarked for demolition by the university, which was buying them up so it could expand. The barn, despite its advanced age, persists as a symbol of regeneration. The Lab died at middle age and is now a ghost in a myth.

ss   What could an old barn and a ritual studies lab possibly have in common? I suppose they're working sites, and they're also retreats from which to contemplate the great expanse. I've known about the Ritual Studies Lab for years but not in much detail. Tell me more.

RG   Even though I call it *the* Lab, there was never a single place.[173] There was one "institution" (the term's too grandiose) which migrated among a series of houses that the university had purchased and slated for eventual destruction in order to make room for new classrooms and dormitories. Lab spaces were typically the living and

dining rooms of 1940s bungalows. Classes held in them were wonderfully, and necessarily, small—a dozen or so students. Other university
units stashed in houses tried to make them over into offices. We didn't.
We tried to honor the spirits of those poor, deceased houses. Sometimes
our ritualized acts of honoring were ludic; sometimes, serious. Whether
anyone "believed in" them or not didn't matter. We made the rooms look
sanctuary- or altar-like. Actually, that's probably overstated. Each one
resembled a cluttered New Mexico *santuario* or a seventeenth-century
cabinet of wonder. Peculiar things hung out of drawers and perched atop
bookcases. Bones and rags and dried flowers hung from ceilings and
walls. As students came and went, year after year, they left gifts, often
handmade or found objects, which became ritual implements or served
as ceremonial decor to be used by the next generation of students.
Drawing on such deposits, I would spin "ancestral myths" about the
forebears of that year's class. From the outside, the labs were mere
dilapidated houses, with bricks crumbling and paint peeling. From the
inside, they were warm nests—at first a little strange, later almost sacred
(in a playful or ironic sort of way). There was no furniture, only a carpet,
typically threadbare. We sat (and played and danced and meditated) on
the floor. "Grounding," I'd say when a student would ask why. "It's for
grounding. That's why we're down here on the floor."

Tell me about the barn at Stonyground. I saw it only once.

ss   It's a grand old timber-frame barn. Its significance lies in what it
represents: the regeneration of rural landscapes through art and agrarian
reform. Is the barn a nest? A cabinet of wonder? Maybe not, but the
ancestors certainly preside. Stonyground is a 150-year-old working farm
renowned for landscape architecture after retired scholar, Douglas
Chambers, inherited the land in the 1980s.[174] It's an old farm taken up
from the Crown in 1850, when pressure for land forced the opening
of the Queen's Bush—last of the region's great forests and home to
Ojibway who had already been pushed out. So, even though the barn
may be the image of stability, the landscape is still evolving out of this
conflicted history. Bruce County is the heart of cattle country in Ontario,
and barns are still the largest structures, although their hold on the land
belies the fact that family farms are under siege.

I first had the pleasure of working at Stonyground in 2002, as part
of a humanitarian initiative in the neighboring town. Walkerton is a
lovely river town, also famous, although, sadly, not for innovation. In
May 2000, Walkerton became the site of a devastating *E. coli* epidemic in
which 7 people died and 2,500 fell ill after spring floods bore cattle
runoff into town wells.[175] I was part of a group of artists who were drawn
to the town, to help.

RG   Tragedy and scandal, on the one hand, and art and innovation, on the other. That's quite the gulf.

SS   Yes, but what Walkerton and Stonyground have in common is their agricultural base, a sensibility tied to the land. The farm, which rests on an incline near the Saugeen River, is one of Bruce County's many farms linked by gravel roads and hardwood bush. At Stonyground, the rural-urban divide is heightened, never easily resolved. There's an immense reach to the place. A working landscape beautified by literary gardens, whimsical plantings, and old implements converted to sculptures transport you in ways the ancestors couldn't have imagined.

All this, a half mile west of Walkerton, is a world away. That leap is part of the charm—and strain—of unconventional labor in a conventional setting. The district (known as "the Bruce") lies far from urban din and is a place of immense quiet and clannish preoccupation with roots. Outsiders are generally suspect; the old ways are revered. Even though the farm exemplifies pioneering innovation, by local standards, Stonyground is still considered odd.

RG   So why go there? And why meddle in Walkerton's affairs?

SS   I didn't know a soul in town, but I come from Bruce County, and I felt the need to respond. So did thousands of others—fresh water poured in from as far away as Fiji. The spring of 2000, I was riveted by the news of helicopters lifting people to hospitals, of schools and businesses shutting down. Half the town's population had fallen ill. Health authorities suspected tainted water, yet families were told to keep pumping water into their sick. We now know that water nearly killed them. The E. coli crisis was the great Canadian wake-up call. If a water tragedy could happen in a bucolic place like Walkerton, it could happen anywhere.

RG   So you initiated the Walkerton Water Stories Project. Why respond to an environmental crisis with stories rather than with science?

SS   I had no idea how to respond at first, but I was drawn to the notion of community restoration,[176] healing after displacement from the very things (cattle and water) that sustain the town. Then, at an ecology and performance conference in the UK, I met artists engaged in grassroots work with whole communities and thought, surely we can do this at home. And I began wondering what might be meaningful to people in Walkerton.

Eventually, a storyteller, visual artist, and I partnered with local citizens groups to found an outreach program called the Walkerton Water Stories Project. The goal was to collaborate with the people of Walkerton on various art forms that could then be toured, to educate other communities. The whole idea was to help the town reclaim its relationship to water. Walkerton has a rich water history dating back 150 years. Storms, floods—they'd seen it all. Yet after coping with calamity for generations, suddenly the town was overflowing with the colonizing narratives of outside experts. Our role was to listen, attend, and facilitate healing by offering people the tools to tell their own stories.[177] We were the diggers and dowsers, drawing local knowledge to the surface, trying to redirect the flow.

RG   How does the barn figure into all this?

SS   It was the restoration site, where all the stories came home to roost. Since the water crisis was directly linked to cattle, it seemed only right to gather for reflection in a barn, to balance the formalities transpiring at the courthouse with alternative inquiries in story, art, and song. So, the hay mow was bedecked with bales and quilts for feasting, a concert by singer-songwriter James Gordon, and a stunning performance by storyteller Mary-Eileen McClear of *Water Finds a Voice*, a piece I wrote based on oral and natural history. The fieldstone stable below housed the remarkable *Water Stories Prints* made by local residents under the guidance of painter and printmaker Wesley Bates, along with the eerie, ephemeral *E. coli Scrolls* and the *Walkerton Life Vest* by guest artist Basia Irland.[178]

What about the Lab? I confess to avoiding it myself, but I know people who swore by it. Wasn't it a ritual-and-arts kind of place?

RG   Like the barn, the Ritual Studies Lab was a place of storytelling, art, and song, and a place to experiment with the elements of ritual—action, space, objects, light, and so on. That's why we called it a lab. We could have called it a studio. There was truth in both labels, the one suggesting scientific research and the other, artistic work. The courses taught there were religious studies courses. For a while, I taught some of them collaboratively with a wandering, ex–Jesuit clown, Ken Feit.[179] Since Lab courses were taught at a provincial (state) university, we didn't dare call the Lab a "sanctuary," but the "the sacred" was certainly our primary subject matter. Ritual studies, like anthropology and other social scientific disciplines, was—and still is—struggling with issues of cultural appropriation and representation, so a basic principle was never to imitate or pilfer existing ritual traditions, even though a particular element might echo a specific tradition.

Lab work was not religious, even though it was *about* religion and required ritual labor. "Ritual-makers," I'd say, "are merely plumbers, specialists in how to do things with water and buckets and mud and toys and masks and . . ." The work of the Lab was to demystify the act of ritual construction and then to remystify it, but in such a way that a student of ritual would never again be tempted to think of ritual as beyond critique.

That was the academic aim—to show how ritual acts could be constructed and subsequently deconstructed. Our approach to ritual was, you might say, domestic rather than ecclesiastical. For the most part, it was down-to-earth rather than lofty, ordinary rather than extraordinary.

But there were exceptions. Near the end of most courses, we'd leap out of the urban university into a rural setting. We'd head to the countryside, hunker down in a barn, hide, then seek, in the woods. We made a radical shift from the ordinariness of classrooms and domestic spaces by creating or finding a liminal space, a place neither here nor there. Because we were working on death rites, we needed not only mystery but also more physical space, free from administrators or spectators. Once we went to a colleague's farm, which had a spacious barn and a crowded cemetery. Another time we used a Mennonite church camp. One time, we used on-campus portables and slept there until campus security caught us.

ss   What did you do in the sessions?

RG   Most of the regular class sessions proceeded in silence or with relatively little talk. There were the usual kinds of reading and writing assignments but only very short lectures of ten or fifteen minutes. There was time for reflection and discussion at the end of each session, but the beginning and middle consisted of "activities," the most generic term I could find. The most frequently asked question was: What are these? Exercises? Games? Rituals? Drama? I would reply, "You tell me." The most interesting moments were those for which we couldn't find a label. Some students would give up categorizing; others would still be driving themselves crazy at the end of the term, trying to classify what we were doing. Some of the activities were adapted from various sources: actor training, martial arts, religious dance, and traditional storytelling; others were made up. The aim was to work with elementals—the stuff—of ritual. So, for example, we might spend a session working with water or earth or a piece of rope or a plastic doll, or we'd circle a story with actions, then circle it again and again.

What about the barn? Your "restoration of stories" is an attractive notion, but what good is a barn, really? Do you ever worry that barns are just a relic of a past, a leftover from dying rural culture?

ss   Actually, barns are all the rage now. Recordings, performances, galleries, and workshops are easily adapted to these wonderfully large, neutral spaces that evoke memories of communal life.

RG   I'm intrigued by the possibility of barn performances and barn galleries, but mainly because such events contradict my experience of actual, working barns. I grew up on a New Mexico farm-ranch where cows, pigs, and mice were slaughtered in the barn.[180] Nobody else went there except my dad and me. The barn was a lonely guy-space; women seldom went there. I can't imagine that Ontario barns are really much different from New Mexico barns.

ss   As a girl, I wasn't even allowed in the barn. Talk about a gendered site. The old adage "The house isn't much, but the barn sure is nice" says it all. Barns remain the dominant symbol of farm communities, in part because it took the whole neighborhood to build one: master framers and dozens of men who worked in teams to raise the timbers, and of course women to feed the whole lot. Historical records, such as my great-great-grandfather's day book, that track the supplies and rhythms of the raisings show how critical the whole process was not only to the survival of a given family but also to the health of the entire community. Work that could not be done alone (especially dangerous work such as thresh-ing, logging, and woodcutting, but also quilting and sewing) led to collective work, social gatherings called "bees." These gatherings offset the hardship and isolation of pioneer life, and the greatest of these were the barn bees.[181]

RG   One of the most shocking sights to me on the night of the Stony-ground performance and celebration was all those tables laden with food. Where I grew up, barns were full of manure, and it was my responsibility to shovel it. The sight of edible things in a place where I expect vile runny stuff was both delightful and disconcerting.

ss   Well, the climax of barn bees was feasting and dancing. Out came the fiddles and the moonlight for the christening of the new threshing floor—an open space in a liminal time, marking the triumph of commu-nal effort. Like building, food preparation was a form of social competi-tion and display. *The Barns of the Queen's Bush* lists as food for a crew of 175 men: "115 lemon pies, 500 doughnuts, 15 cakes, . . . 16 chickens, 3 hams, 50 pounds roast beef. . . ."[182] Adapted barns, such as the one at Stonyground, make it possible to revive the spirit of such festive rituals.

RG   So, the food at Stonyground wasn't just fuel; it was also perfor-mance. The barn and the grounds became a work of art.

ss   Yes, but there's another, less romantic side to the image of these barns as sacred spaces. They're also barriers that block out as much as they contain, big boxy structures that signal the reclamation of the bush and the triumph of human ingenuity over the wild. Like the grid-shaped landscape over which they preside, barns mark the ascendancy of right angles over randomness and chaos. The problem now is that the agrarian culture that once determined the destiny of field, wood, stone, and cattle is in decline;[183] hence the need for new myths and rituals from old.

It might interest you to know that long-term plans for Stonyground include conferences and workshops, which means the barn may one day function as a lab. But if labs are the prototype for contemporary knowledge-gathering, then why did you lose the Ritual Studies Lab?

RG   I didn't quite lose the Lab. It was gobbled up by a landlocked, therefore land-hungry, institution. I wanted a lab with no chairs, no desks, and no equipment—a bare room. And universities cannot stand bare rooms. To create any kind of experimental space at a university, you have to call it either a lab or a studio and fill it with expensive equipment. I would have preferred to call our space an incubation chamber, a place where one sleeps in search of a revelation or vision. Since such chambers died out in ancient Greece, I knew I would never get away with dubbing the place "The Ritual Studies Incubation Chamber." So it was a coin toss between "lab" and "studio." In the end, I went with "lab," echoing perhaps the Polish Theatre Lab directed with Jerzy Grotowski. When he invited me to Poland, Grotowski was working with ritual, although it took in him twenty years to admit that out loud.[184]

ss   Was the association of the Ritual Studies Lab with the Polish Theatre Lab explicit?

RG   No, I wasn't doing theater. Besides, the university administration, not unlike the communist Polish government, would never have tolerated whirling with Sufis in the dark forest or trance dancing with Haitians in a barn. The Polish Theatre Lab was originally in an urban theater, but by the time I went there, Grotowski was carrying out his international experiments in a rural area that crisscrossed an old German-Polish border. The German trees stood all in a row, plantation style, and the Polish trees were randomly planted. As we whirled in the dark, we could always tell when we were passing from the one territory to the other. If we whirled long enough, the birds and deer would start to follow us, unafraid. This was Grotowski's Tree of People Project; he was experimenting to see if people of different religions, cultures, and nationalities could interact ritually without talk or discussion.

ss   When your Lab shut down, you didn't take it on the road, yet there's such hunger for experiential learning. Don't you have a responsibility to continue in some form?

RG   In the current intellectual climate, I don't trust the hunger. The shift from experience-hunger to grade-hunger has been remarkable and pronounced. I love road shows. I've studied a few, such as turn-of-the-century "Native" medicine shows, as well as Tibetan Buddhist monks on the circuit, but the last thing I want to do is to conduct a road show. Road shows are just exotic forms of evangelism. I don't like working with unprepared audiences. I don't like the "stir 'em up and leave town" ethic. It's easy to create deeply moving experiences that can't be sustained beyond a weekend, highs that can't really be integrated into everyday life. But I have no interest in stoking the fires of such experiences. I prefer working with groups that are together for longer periods than a week. In Lab courses I would have a twelve- to thirteen-week term—occasionally even a twenty-six-week one—in which to get to know participants. In some cases I would continue working with them across their universitery career, a three- or four-year period. I feel like I'm better able to act responsibly across longer periods of time than in brief periods, which, almost by definition, invite irresponsibility. Ritual requires time to be ingrained, even more time to be constructed or critiqued.

Anyway, to answer your question: I would, in fact, teach other lab-style courses if the circumstances were right. Since they are not, I'll watch and wait.

ss   By ritual standards, your courses were short, even though by work-shop standards, the Lab was long-lasting.

RG   That's true, but I was not trying to equip students with new rites to displace old ones. I was trying to get them to think about the processes of ritual construction and ritual criticism. In this respect, activities in the Ritual Studies Lab were consistent with the standard university agenda, to get people to think analytically and critically. Instead of trying to create experiences that wowed participants, I would break up such experiences by teaching students to step out of them in order to critique and reflect on them. I was trying to normalize the cycle of creativity, participation, and critical reflection so that all three moments in the process required each other, belonged together. I wasn't trying to create an alternative tradition but generate an alternative attitude.

ss   Your attempt to normalize that cycle is controversial, right?

RG   For sure, but not so much in the Lab or at my own university as in scholarly circles. The mere phrase "ritual criticism" raises hackles,[185] and the very title of my book *Ritual Criticism* has stirred up trouble.[186] In that book I argue against standard definitions and theories of ritual insofar as they ignore or preclude the creative and critical processes that suffuse ritual. Ritual is usually defined as traditional, not creative; therefore it is supposedly beyond criticism. But it isn't, not really. Evaluating ritual activity is a normal part of ritual enactment.[187] People are always complaining about, revising, or trying to improve weddings, funerals, and other kinds of ritual. The criteria are contested, but so are the criteria for making moral or aesthetic judgments.

For me, the real problem in both the Lab and in actual ritual circumstances isn't theory or definition; it's time. There just isn't time for adequate ritual planning or ritual evaluation. Ritual is time-consuming, so it doesn't easily fit into a consumer society's cost-effectiveness models.

SS Time is critical, isn't it? Our work in Walkerton was far too compressed. People were just beginning to make the connections when it was time to wrap things up and hit the road. The whole question of time is aggravated by grant cycles and expectations about what are reasonable periods of preparation, production, and critical reflection. For this kind of ecological and cultural restoration to succeed, we need sustained periods of contemplative work based on ritual cycles of time. Interdisciplinary teams of artists and scholars need to work together in long-term residencies, so there is actual time to dwell. Having too little time borders on irresponsibility. The question of how to work in community raises not only research and pedagogical issues but also ethical ones.

RG You're right. Not long ago, at Union Theological Seminary in New York City, theologian Tom Driver, performance theorist and practitioner Richard Schechner, and I had a public discussion about performance. One of the central questions was about the relationship between ritual and ethics. The ritual-ethics connection is a major theme in Driver's *Liberating Rites*.[188] Now that he's retired from teaching, he's become a dedicated social activist, so one of his questions to Schechner and me was, "Why don't you spend more time on ethics in your ritual theory and pedagogy?" I understood why he posed the question.

I have interest in ethical issues—the environment, social justice, gender equality—but I've never made them a central focus of my own research and writing. One reason is because North American culture, which is so Protestantized, has a pronounced tendency to reduce everything, including religion, to ethics. As a result, it's hard to get people to focus on ritual. Everyone wants to reduce ritual to ethics or politics or psychology. So, I've made it my business to focus stubbornly on ritual itself.

SS Ah, yes, you yourself are a product of Protestant formation, so you understand it well. Do you have no interest, then, in applying ritual to ethical problems?

RG Sure, I do. For example, I was involved in the repatriation and reburial controversies. I'm interested in the ethical and ritualistic problems of reburying the excavated remains of Native people. I don't avoid such activities either in class or in writing, but I typically become interested in them as ritual problems first, not as ethical issues. Once you become immersed in such a problem, then there really is no separation between its ethical and its ritualistic dimensions. I suppose I'm saying that the ritual-ethics distinction is just a gestalt question, a matter of which you cast as figure (or center) and which you make ground (background). Driver tends to put ethics in the foreground and cast other things in the background. I tend to put ritual in the foreground and cast everything else in the background. In both cases, ritual and ethics are integrally related, but the emphasis is different. In a sense, my whole academic career has been about trying to perceive absolutely anything in the world through the lens of ritual. I've taken up all sorts of issues, always relating them to ritual. I'm not saying that I experience the world that way, only that I have experimented with what you might call a ritual view of the world.

When you went to Walkerton, did you have an ethical agenda? Were you trying to change the world under the force of a moral imperative?

ss   We went in two years after the crisis, to tap the communal imagination. Before that, people were just trying to survive. Yet for all our good intentions, we had a hard time making ourselves understood.

RG   That's not surprising. Would the town council have been thrilled to hear that you were "divining," listening to wells and ditches?

ss   No, we didn't burden them with that piece of information; having artists underfoot was bad enough. The trouble was, we were asking people to remember what they most wanted to forget: "Stories, what for? You're rubbing salt in the wound."

So we began talking about natural (landscape) history and cultural (people) history, asking how the Water Stories Project could bridge the two. Tradition and stewardship are crucial to farm communities; collecting, preserving, and reviving local knowledge of the land is (or should be) part of environmental stewardship and ecological restoration. So, just as you wanted the Lab to focus on the elements of ritual, we wanted to get at concrete experience, the details and images embedded in telling stories. Our perspective was: People need good water stories as much as they need good, clean water.

What the project underscored for me is how much more work is needed to get this message across. People aren't making the connection. Simply put, we need dramatically better ways of linking human and landscape stories.

RG   Or landscape spaces and human stories. . . . Around the university there's much discussion about ethical issues, but little of that discourse has anything to do with the ethics of built, on-campus spaces. University ethics these days focus mainly on gender, safety, or accessibility. There is plenty of discussion about dangerous spaces and dangerous substances, but the talk, as well as the action, is driven by the fear of lawsuits. Almost never do you hear a discussion of the ethics of a space as common as the classroom. One hears complaining about classroom functionality or lack of it, comments on a building's aesthetics (university architecture being what it is), but little is said about either the ritual or the ethics of building, inhabiting, or tearing down such places. The Ritual Studies Labs were pulled down unceremoniously except for the gestures I committed (as if they were crimes) shortly before demolition.

ss   Such as?

RG   Such as burning leaves, rescuing old doorknobs, giving away ceremonial paraphernalia to the poor, saying good-bye to rooms. These were not acts commissioned by the university's ceremonials committee or authorized by the institution. They were surreptitious acts of guerrilla ritualizing committed, probably, in violation of some fire code or other rule.

ss   So the space and objects were sacred?

RG   I never labeled them as such, but they were special, for sure. If you had asked some students, they probably would have called them sacred. Lab spaces were special to me and a few others, so I sometimes felt sadness, nostalgia, or anger when the buildings were demolished. At the end of a course, there was always a rite of exit. We would say good-bye to the space itself. I never viewed our nests as mere public classrooms. But does that make them sacred? Calling an act sacred is a little like declaring one's own deed to be just. I prefer to leave it to others to confer the ultimate-value labels. By the standards of university ethics, the truly sacred spaces are those in which the most energy, imagination, and money are invested, namely science labs, ball courts, and business classrooms.

ss   Strange, how easy it is to overlook the juxtaposition of sacred and profane. Isn't water sacred? Isn't that what we mean by "pure"? In Walkerton, Well Number Five once stood in a grove of trees, right next to the farmer's field that flooded during that deadly deluge. Now the well house is gone, and the site is razed, yet here's a site crying out for restoration.

Mary Douglas defines evil as matter out of place, and the water tragedy begs for this kind of analysis.[189] E. coli 0157 is a bacteria found in cattle feces, and it's deadly to humans. When cattle runoff failed to be purified at the water treatment plant, tainted water flowed right from people's taps. The contamination that began with eroded boundaries between local sources of sustenance (cows and water, farms and wells) led to the discovery of astonishing transgressions, ranging from misplaced wells to forged documents and breach of trust. Can we really fathom sacred space unless we understand boundary transgression and displacement? Only then can restoration—ecological, cultural, and spiritual—play its rightful role.

What's left of all the groundwork you've done? Do you see signs of the Ritual Studies Lab's influence? Does anything from it survive?

RG   The people who experienced it are all in diaspora now, afloat on the great sea of undifferentiated, global secularism, ritualizing as best they can. Some of the objects are still around. Not long ago, I handed a mat and a cushion to a former student, saying "This is the dismembered body of the Ritual Studies Lab." He was Catholic enough, and Buddhist enough, to laugh and be grateful for both the action and the words.

SS   Is that how you wanted it all to end?

RG   Well, death being what it is, institutions have life spans. The Lab had a good life of thirty years. That's almost my entire academic career. So I can't complain. And stories trickle back. Students who are now nurses or doctors or chaplains or parents say they find multiple uses for the ritual sensibilities cultivated in the Lab. Sometimes the consequences actually seem to match my intentions, which is more than one can say about learning situations in which there is more talk than action.

Anyway, you're asking a hard question: What does it all amount to? Will it last? Let me ask you a parallel question. After the performance of *Water Finds a Voice* levitated the barn—and I think it really did—did local people absorb it? Does this narrative-ecological practice that you instigated continue? Or, more pointedly, can such impulses survive rural inertia any more than ritual impulses in the Lab can survive the reconstruction of university culture on the basis of business models?

SS   As much as I'd like to say yes, the answer is no. Walkerton lacks the infrastructure to support this kind of work. For two years, we ran the project out of our partner group's environmental resource center, but that has had to close its doors. People are drained—exhausted from stress, economic hardship, and health problems but also from conflicting stories about what their community has become. And, too, innovation is tiring. It's momentarily exhilarating, because you're working with a dilated consciousness, but you can't sustain intense creativity without support. The irony is that the Water Stories Project was possible precisely because of the fissure, the enormous pressure, the water crisis had created. For the next phase of touring the arts, lecturing, writing, and so on, we had to get fiercely pragmatic. So goes the routinization of charisma.

RG   Sounds bleak: The Lab's folded, and the barn is empty. Maybe some momentary celebration will wake them up or set another round of spiritual creativity in motion, but it will all just die down again.

ss   But isn't that as it should be? Our work is tied to organic cycles of focus and diffusion. Don't you say somewhere that ritual is episodic? You can't be in a state of hyperproductivity all the time. So for now, we rest, read, and write. Who knows what will arouse us next, what lurks just around the bend.

IO

Ritual Theory
and the Environment

Between 1992 and 1994 I taught at the University of Colorado as a visiting professor. Shortly after my arrival, I attended a conference on the environment organized by Vine Deloria Jr., author of many books on the conflicts between indigenous religions and Western worldviews. William R. Jordan III, who later wrote The Sunflower Forest: Ecological Restoration and the New Communion with Nature,[190] was also in attendance. The conference, which provoked my interest in ritual and environmental issues, brought together Native people and non-Native environmentalists, many of the latter expecting to celebrate their common values. Instead, differences quickly polarized the group. Clearly, multiple languages, sensibilities, and values surrounded the topic.

Like Siamese twins, this chapter and the one following it were attached at birth. For the health of each, they had to be separated subsequently, although signs of the original unity are still visible in both. The first, unpublished version was plagued with two distinct voices, the one more theoretical, the other, more poetic. For months I tried to integrate the two, but the effort failed, so I resorted to surgery. In this chapter, I lay out an argument, the contours of which are complete, even though the chapter really foreshadows a book-length work that would probe more deeply into the connections among ritual studies, cognitive psychology, and environmental planning.[191]

We are in a mess. The ecological fabric has been ripped, and the fleet-of-foot rescue teams have arrived already. The not so fleet are still on their way. Some passersby are fleeing the scene. A few are stopping to offer advice and band-aids, even bulldozers. Other, less metallic, resuscitation devices are showing up too—among them, ritual.

Few people consider rites an effective means for saving the planet from environmental destruction. Ask the ordinary person, "Should we expect anything of environmental significance from ritual or performance?" and the reply will probably be, "No. Why would anyone even raise such a question?" Yet, we are witnessing the emergence of groups and individuals who consider it obvious that ritual is one, if not *the*, answer to the environmental conundrum. They consider it urgent that humans learn, or relearn, ritual ways of becoming attuned to their environments.

For example, the story of evolution is being told as myth and used as a script to inspire ritual activities. Miriam Therese McGillis leads the Cosmic Walk, a symbolic reenactment of the epic of evolution as told by Brian Swimme and Thomas Berry in *The Universe Story*.[192] Participants meditatively walk a path marked by a coil of rope representing the chronology of earth's emergence and evolution.

Ecological restorationists such as William Jordan III are attempting to spark the ritualizing of pragmatic actions, such as prairie burnings, that restore degraded environments.[193] *Restoration Management & Notes*, a publication that Jordan edited, issued an playful but serious call for scientist-shaman-performer-storytellers who might help construct eco-rituals:

> Immediate opening for people who know the story of the earth and can tell it in a compelling manner. Candidates must be initiated into one or more of the contemporary scientific mysteries (physics, chemistry, geology, biology, ecology, climatology, cosmology, astronomy) and be willing to share the meaning of what they know. Ability to celebrate the rituals of the scientific tradition essential. Chanting and drumming skills useful, but not required for entry level position.[194]

Australian John Seed has designed an event called the Council of All Beings. He and Ruth Rosenhek lead a series of "re-earthing" rituals and workshops, some of which include a welcoming of species and an honoring of local indigenous people, as well as mourning and bonding exercises. Seed and Rosenhek believe that people will act morally and politically on the planet's behalf if they experience the depth of their own planetary despair and cultivate a felt connection with the earth and its creatures. In a culminating phase of one event, participants arrive masked as animal "allies." When the event concludes, folks take off their animal selves and assume their usual, human masks, thereby learning that "human" is just one among many masks that animals wear.[195]

A few mainline religions too have begun constructing environmentally oriented rites. Buddhist monks in Thailand, for instance, are ordaining trees, thereby making them into Buddhas and forcing bulldozer drivers into a crisis of conscience over clearcutting the land.[196]

Artists too are working in concert with some of these movements. Canadian composer Murray Schafer has been engaged in what he calls "theatre of confluence."[197] In wooded rural areas, a series of ritualized musical performance rites called *Patria* (homeland) began in 1966 and continues today. It aims at nothing less than a recovery of a sense of the sacred, one not bound to either the anthropomorphism of Christianity or Renaissance humanism. Schafer writes:

> We need to breathe clean air again; we need to touch the mysteries of the world in the little places and the great wide places; in sunrises, forests, mountains and caves and if need be snowfields or tropical jungles. For too long the clement temperatures of our theatres have neutralized our thermic sensibilities. Why not a concert under a waterfall or a dramatic presentation in a blizzard? And why should we not feel the rain on our faces when we sing or a distant mountain throw back to us the voice we have just sent out to it? Why do we fail to notice the grass at our feet, the darkening of the sky or the sharp green eyes in the night air? Here are the divinities of our holy theatre, now so exceptional for having been ignored so long as to be overpoweringly real. These are the miraculous arenas of living drama inviting us to interaction; and the experience is absolutely free.[198]

Accordingly, Schafer conducts events in the woods that might be loosely called musical, but really they are ritualized enactments in which world mythology provides much of the content and in which landscape is a primary actor.

The surge of popular interest in the ecological possibilities of ritual is fed by a rich, publicly consumed ethnographic literature, some of which depicts rites as a primary means of being attuned to the environment. An environmentally attuned ritual sensibility is not characteristic of every indigenous ritual system, but it is, or was, of many small-scale ones. The import of this ethnographic testimony is that ritual participants believe ritual activity enables them to cultivate a bond with animals and plants, even rocks, mountains, bodies of water, and other holy places. In such societies people are expected to behave environmentally with humility and receptivity. They realize that they are not more powerful than other creatures, so the human task is not only to use creatures but also to be receptive to their teachings. In the traditional world presented by ethnographies, what we in the West think of as nature is animate. In rites, animals and plants and places are addressed with respect as equals, even superiors. Animals and plants and places are people too. So the nature/culture divide either does not exist or is not so pronounced as it is in technocratic societies. In Native and alternative circles, ritual performance is a primary way of becoming attuned to the planet and, attuned, people behave more responsively, thus more responsibly.

In ritually attuned cultures, animals and plants are also food. With apology, song, and prayer, they are killed or harvested, then distributed and eaten.

Animals, like exceptionally generous people, give themselves to hunters, and hunters are the kin of animals. But hunters also track, stalk, study, and strategize. The environmentally attuned ritual attitude, then, does not preclude a pragmatic attitude. Prey are persons, but they are also targets for arrows.

The ethnographic testimony reminds us at the outset that rites are not necessarily nice or foolproof. The animals become angry when they are shot out; the fields rebel when they are overharvested. Although rites attune, they do not do so perfectly or harmlessly. Thus, not all Native people in every place and time are "natural ecologists." Rites not only can attune participants to nature but can also insulate people from nature or make "others" seem different from "us." Rites can become ends in themselves or tools for wreaking environmental and social havoc. Everything depends on which people at which time in which specific place are engaging in which ways of ritualizing their relations with nature.

Responding ritually to environmental crises is not typical of the religious mainstream of the Euroamerican West. When religious liberals, for example, make their peculiar offerings, hoping to appease the ravaged planet, they typically bring ethics, statements about what ought to be, hoping to stem the tide of what is. The currency tendered usually does not consist of plans for renewed cities, scientific procedures aimed at stemming the tide, or musical scales calculated to earn the affection of plants and animals. Rather, codes of moral behavior are the obvious means. If rites are on the table at all, they are there only to buttress moral persuasion. Rites are construed as variables dependent upon, and illustrative of, moral values and religious beliefs.

It would be difficult to deny that ethical reformulations and new laws are essential to the protection of the planet. Who would not subscribe to the sonorous principles of the Earth Charter?[199]

- Do not do to the environment of others what you do not want done to your environment.
- Respect Earth and all life. Earth, each life form, and all living beings possess intrinsic value. . . .
- Share equitably the benefits of natural resources. . . .
- Treat all creatures with compassion. . . .

It is worth being in concert with the aims of the Earth Charter, but the striking feature of religiously attuned environmental activism is the recurrent, liberal-Protestant-sounding assumption that the obvious way to proceed is by formulating ethical principles and then putting them into action by drafting laws and challenging political institutions.

This strategy is necessary but insufficient, because moral principles and new legislation do not by themselves ground worldviews or form attitudes. Attitudes are not merely emotional, nor worldviews merely intellectual. Each collaborates with the other in determining how people act, what they perform, and therefore how they behave. A sailboat's attitude, its tilt, is the result of a complex negotiation among wind, water, and rudder. Human attitudes, too, are complex expressions of one's characteristic tilt in and toward the world.

Asked whether ritual is good for the environment, I am inclined to say yes, but for attitudes to become definitive, they must be cultivated by practice, and the name for sustained, value-laden attitude practice is ritual. In ritualizing, human beings discover, then embody and cultivate their worldviews, attitudes, and ethics. Rites are not only about confirming views that people already hold but also about divining new ways to behave in changing circumstances.

The notion that rites might have an ecological function can sound outrageous even to religious studies scholars and theologians. Typically, both groups treat ritual as having expressive value but not causal force or formative power. For instance, Sallie McFague in *The Body of God: Toward an Ecological Theology* does not include a single index entry on ritual, ceremony, liturgy, or worship. If one asks, What are all those bodies in her book *doing*? the answer is that they are thinking, imagining, and acting ethically. What they are *not* doing is ritualizing. The connection between ethics and ritual is not at all obvious in the popular mind, in religiously motivated environmental activism, or in ritual theory.

Ritual Theory, Performance, and Efficacy

If one turns from liberal religious ethics and theology to functionalist ritual theory and poses the ritual-and-environment question, the answer is, likewise, not an obvious yes. Rather, it is: No, ritual has no significant connection with the environment. Rather, ritual is a way of maintaining the social-political status quo and of keeping in power those who are already in power.

Theorists of ritual are no better equipped than religious liberals to make sense of environmental ritualizing. Few theories accommodate the facts of ritual change, ritual innovation, and ritual performance. Theoretically speaking, it is not at all obvious that one should speak of ritual, arts, and performance in the same breath, much less bring ritualistic, artistic, and performative sensibilities to bear on environmental problems.

Prior to Victor Turner's writings, students of religion and anthropology had been taught to think of ritual and performance as opposites rather than as cousins. Performance was one thing, ritual, another. Performance was entertaining and ritual, serious; performance was pretend and ritual, real. Performance was fictive and subjunctive, shot through with as-ifs, while ritual was believed in—absolutely and without question. As a result, many, both inside and outside the academy, considered ritual religious, traditional, unchanging, and largely maladaptive, whereas performance was irreligious, experimental, theatrical, and adaptive, although sometimes to the point of being fad-driven.

Even theories that seem to embrace performance are not necessarily con-genial to it. For instance, Stanley Tambiah proposed a performative definition. Ritual is

> a culturally constructed system of symbolic communication . . . constituted of patterned and ordered sequences of words and acts, often expressed in multiple media, whose content and arrangement are characterized in varying degree by formality (conventionality), stereotypy (rigidity), condensation (fusion), and redundancy (repetition).[200]

Tambiah recognizes that rites are adapted locally and that they have vari-able components, but he defines ritual as rigid, redundant, and formal, making it difficult to think of it as related to performance, since performance is often associated with the creative, experimental, and playful. The danger, as I see it, is not that of studying rites which are in fact rigid but in granting this character-ization of ritual definitional status and thereby implicitly setting ritual against performance, play, and creativity.

In addition to disagreeing about ritual's creative and adaptive possibilities, theorists are divided over its efficaciousness. Some are willing to consider a rite an effective tool for achieving a specified end, usually a social or psychological one; others argue that rites cannot be properly said to "work" at all. S. G. F. Brandon, illustrating the first predilection, defines ritual as "action of an imita-tive or symbolical kind designed to achieve some end, often of a supernatural character, that could not be achieved through normal means by the person who performs it or on behalf of whom it is performed."[201] Some would say that when a rite aims at observable results (even if by mysterious or supernatural means), it is more properly labeled "magic."

Other theorists regard the question, How do rites work? as nonsensical. The assumption of ritual efficacy, they say, misses the point in the same way it would it would be a mistake to ask whether a piece of art "works." Liturgical theolo-gians, for example, regularly define liturgy so as to remove it from means-end reasoning. Worship rites, like works of art, are not supposed to work or cause; they just are. So the theoretical dilemma is this: Neither what ritual *is* nor what ritual *does* seems appropriate to the task of environmental restoration.

But there are alternative theories. Theater director Richard Schechner cir-cumvents the dilemma by treating performance as the "showing of a doing."[202] By this definition, both ritual and theater qualify as kinds of performance. The difference, according to Schechner, is that ritual performance emphasizes effi-cacy, whereas theatrical performance highlights entertainment, even though ritual also entertains and theater also effects. His view of ritual performance would allow for the possibility of creative and adaptive ways of responding to planetary and environmental dilemmas. If one can assume that ritual efficacy and ritual creativity are possibilities, it becomes easier to understand why people might carry ritual impulses to scenes of environmental degradation.

Definitional wrangling is largely beside the point unless one inquires into its theoretical foundations. If ritual is to have anything more than a buttressing role, dependent for its worth on the moral prescriptions that it acts out or the groups that it consolidates, there is need for an alternative conception which articulates ritual's roots in human biology and the natural environment. Simply redefining ritual so that its performative aspects are more obvious is necessary but insufficient.

By the conventional account, ritual is cultural rather than natural. It is not at all the sort behavior one *cannot help* doing. Ritual is not like eating, sleeping, digesting, and breathing, or even copulating and speaking. Ritual is optional— one can choose *not* to engage in it. Whereas being alive requires eating and sleeping, it does not require ritualizing. Even if one claims that humans and other animals exhibit an inherent urge to ritualize, responding to that urge is optional, and because it is optional, ritualizing is cultural rather than natural. The dichotomy, cultural versus natural, is familiar. It is a staple of Western thought with its dualistic tendencies.

In my view, it is wrong to overstate the separation between culture and nature, since a less polarized view is possible. In fact, it has survival value. One can argue, for instance, that it is perfectly *natural* for humans, given their upright postures and large brains, to be *cultural*. Or one might point out that cultural activities, when sustained for a sufficient time in the right environmental niche, can have genetic, which is to say, evolutionary, consequences. In other words, even though a noticeable cultural/natural *distinction* characterizes much human behavior, it is unnecessary to think of it as *an impassible divide*. We might imagine it as a membrane rather than a chasm or wall. The distinction between things cultural and things natural is relative rather absolute, so it is conceptually possible that ritual (like language but unlike digestion) is both natural and cultural—a cultural edifice constructed on a natural foundation.

According to a few alternative theories, ritual behavior is not an archaic or merely expressive device that groups add to their usual activities in order to provide group cohesion or to shield the powerful from the deprived. Rather, ritualization is hardwired into the structure of the brain and nervous system, a function of primate biological hardware rather than of merely human, cultural software. Even if one tries to escape explicit rites, tacit ritualization nevertheless emerges unbidden. If, for instance, people do not initiate their youth into adulthood, young peers will (perversely in all likelihood) initiate themselves. By this account, all social behavior is not only ritualized but *necessarily* ritualized. In ordinary interaction, ritualizing, like dramatizing, is a universal, a given among humans and other animals. Our very biosocial being is dependent upon these twin foundational activities. Even if people avoid formal rites and stage plays, they cannot escape ritualizing and dramatizing. These impulses are essential to being human; they permeate human actions the same as they do the mating and aggressive behavior of birds and fish.

Ritual and Biogenetic Structuralism

The foundation for an ecologically relevant theory of ritual has already been partly laid. In 1965 Julian Huxley organized a discussion of ritualization among animals and humans, the proceedings for which were published in 1966 by the Royal Society of London.[203] The transactions of that conference are important documents for considering ritual's relation to the environment. In attendance were an unusually large number of thinkers whose ideas would shape ritual theory for the next several decades. Among them were Konrad Lorenz, Victor Turner, Desmond Morris, R. D. Laing, Erik Erikson, Edmund Leach, Myer Fortes, and N. Tinbergen. Huxley proposed this formal definition:

> Ritualization may be defined ethologically as the adaptive formalization or canalization of emotionally motivated behaviour, under the teleonomic pressure of natural selection so as: (a) to promote better and more unambiguous signal function, both intra- and inter-specifically; (b) to serve as more efficient stimulators or releasers of more efficient patterns of action in other individuals; (c) to reduce intra-specific damage; and (d) to serve as sexual or social bonding mechanisms.[204]

He also offered a shorter definition: ". . . the adaptive formalization and canalization of motivated human activities so as to secure more effective communicatory ('signalling') function, reduction of intra-group damage, or better intra-group bonding."[205]

Huxley thought that ritualization (as distinct from ritual) was a biosocial asset rather than a liability. It had survival value. Ritualization was not, as Freud had seemed to imply, dysfunctional. Huxley knew there were differences between human rites and animal ritualization. He assumed they were the result of human ritual's basis in cultural rather than genetic transmission. But he was also insistent that there are important continuities.

Now, after the turn of the millennium, it is more common to assume continuities between animal ritualization and human liturgy, the "bottom" and "top" ends of the ritual spectrum.[206] Among those espousing such a view are anthropologist Charles Laughlin and psychologist Eugene d'Aquili, along with several of their colleagues. By the 1970s they were articulating some of the strongest theoretical arguments in favor of ritual's adaptive import and its fundamental rootedness in the human brain and nervous system. They refer to their theory under various labels, most commonly neuropsychology, neurophenomenology, or biogenetic structuralism. The theory is a confluence of ideas from evolutionary, biological, genetic, ecological, neurophysiological, structuralist, psychological, ethological, and phenomenological thinking. Methodologically, the biogenetic structuralists espouse a wedding of what they call "mature contemplation" (a species of ritual activity) with neuroscience. This combination, they argue, is the most holistic form of consciousness and the most effective means of conducting scientific research.

To invoke terms from structural linguistics, the biogenetic structuralists study *competence* rather than *performance*. The objects of their theorizing are the underlying (or, backstage) structures presupposed by frontstage (or, performative) activity. And these structures are, in their view, systemic, universal, and usually imperceptible to actors (hence, their metaphor "deep" and my metaphor "backstage"). Like rules of grammar, they must be inferred from actual, up-front usage, that is, performance. Accordingly, performance is regarded as a surface *transform* of these deep, or preconscious, structures.

The biogenetic structuralists have tendered several variations of their definition of ritual. A typical one holds that ritual is

> a sequence of behavior that: (1) is structured or patterned; (2) is rhythmic and repetitive (to some degree at least), that is, tends to recur in the same or nearly the same form with some regularity; (3) acts to synchronize affective, perceptual-cognitive, and motor processes within the central nervous system of individual participants; and (4) most particularly, synchronizes these processes among the various individual participants.[207]

Two of the biogenetic structuralists' most far-reaching claims are (1) that ritualization is hardwired—not only cultural but also a necessary function of the biological system and (2) that ritual activity is evolutionarily functional rather than dysfunctional. Ritual, they say, emerged along with encephalization and is crucial for both the control and the transformation of consciousness. Employing various driving mechanisms such as drumming, chanting, dancing, and ingesting, as well as ordeals and privations, rites are means of retuning, or returning balance to, the autonomic nervous system. Ritual activity facilitates the penetration and embodiment of symbols into human selves and societies, thus entraining the symbols into an effective system. In short, there are remarkable similarities between the propositions of biogenetic structuralism and ethnographic testimony concerning ritual's environmental significance.

The biogenetic structuralists posit a drive toward wholeness in all biological systems, and they consider rites a primary means for achieving both social and neuropsychological wholeness. Ritual practices facilitate in the brain a simultaneous discharge of the ergotropic (excitation) and trophotropic (relaxation) systems, thereby coordinating them into a larger whole.

The biogenetic structuralists stop short of claiming that rites are the *only* means of practicing wholeness and interconnectedness. And since they say many of the same things about play and contemplation as they do about ritual, it seems that ritual is not the exclusive agent of wholeness (unless, of course, both play and contemplation are conceptualized as kinds of ritual).

Although I consider biogenetic structuralism a major, provocative theory of ritual, I have three reservations about it:

1. The biogenetic structuralists' claims are more appropriate to some kinds of ritual than to others. What they say about ritual's ability to affect the nervous system and brain applies mainly to trance dance and meditation, the top and bottom ends of the scale of ritual exertion. These two activities require, respectively, either sustained exertion and driving or else the stilling of physical and mental activity. More than mainline worship and decorous liturgy, these kinds of ritual activity stimulate the extremes of the autonomic nervous system, thus facilitating the "crossing over" that biogenetic structuralists treat as the primary biological virtue of ritual. So, unlike the biogenetic structuralists, I would distinguish quotidian ritualization from formal rites, and I would not claim that ritual *in general* attunes, only that *certain kinds* of rites, under certain circumstances, attune.

2. However true it may be that certain kinds of ritual activity can precipitate measurable changes in brain functioning, this fact alone does not mean that ritual is either necessary ("hardwired") or a good thing. As far as we know, there is no "ritual gene," and if sonic driving synchronizes the activities of brain hemispheres, such synchrony may serve evil as readily as it serves good. One can ritually destroy an ecosystem as surely as one can ritually redeem it.

3. There is also the obvious fact that some cultures minimize ritual while others maximize it. In my view, there is not yet a demonstrable connection between the amount of ritualization and the degree of either mental health or ecological sensitivity. So I am less certain than the biogenetic structuralists that ritualization is hardwired, and I am more insistent on the necessity for an ethical critique of ritualistic means. Even though I take issue with the ethics-first or ethics-alone strategies of religious liberalism, I do not assume a ritual-ethics *dis*connection either.

Ritual and Ecological Anthropology

Another key source of theorizing about ritual and the environment is the writing of anthropologist Roy Rappaport. Sometimes he is referred to as an ecological anthropologist and his theory, as an ecological theory of ritual, but the label is not entirely accurate. Some of Rappaport's writing is certainly informed by cybernetic and ecological perspectives, but when he writes more generally on ritual and liturgy, much of his ecologism is displaced by formalism. Unlike the biogenetic structuralists, he claims to study the "obvious" (or performed) rather than the "deep" structures of ritual.

The second edition of Rappaport's *Pigs for the Ancestors* was quite concerned to correct the excessively ecological misreading of the first edition. Rappaport says his demonstration of ritual's crucial role in regulating Maring ecology does not imply that ritual plays such a role elsewhere.[208] His early claims about ritual's ecological function were, he says, culture-specific, a matter of empirical observation of Maring warfare, ritual, and exchange, rather than a general assertion about the function of ritual everywhere. He does not claim, for instance, that the mass and the synagogue Sabbath service help balance the ecosystems in which they are enacted. So, labeled more accurately, Rappaport's later wrork is a formalistic theory of ritual articulated in the context of an ecological worldview.

The concluding chapters of his final book, *Ritual and Religion in the Making of Humanity*, do not say that rites *in fact* exercise ecological functions, rather that they *should*. The ecological framing of his formalistic theory is prescriptive rather than descriptive. Rappaport's ethic assumes or requires a ritual grounding. He articulates what he takes to be the logical (rather than empirical) entailments of ritual form. And his formalism leads to an explicit universalism which resembles that of the biogenetic structuralists. However varied and culture-bound the *contents* and *purposes* of a rite, Rappaport says, ritual *form* is universal:

> [Ritual,] the performance of *more or less* [my emphasis] invariant sequences of formal acts and utterances *not entirely* [my emphasis] encoded by the performers, logically entails the establishment of convention; the sealing of social contract; the construction of the integrated conventional orders we shall call *logoi*; the investment of whatever it encodes with morality; the construction of time and eternity; the representation of a paradigm of creation; the generation of the concept of the sacred and the sanctification of conventional order; the generation of theories of the occult; the evocation of numinous experience; the awareness of the divine; the grasp of the holy; and the construction of orders of meaning transcending the semantic.[209]

This is Rappaport's most comprehensive summary statement. A staggeringly complex assertion, it takes him a book's worth of exposition to clarify. His theory is the most doggedly "ritocentric" of current theories of ritual. For him, not only the sacred and religion, but also social convention, morality, and cosmology are entailments of ritual. Ritual is *the* basic social act.

The "more or less" and "entirely" of his definition are concessions to the possibility of ritual change, revision, and creativity. In my view, they are fragile patches on the dike of his theory. They allow him to make concessions to more processual theories without having to take such alternatives with sufficient seriousness. For instance, he does not really engage the major alternative to his own view of ritual, that of Victor Turner. Whereas for Turner ritual is essentially creative, for Rappaport ritual is essentially conservative.

But both agreed that ritual, whatever else it is, is performative. Without performance, Rappaport says, ritual is merely a dead artifact. Ritual exists properly, fully, in the performing of it. He takes considerable issue with those who believe that myth and ritual express the same thing, just in different media. Since many theorists talk as if ritual had other functional equivalents (social structures capable of doing the same work), Rappaport's is an elevated conception of ritual. He makes ritual not merely interesting or even important but *necessary* for human social survival on the planet. Ritual, he insists, is the *only* way certain kinds of meaning can be expressed. The performative ritual form contains a meta-message—a declaration of certainty and sanctity—that no other form can or does.

Rappaport does not think performance is unique to ritual, so he compares it with dramatic and athletic performance. He makes the usual contrasts: participating ritualistic congregations versus spectating theatrical audiences; ritual's establishment of invariant orders versus theater's problematizing of such orders; ritual's earnestness versus theater's playfulness. And so on. The comparisons are conventional, but the conclusion is controversial, namely, that ritual, drama, and athletics are not equal partners. Drama and athletics are sanctified by their association with ritual, not the other way around. Logically and formally (not necessarily empirically), all other kinds of performance are subordinate to ritual performance.

For Rappaport ritual is "a performative," by which he means a conventional procedure for achieving a conventional effect. Ritual is a complex, not a simple, performative, since one of its primary tasks is that of *establishing* conventions of obligation. Since ritual not only uses convention but also actually establishes it, ritual is, properly speaking, meta-performative. So the sense of the term "performance," as Rappaport uses it, is not only, or even mainly, theatrical. Rather, like J. L. Austin, Rappaport considers a performative to be any embodied accomplishment or doing. "Participants [in rites] enliven the order that they are performing with the energy of their own bodies, and their own voices make it articulate. They thereby establish the existence of that order in this world of matter and energy; they *substantiate* the order as it *informs* them."[210]

Whereas Turner and Schechner use the notion of performance as a wedge against the solidity of the prevailing metaphors of structure and text, Rappaport understands "performativeness" (his term) to be the means of establishing, rather than challenging or undermining, social convention. To perform a rite is to establish and accept a canonical order. Acceptance, by his definition, is not a private state of mind but a fundamentally social, public act.[211] Acceptance, he argues, is intrinsic to ritual performance, and one is bound by it even when violating it, just as one can break a law while acknowledging its validity.

For Rappaport, ritual is *the* paradigmatic means of establishing obligation, thus of generating social and ecological order. Ritual is *the* basic social act without functional equivalents. "In sum, ritual is unique in at once establishing conventions, that is to say, enunciating and accepting them, and in insulating them from usage."[212]

Holiness and sacrality are the ultimate social-environmental insulators. For Rappaport, holiness is inexpressible, but sacrality is "that [discursive] part of the holy [which itself is nondiscursive] that can be expressed in language and that, as it were, faces conscious reason and discourse."[213] In this terminological division of labor, the holy is characterized largely by recourse to Rudolf Otto's phenomenology, except on occasions when holiness is given a reductionist twist by being spoken of as a "product of emotion."[214] Rappaport renders Otto's phenomenology of the holy in such a way as to make ritual performance the origin of religion: "Divine beings . . . remain nothing more than inductions from mystified performativeness."[215]

For Rappaport, religion and ritual, however adaptive and necessary for human survival, are mystified modes of human, utterly human, performance. Even though he makes other statements that seem to contradict this view, the logic of his argument echoes the claims of Ludwig Feuerbach and Karl Marx. For instance, he says, "The vitality that the worshiper feels in the divine object is his own projected upon what he takes to be other or 'concompassing.' Ritual, then, is possibly the furnace within which the image of God is forged out of the power of language and of emotion."[216]

In sum, for Rappaport, ritual is essential to planetary survival not because God created it but because it created God. Rappaport credits ritual generally and liturgical order specifically with the origin of God, religion, rationality, morality, and language. Ritual is *the* self-contained, self-regulating system, hence its importance in modeling social and ecological systems.

There is a stunning paradox at the heart of Rappaport's sweeping vision. On the one hand, ritual utterances ("ultimate sacred postulates") are vacuous; on the other, they are the paradigms of cultural creativity and environmental regulation. On the one hand, liturgies are not "encoded" by performers. On the other, social actors construct meanings.[217] If this is not to be a blatant contradiction, readers of Rappaport must posit two distinctly different points of view, that of liturgical performers who do *not* know that they are constructing meaning, and that of scholars who *do* know that ritualists construct both meanings and gods.

Rappaport crystallizes these two points of view into two models, "cognized" and "operative." Liturgies, in his view, are cognized models. They are emic, issuing from ritual participants. Operative models, on the other hand, are etic; they are the explanatory schemes of theorists. Neither model *is* the environment; both attempt to comprehend it. Both are maps that can never coincide entirely with each other or with the territory to which they refer.

Rappaport's "anthrocentric theology" (my term) is perhaps encapsulated in the single phrase "fabricated sacred truths."[218] It is common to assume that the sacred precludes fabrication and that anything fabricated cannot possibly be sacred. But Rappaport is utterly serious about both adjectives and about holding them together. The outcome is an ironically sacral anthropology that has many of the features of a theology.

Rappaport's conservatism regarding ritual arises in part from his holding Romer's rule as an ultimate sacred proposition in his own theoretical system. Romer's rule states that "the initial effect of an evolutionary change is conservative in that it makes it possible for a previously existing way of life to persist in the face of changed conditions."[219] Rappaport says nothing about subsequent (as opposed to initial) effects. Holding this rule to be the case in the evolutionary, biological world, Rappaport seems also to believe it true of the sociocultural world. Thus, he not only views ritual as conservative, his view of ritual is conservative.[220]

On the surface, it seems that Rappaport's definition and theory might render ritual utterly antiecological, incapable of adaptive change. But Rappaport is quite aware that conventions must be flexible and adaptable for humans to survive. For him, however, the proper location of flexibility and versatility is in language. No longer reliant exclusively upon genetic change, humans adapt by using symbolic means, especially language. The problem with language, he observes, is the lie, the fact that symbols can be divorced from what they signify. With language comes the possibility of lying and disorder, of disordered versatility, innumerable possibilities.

The role of ritual action is opposite that of language. Ritual is the means of grounding change, establishing order, and ensuring certainty in an uncertain world, whereas language is the means of adaptability and change but also of lying. Rappaport, it seems, does not take seriously the possibility of the gestural (as opposed to the linguistic) lie.

Rappaport seems intent, even desperate at times, to defend, restore, or invent ritual's authority, hoping it can close the maws of several great beasts: desertification, ozone depletion, species extinction, and environmental degradation.[221] Against the Goliath of quality-denying, "monetized" epistemologies based on cost-benefit analysis (which he clearly considers maladaptive), he marshals the slingshot of ritual, hoping its emphasis on complementarity and reciprocity can displace the forces of disintegration. The difference between Rappaport and me is that he believes he is describing "the obvious aspects of ritual," whereas I believe he is prescribing a long shot, asking readers to take the risk acting on the assumption that ritual can do something.

Rappaport is more willing than most anthropologists to admit that the very idea of ecology is as much a religious conception as it is a scientific hypothesis:

Ecosystemic conceptions which, in some non-Western societies, approach ultimate sacred status, are thus worthy of high sanctification by the religions of the West as well. High and explicit sanctification of such conceptions and the actions they encourage not only might contribute to the preservation of the world's wholeness in the face of pervasive fragmenting and dissolving forces but could contribute to the revitalization of those religions in an age of increasing skepticism and cynicism toward them.[222]

Rappaport uses the idea of an ecosystem not just as a scientific hypothesis but as an active intervention, a guide for how to act in the world. And ecological thinking, he is sure, requires ritual performance. "Weakened or not, ritual and related forms of action should not be ruled out of attempts to establish a new Logos grounded in the concept of the ecosystem."[223] Rappaport goes even further. For him, humanity "is that part of the world through which the world as a whole can think about itself."[224] So ritual performance is not merely a means for humans to illustrate ideas about the environment. Ritualizing is the way the world itself tries to ensure its own persistence. This is a deeply provocative suggestion, coming as it does from one of the United States' most respected anthropologists.[225]

Is Ritualizing Good for the Planet?

Is ritualizing good for the planet? Ritual studies does not give an unambiguous answer to the question. Whereas conventional ritual theory and mainline post-Protestant practice do not even raise the question, much less support the claim, some indigenous peoples, a few alternative practitioners, and a small group of provocative theorists suggest otherwise. They have not *proven* that ritual is good for planetary health, but they have envisioned this possibility and argued its plausibility on the basis of well-grounded but speculative theory.

Western scientistic and technocratic true believers look with skepticism on the claims of ritualists who emerge from ethnographic literature. At best, their testimony is soft rather than hard evidence. Ethnographic reports present stories, beliefs, descriptions, even tacit hypotheses, but not demonstrated facts or replicable conclusions. So the best one can claim, and still honor the sacred tenets of scientism, is that certain kinds of ritual practices *may* have survival value. They *may* enhance adaptability and thus the longevity of the human species on the planet earth.

One must reiterate the "may" as long as we have not eliminated the alternative, namely, that deeply ritualized human life can render participants one-dimensional, stereotyped, and inflexible—in short, maladaptive. If "stereotypy" (to recall Tambiah's term) were ever a virtue in some other place and time, it is, in the Darwinian universe that many of us inhabit, a vice. Loss of postural and gestural diversity and flexibility would not stand us in good stead with Natural Selection, the reigning deity of the current Darwinian myth.[226] Loss of bodily or cultural flexibility, like loss of cultural and biological diversity, would jeopardize human health and longevity. If ritualizing implies rigidifying, we may be courting earthly extinction rather than planetary salvation by engaging in it. So everything depends on which kinds of ritualizing we practice and which kinds we forgo.

In my view, the convergence of ethnographically recovered indigenous views with ecological and neurobiological theory was one of the most promising of the last century, but it remains incomplete. There is need for synthesis, teasing out implications, critique, and the reformulation of basic definitions of ritual. For me, religious ritual is the predication of identities and differences (metaphors) so profoundly enacted that they suffuse bone and blood, thereby generating a cosmos, an oriented habitat. In such rites people enact a momentary cosmos of metaphor. Ritually, people do not dance merely to exercise limbs or to impress ticket buyers with their skills or even to illustrate sacredly held beliefs. Ritualists dance, rather, to discover ways of inhabiting a place. This is the noetic, or the divinatory, function of ritual; ritual helps people figure out, divine, even construct a cosmos. A cosmos is not merely an empty everywhere. It is an everywhere as perceived from somewhere, a universe as construed from a locale. A cosmos is a topocosm, a universe in this place, an oriented, "cosmosized" place, a this-place which is also an every-where.[227]

Cosmologies are as important for what they tell ritualists *not* to perform as for what they tell them *to* perform. In the middle-of-the-road world many of us inhabit, we are not, in ritual circumstances, supposed to sweat, stay up all night, sleep in the sanctum, enter trance, or let wild sounds escape the throat. All rites, even the holiest of liturgies, express time-bound values and space-bound peculiarities. They are suffused by the same spiritual and intellectual pollution that we all breathe in order to stay alive. So neither ritual theories nor ritual systems are free of the obligation to serve the ground we walk on, the water we drink, the air we breathe. Like Rappaport, I am speaking about what rites *ought* or *might* do. We will not know what ecologically attuned rites *actually do* until we thoroughly embrace sustained ritual experiment and critique.

II

Performance Is Currency

Prior to publication, this was a script for oral performance. Publication required the decorum, the civilizing influence, of those speed bumps we call paragraph breaks.[228] Even though the original script was not written as poetry, it looked more or less like poetry on the page. It looked that way to assist the eye in keeping up with a mouth fondling words in an incantatory way. The performance was preceded by the showing of a scene from The Music Man, a 1961 film in which Robert Preston plays the huckster, Professor Harold Hill. He conjures up parental fear that the young men of River City, Iowa, are going to hell in a handbasket unless they stop playing pool and join the big brass street band that he proposes to lead despite his abysmal musical ignorance.

A young woman asks poet, environmentalist, Buddhist Gary Snyder: "If we have made such good use of animals, eating them, singing about them, drawing them, riding them, and dreaming about them, what do they get back from us?"

". . . Excellent question," replies Snyder, "directly on the point of etiquette and propriety, and putting it from the animals' side. The Ainu say that the deer, salmon, and bear like our music and are fascinated by our languages. So," continues Snyder, "we sing to the fish or the game, speak words to them, say grace. Periodically, we dance for them. A song for your supper. Performance is currency in the deep world's gift economy."[229]

This line is the torah fragment around which I build a fence, the plenary axis I circumambulate. When I first read it, I scribbled questions in the margin: What? Animals care about performances? What kind of performances? Currency? Performance has cash value? Deep world? What's that—a place below this one? And, what do you mean, gift economy? This is a dog-eat-dog, country-eat-country global economy.

Daily newspapers and popular books are riddled with eco-factoids:

- We are extinguishing ten thousand species each year.[230]
- We are destroying the rain forests, earth's most luxuriant life system, at the rate of one acre per second.[231]
- So few farmers are there now that the U.S. Census Bureau has quit counting them as a category.[232]
- Humans have destroyed enough species that it will require a full 10 million years for the planet to recover—twenty times as long as humans have already existed.[233]

Chant a few eco-factoids a sufficient number of times and either you begin to pace, or you become strangely calm. Either you levitate into an apocalyptic frenzy, or you drop down into a surprising stillness.

A few centuries ago we graduated from homicide, patricide, matricide, and suicide, to genocide. Now, we're on to bigger deeds: ecocide and biocide. To destroy a life, even a bevy of lives, is one thing; but to destroy entire species, the genetic templates, the utter seeds of life is quite another. This life-on-earth arrangement is likely a rare, if not a one-shot, deal, but we, our very selves, have become the gravest danger to this tumbling, swirling, teeming entanglement we call life.

Ecocide is slower than homicide but surer, because it is total and irrevocable. War between nations is dramatic and destructive, but industrial waste, lacking the drama, is as deadly. The game of eco-eightball may look benign (because there's always some warranty promising to repair any damage with a technocratic fix), but techno-fixes are patches on a crumbling dam. So we are in dire need of some foolish vision, some brassy, instrument-free band to keep the old boys club occupied, away from the lakes and bays and nesting grounds.

The soiled state of the global nest is just as evident in the fate of ritual as it is in the blitz of eco-factoids. Our choreography, naturally, apes our cosmology. A few years ago, my family and I were invited to an outdoor service. Ecology was in the air and the pastor smelled it. It was time this particular Christian tribe risk a little sunburn on the pale forehead. So the congregation moved all the chairs outdoors, leaving their sacred, suburban canopy empty for that particular Lord's Day.

It was an awkward spectacle, clerical robes blowing up thigh high, bulletins flying, chairs tipping this way and that on the uneven slope, adults squinting in the sun, and kids, invited into action by fresh-cut grass, romping and rolling. . . .

Despite the claims of the sermon, everything about that performance (except the oatmeal molasses brown bread from the hand of the pastor's mother) was a testimony to alienation from the environment, to the utter unsuitability of this liturgy to this place. The pastor held an ecologically respectable view of the universe, and she did distribute her mother's homemade oatmeal molasses brown bread instead of paper-thin wafers, but this liturgical celebration dishonored the dirt upon which it was done.

The state of the world nest is reflected in the failure of the old "services" to service that nest. Liturgies around the world have been caught in the act of doing disservice to the planet. Ritual disservice to the planet—ponder that.

Performance

You wouldn't expect it, would you, for performance to be anybody's answer to the question: How can we save River-City-Bay-Town-Mountain-Village from death by conspicuous overconsumption? Unless, of course, we are required to entrance the plants and animals with our song and dance.

The question of planetary survival is a conundrum, a koan. A koan is not just a cute riddle, a brainteaser for Buddhists. A koan is a bottleneck-in-being, a belly full to meditate upon for the duration. The incantation, "Performance is currency" implies a koan-like question: What action, rightly performed, can save the planet? This koan of planetary performance, let us call it, when it is properly contemplated, should burn like a jalapeño in the belly of the soul.

If you are among the quick-witted, you may think you already have the answer, and it is: "There is no such action." But if this is your reply, you are too quick for your own damned good. A koan, it's true, is an impossible question, but, as a dutiful disciple of the earth, you must answer it, not evade it. In fact, you not only must answer correctly (for your heartbeat and breath cycle depend upon it), you must embody your reply. The reply can't be evasive or merely verbal. If your reply is that there is no answer at all, or that there is no gesture performative, ritualistic, or otherwise that could possibly save the planet, then the master, the lord of the beasts, sends you back to square one to meditate on the koan of planetary performance.

As long as performance is confined to performance halls, performance is no answer to the problem of saving the planet from toxicity and species evacuation. The best that aesthetic art can do is to mime the problem.

The same is true of religious religion and scientistic science. The problem lies in the sectoring and the scissoring. In the sectored-and scissored-up world, performance is one thing, religion, another. Performance is entertaining and religion, serious; performance is pretend and religion, real. Performance is fictive and subjunctive, shot through with as-ifs, while religion is believed—absolutely and without question.

But Gary Snyder, our testy teacher whose aphorism I am shamelessly and publicly milking, assumes no such divisive dualism. He keeps performance together with religion; singing to the fish together with saying grace. In the deep world, ritual enactment and theatrical performance are not enemies; they are cousins, kissin' cousins.

So what kind of performance could possibly gain the attention of the creatures and thereby save the world? If you consider the world from the animals' point of view, the answer is obvious: Performances in which the performers are animals, human and otherwise. Coyotes and baboons are as narcissistic as we are. Why, they'll trade their skins to witness good singing and dancing. Performances are currency only if they are deep-world performances, and they are deep-world performances only if their metaphors are embodied—radically, to the bone, to the quick.

To dance the peacock or play the snake, you must become the peacock, be the snake. A deep-world performance is one in which performers are so drastically identified with the objects of their performance that there is no difference, even though everybody knows animals and humans are different.

Such a world can be frightening. Why, when your very lawn or your beloved garden—object of costly love and chemical affection—rises up against you, subjecting you to tough, inquisitorial questions, well, what can you do but tremble?

Fearing the magic that always arrives on the heels of drastically embodied metaphors, people are tempted to resist the call to right ritualizing by setting performance and ritual in opposition.

Ritual is religious, traditional, unchanging, and purged, by god, of magic. Accordingly, performance is irreligious, experimental, theatrical, and, shame upon its head, fad-driven.

But the congregation of earth creatures has no use for squeaky-clean, safe religion and just as little use for aestheticized entertainment purged of harmony, humility, and prayer. Neither earns the applause of butterflies and milkweed.

Currency

Another surprise: Ecology activists, especially poetic Buddhist ones, don't talk much about money. But consider this: Currency is any medium of exchange, the stuff which, though worthless in itself, we work for, buy with, die for. Currency: paper that stands for gold or silver which in turn stands for food and shelter and air and water. Currency: the symbolic stuff with which we buy our way out (or in).

When sneaky Snyder teases us into believing that performance is currency, he isn't talking about box office revenues, or the sort of performance the governments have in mind when they declare that grants to universities will hereinafter be dependent upon multiple performance indicators. He's saying performances themselves are currency. The performances, not the money, are what earn the attention, the grace, and the forgiveness of the animals and plants and spirits, the council of all beings.

The reigning view is that science and technology, allied with industry and commerce, can mint the currency with which to buy our way out of the ecological mess. But, of course, the ecological mess is bigger than science, because scientists (like the rest of us) are smaller than the universe. Earth contains science and scientists, not the other way around.

The world's planners and managers like to construe the state of the planet as a problem with a solution. But solutions are discrete and specific, whereas the eco-crisis is systemic and pervasive; it implicates the whole, not just some part such as the sludge in the Great Lakes, the air over Mexico City, or salmon who refuse to run West Coast streams in British Columbia. So a planet-saving performance requires the participation of the entire council of creatures, not just some special class like scientists or priests or band leaders or professors or artists or even humans.

There is no ecological problem—except earthly extinction, which is to say, problem solving is the wrong model. We will never know enough in time to solve the earth's human "problem." To echo Yeats, we can embody truth but we cannot know it. A problem assumes a problem solver who stands apart from the problem. A problem concerns some thing *in* or *on* the earth. A crisis concerns the fate *of* the earth.

The difficulty, then, is not with this trombone or that violin but with the whole concert, in fact, with the music that underscores it. There is only one concert playing on stage-earth, and we have no choice but to play together. So, by all means, let there be scientists and technicians in Mr. Music Man's big brass save-the-planet band, but also call the bricklayers, boom operators, old cranks, young crickets, and master tinkers.

Some scientists fret that so many nonscientists are showing up on an already overcrowded stage. Other scientists welcome the tinkers. On the one hand, the talk becomes fuzzier. On the other, the arrival of ritual-makers and musicians, parading Fundies and becaped witches, game animals and domestic vegetables makes the medicine show a lot more entertaining as the music, the squawking, and the metaphors begin to flap and fly. The currency-confusion is godawful. What's the medium of exchange—formulas and equations? Or musical scores and incantations?

When religious people arrive at the ecological market where planetary salvation is up for auction, they usually arrive with a wallet full of moral currency. They typically tender ethics, statements about what ought to be, hoping to stem the tide of what is. The currency of religion, as well as religious studies, is not rules of scientific procedure or musical scales but canons of belief and codes of behavior.

A series of conferences was held at Harvard. Out of them emerged the Forum on Religion and Ecology[234] and several volumes on the environmental contributions of the multinational religions. A remarkable feature is how much attention the volumes pay to beliefs, myths, ethics, and worldviews and how little they attend to ritual and other kinds of performance. The Forum's brochure describes its mission as that of "highlighting the important roles religious traditions play in constructing moral frameworks and orienting narratives regarding human interactions with the environment." Even though the brochure mentions ritual practices, it rapidly drops the topic to return to the theme of a "distinctive ethics of respect for nature."[235]

The framers of the Earth Charter are ethically preoccupied too. They speak of their carefully hammered out ethical principles as "soft law." They hope nations and other human groups will give these principles teeth by transforming them into "hard law," the kind you are fined for violating.

For sure, ethical reformulations and new laws are required to protect the planet. And we could do worse than subscribe to the sonorous principles of The Earth Charter:[236]

- Do not do to the environment of others what you do not want done to your environment.
- Respect Earth and all life. Earth, each life form, and all living beings possess intrinsic value. . . .
- Share equitably the benefits of natural resources. . . .
- Treat all creatures with compassion. . . .

The Earth Charter is a generically religious document. "Earth" is capitalized, and the principles echo those of several faith traditions. Charter principles are lofty and worthy, but can they create the realities they aspire to? Probably not. That's why the framers of the Charter hope to inspire legislation, "hard law."

I'm in concert with the aims of the Forum on Religion and Ecology and of the Earth Charter, but what strikes me about these and other examples of religiously attuned environmental activism is the recurrent, liberal-Protestant-sounding assumption that the obvious way to proceed is by formulating ethical principles and then putting them into action by challenging political institutions.

The strategy is necessary but insufficient, because moral principles and new legislation don't—by themselves, disembodied—change attitudes. Attitudes and worldviews are related; each conditions the other. Attitudes are not merely emotional, or worldviews merely intellectual. Each conspires with the other in determining how we act, what we perform, and therefore how we behave.

Deep World

Performance is currency in the deep world. . . . What is this "deep world"? Surely not some place below the ground, or some supernatural envelope surrounding ordinary reality, not even the human unconscious (which we in the psychologized West imagine as deep within the psyche).

We in the sectored-and-scissored West are habituated to dividing things into warring camps: shallow world/deep world, this world/the other world. The philosophical label for this particular form of deviance is dualism. Our dualistic tendencies lure us into setting part against whole, part against part. Dualism is not the mere making of distinctions but the setting of them in hierarchical and antagonistic relation to one another and then assuming that one of the two parties is not necessary while the other is.

Dualism lives in the marrow and blood; it's taken root in languages and brains. But Earth is declaring dualism taboo. Earth people are recognizing that the survival value of a scissored-and-sectored cosmology is diminishing at an ever-increasing rate. We have stumbled over the obvious: The ankle bone is connected to the shinbone is connected to the knee bone is connected to the thigh bone is connected to the planet Jupiter is connected to the crawling things beneath the sod is connected to the price of Canadian lake water exported to Japan.

So we're pausing to take stock. We're asking: What's the cost of stashing science in labs, art in galleries, education in universities, government in parliament buildings, and religion in temples?

Answer: The cost is the rarification of religion, the preciousness of the arts, the bureaucratization of government, and the reign of technocratic scientism throughout the land.

If there is to be an enduring deep world, some superseamstress somewhere must find a needle capable of stitching together the swatches.

The deep world, then, is not the opposite of the shallow, or this, world. Rather, it is—now you may choose your metaphor—the center of the six directions, the kingdom of God which is among you, nirvana which is no place other than samsara. In short, the deep world is the planet, whole cloth, earth's space and history, all of a piece. The deep world is this very world on occasions performative, when creeping, crawling critters and tenacious, clinging weeds join things vegetative, hopping, and contemplative to sing and talk and dance and eat together with the beclothed, us humans. That's deep.

The deep world, because it is an imagined, performed cosmos, is momentary and occasional, but it is also metaphorically and utterly real, as real as anybody's smokestack or weed whacker. The deep world is fed on things sprouting in the dark root cellar of the human animal's imagination.

Participants in international religion and ecology discussions sometimes recognize that more than ethical principles and just laws are needed, that deep-world transformation is necessary. One religious studies scholar declares, "As a Buddhist, I would emphasize that inner personal transformation is most basic."[237] For her, consciousness is the deepest, or most fundamental, layer. The logic seems to be: A change in consciousness eventuates in an explicit ethic, which in turn inspires ecologically sensitive laws, which in turn bring about collective and institutional compliance, thus transforming the planet into a just and sustainable environment.

But spiritual change alone makes no more sense than legal change alone. It is as profoundly counter-ecological to posit consciousness or spirit as basic as it is to claim that law or matter or production is basic. Neither survives for long without the other.

The urgent task, then, is not in deciding which is deepest, spirituality or politics, religion or theater, but learning how to nurture such an attitude of interconnectedness that *we* are no longer the aliens on the earth. We human creatures have always tended to levitate off the planet. By thinking, emoting, imagining, calculating, and inventing, we rarefy ourselves into the ether, fancying that we are not food. But if we cannot learn to be food, our species will become a dead-end branch on the evolutionary tree. So the question is how to ground ourselves, admit that we are food, and become the animals we are.

Gift Economy

Performance is currency in the gift economy. A gift economy is a ritual economy, a performative means of exchange in a stitched-together, bricolage world. A gift economy is related to *the* economy, but it's not identical with it. A gift economy has a certain holy foolishness to it. In *the* economy, gifting would seem an unlikely answer to the "problem" of ecological disaster. *The* economy is supposed to be sufficiently rational that, having conducted a calculation of risks and benefits, one can cash into it. The gift economy, however, originates with a giveaway, a proffering of gratitude magnanimous, of play excessive and impractical.

To the council of all beings, bodied and disembodied, masked and unmasked, the gift economy makes a certain ridiculous-hilarious-utterly-essential sense, and it assumes the necessity of loss, even of deliberate and celebrated loss, of sacrifice, of giving up what you'd rather keep.

The economy would never countenance offering African beer to ancestors already in the ground, spilling the blood of perfectly edible Haitian chickens, yielding up only begotten sons, giving away first fruits, or promulgating a jubilee cancellation of third world debt.

In a gift economy, the animals are willing to trade their very skins and feathers for a song and dance. So the people-dancers and the people-singers must condescend to trade *their* skins and *their* masks for those of animals or plants or water or clouds.

What the creatures have to lose in the gift economy is their lives. What the people have to lose is their false sense of themselves as superior.

Deep-world performance transpires any place where a gift economy, even temporarily, undermines—or better, suffuses—"the" economy. But what kind of performance is appropriate to a gift economy? It's easy enough to say: Do the dog. Wiggle the worm. Howl the jackal. Admit to being fodder or cabbage or bran.

Ritually speaking, we are not only what we eat, but also what we sing, proclaim, dance, chant, drum. If I am what I sing, what will singing this song make of me? If I am what I dance, what will doing this dance make of me? These are gift-economy, ritual, questions.

The peanuts in the gallery only care if the dancing and eating and singing make of us, plants. The snaky creatures of the orchestra pit only care if the dancing and eating and singing make of us, animals. The earth only cares if the dancing and eating and singing make of us, earthlings.

If we can't earn either the respectful silence of carrots or the applause of vultures, we won't survive the third millennium. Like all performers, we are radically dependent upon our audience. So drastic is our dependence upon the council of creatures that *they* are the real auditors of earth's books. *They* are the true congregation, the real tribe, the original extended family. And the kind of performance *they* require is ritualistic. The only kind of performance capable of saving the planet is the kind worms applaud with their peculiar sort of silence, the sort to which geese respond with bawdy squawking and clacking (silence and racket being earth's main gestures of approval).

Planetarily significant performances transpire in times and places where the deep-gift economy is actualized, because these are the only spaces where geese and worms and bears and bugs are welcome as congregants.

Snipes and turtles and other creatures rooted or bipedal are utterly fascinated with human performances in which they themselves appear, and they can *only* appear when ritualizing humans sacrifice their sniveling little dignities in order to don skins that the creatures sacrifice.

Just as the pool-playing boys of River City, Iowa, need a big brass band to stem their lapse into delinquency, so we ought to dress in the plumage of deforested pines, make offerings of Erie water, and meditate beneath the bridges of the Don Valley Parkway.

Too grandiose? Too full of bilgewater and balderdash? Well, okay, for the likes of us who've made it to the twenty-first century, it may be that ritual is possible only in a ludic-ironic-metaphoric, clowny-subjunctive-disjunctive fiddledeedee mode. But embraced-to-the-point-of-embodiment, metaphoric-ironic ritualizing, however perverse and silly, is a way in.

The deep world is stitched of metaphors, and if you cut them loose from one another and yourself, you skin the world, peel it like an onion. No net of metaphor, no earth. No earth, no place for an audience to stand. No place, no performance. No performance, no performers. No performers, no students of performances entertaining and efficacious.

We are engaged in a global conflict over metaphor. The mere-metaphor school is content, thank you, to leave metaphor a mere turn of phrase; these folks aren't about to chant their metaphors, much less inhabit them. The deep-and-drastic school, on the other hand, insists that metaphor is not empty talk, that world metaphors should be practiced, so convincingly embodied, that even alpha male apes can't be sure if those strutting on the stage are animals, or men, dressed up like animals, so convincingly performed that even the muses can't decide whether those are goddesses or women gussied up like birds.

Ritual is the predication of identities and differences (metaphors) so profoundly enacted that they suffuse bone and blood, thereby generating a cosmos (an oriented habitat). In rites we enact a momentary cosmos of metaphor. A cosmos is not merely an empty everywhere. It is an everywhere as perceived from somewhere, a universe as construed from a locale. A cosmos is a topocosm, a universe in this place, an oriented, "cosmosized" place, a this-place which is also an every-where.

Each cosmos has its characteristic lilt: If your universe is a womb, your rites go rotund; they moan, slip, and slide. If your universe is an orderly, law-abiding, clocklike place looked after by a kindly watchmaker who prefers really, really big grandfather clocks, your rites will run regular as clockwork, be performed as if ritual were, by definition, repetitive, orderly, stately, vertical, and by the book.

Cosmologies are as important for what they tell ritualists *not* to perform as for what they tell them *to* perform. In the middle-of-the-road world many of us inhabit, we are not ritually supposed to sweat, stay up all night, sleep in the sanctum, enter trance, or let wild sounds escape the throat.

Otherwise, the critters might arrive in droves, and mama earth might heave her big buttocks smack into the middle of our decorous assemblies. In the middle-of-the-road world, entranced, drum-driven bouncing, and trembling buttocks are out. So is just sitting, eyes down as if quieted belly buttons and round cushions matter.

All rites, even the holiest of liturgies, express time-bound values and space-bound peculiarities. They are suffused by the same spiritual and intellectual pollution that we all breathe in order to stay alive. Even so, ritual systems are not free of the obligation to serve the ground we walk on, the water we drink, the air we breathe.

With rites we have served gods; now, with rites let us serve the ground, the air and water, the frogs and rutabaga, even our cranky ancestors buried book-in-hand in six feet of clay.

What might it look like to turn book-serving liturgies into earth-serving ones? In Thailand, where the rate of deforestation is exceptionally high, monks have begun ordaining trees. By ordaining these upstanding ones, the monks inspire bulldozer drivers to stop, chainsaw cutters to balk, and developers to reconsider. Thai "ecology monks" are crossing the line that has traditionally kept them from political involvement. Would you cut down a seventy-year-old, fifty-foot tree-priest in his prime?

Clearcutting in Thailand had become so extensive that monks began preaching about the suffering of trees and land. In order to sanctify forests so wildlife and plant life would be protected, the monks began hammering old Buddhist rites into new activist ceremonies.

In the 1970s, after his ordination, Phrakhru Pitak began to notice the deforestation around his home and the consequent damage to watersheds and local economies. He began to preach against the destruction but found that the villagers, even those who believed him, went home from temple services only to continue clearing the land. Moral admonition was not enough. So in 1991 he ordained a tree, wrapping it in monk's robes. To down an ordained tree would be to kill a sentient being and incur religious demerit.

At first, the monk led people in sprinkling holy water on the trees. Later, he upped the ante by requiring village leaders to drink holy water in front of a statue of Buddha by a tree. This way, community leaders ritually enacted their identification with the tree, and thereby pledged themselves to its protection. Sometimes, posted on an ordained tree would be a sign saying, "To destroy the forest is to destroy life, one's rebirth, or the nation."[238] Sincere Buddhists don't want to tamper with their rebirth.

This improvised ritualizing is now attracting upstanding citizens. As a result, the Thai debate is no longer purely political but also moral and religious. The metaphoric act of ordaining trees has made it so. If trees have Buddha nature, to saw one down is to slice yourself in half. Now, it costs moral and religious capital to lay low the ancestor-teacher trees.

The so-called world religions claim to have a repository of wisdom that can help save the planet from ecological destruction. But the large-scale, multinational faiths have been slow to mobilize, and they are typically saddled with environmentally hostile or indifferent myths, ethics, and rites.

Religious leaders are now scouring the scriptures in search of images capable of inspiring ecologically responsible behavior. The big religions are defending their traditions against attacks that blame them for the sorry state of the environment. In self-defense, they launch criticisms of economic greed and human failure to exercise stewardship of the land.

The monotheistic traditions bear a large share of the blame, because of their entanglement in Western ideologies of natural domination and dualistic separation. The truth is that none of the large-scale religions has resources adequate to the crisis. None of the "world" religions is an earth religion. The nonlocal religions are in no better shape than the multinational corporations. Because so much pollutes the spiritual environment, cleaning it up is every bit as urgent and challenging as cleaning up the physical environment.

The ecological question can be posed politically, biologically, economically, legally. I have put it ritually by asking, What gesture can save the planet? You, of course, know this is a silly question, a trap. You're educated, smart enough to know that by calling the question a koan, I'm either sidestepping or teasing you. I am trading on what I surmise about readers, that you are devotees of the well-posed question. There is nothing finer in the reading-and-writing life than a question that requires a koanic response, that is, a disciplined and passionate identification with the question.

So again I put it to you: What gesture, rightly performed, might be so compelling that the creatures would be entertained and thus, the planet saved? We can put it in other, more local ways: What does the south shore of Lake Erie ask of men on Tuesdays? Women on Thursdays? Why is the Rio Grande weeping? Where on Highway 7 should the northbound tundra swans land during rush hour?

I'm sure you have your own environmental koans, conundrums in need of direct action but also of divination and contemplation. Just remember that the point is not to turn cute phrases or to moralize but to identify yourself bodily and attitudinally with the questions. Otherwise, the grackles and sparrows won't give a rip about our celebrations, liturgies, meditations, and performances.

A koanic attitude practiced ritually helps participants divine a way of acting that resonates with the world. Ritually, people don't dance merely to exercise limbs, impress ticket-buying audiences, or even to illustrate sacredly held beliefs. People who dance in a sacred manner do so to discover ways of inhabiting a place. (This is what we call the noetic power of a rite.) If we ritualize *only* to confirm what we already know, our ritualizing is in a state of decay.

So here's the pitch. Here's what I'm trying to sell you on instead of a brass band: Just as there is an emerging global culture overtop local cultures, and civil religion alongside denominational religion, so there are emerging global ritual gestures boiling up under the liturgies of specific religious traditions. The Olympic Games are the grandest example. So a global earth rite parallel to a global ethic in the Earth Charter is not an impossibility (even though the notion is as ridiculous as that of a salvific street band whose leader is a musical ignoramus).

A few decades ago we'd have thought it ridiculous to consider drafting universal, ethical declarations. We'd read enough history and anthropology to know that different societies have different values and differing ways of doing things. We'd have said that only a powerful act of coercion could bring about a global ethic. But a global ethic is now on the horizon. Maybe it will require another millennium for every nation to sign on, and such an ethic will not be framed without compromise, but there is a surprising consensus in documents such as the Universal Declaration of Human Rights. So, why not an earth-embracing, earth-encircling rite?

If that's too grandiose and you worry about a globalized rite for the same reasons you've become suspicious about globalization and multinational corporations, then ritualize in your own back yard. Literally. Physically. Bodily.

For now, imagine just a single gesture or posture that might become the seed of a rite. Make it one worth doing, or holding, over and over. This is ritual, so again, again, and again. Even when no one is watching: again.

What is the shape and duration of your gesture? What's the basis of your posture? Sacred texts are too tendentious a basis, so what else might a gesture to the creatures be based on? In what posture would we not scare them away, would they not fear to creep up on us?

The universe is curved, they say, just closed enough to maintain cohesion, just open enough for transformation and creativity. So why not a curvaceous gesture based on the shape you imagine the universe to have?

Now, this brass-band-foolish gesture not only has to make the monkeys laugh loud enough that the hyenas and dingos come to see what's up, it must be a practice that helps people root themselves in the planet like old trees worthy of ordination. It should be a gesture so simple and profound that, even if it doesn't attract the hordes or save the planet, you'd keep doing it anyway, hoping to hear cabbage heads chuckle and frogs titter, because performance is currency in the deep world's gift economy.

So . . . What are you imagining? Bowing like a Muslim at prayer (but sneaking in a ground kiss)? Standing, Navajo-like, thrusting your child high so the rising sun can see? Circumambulating a tree in your back yard until a circular path is worn deeply into the ground? Washing each of your neighbors' feet each time they enter your front door? Maybe you are curled up, your head in Big Mama's lap. Or maybe you are handing a clear glass of water, without spilling a drop, hand over hand over hand down the serpentine miles of a river's course. Perhaps you are prone, lying on the warm desert sand, your arms spreadeagled so that from on high, a god's eye or cloud would spy only a tiny swatch on the landscape.

A sustainable gesture to the creatures is possible only by a dialectical dance. So grab your partner and all go round. Leap locally to the left. Leap globally to the right, all at the very same, very curvaceous time. This is a riprap romp, a locally global medicine show.

If exercising your imagination this way makes you feel foolish, a little like you're pretending to be the leader of the band when you never went to music school, a little suspicious that ritual gestures and postures are as useless as, what? a roll of waxed toilet paper, well, you can relieve yourself of this self-conscious foolishness by chanting.

By now, surely, you know the words. . . .

Notes

1. Originally published as Ronald L. Grimes, "Ritual and the Media," in *Practicing Religion in the Age of the Media: Explorations in Media, Religion and Culture,* ed. Stewart Hoover and Lynn Schofield Clark (New York: Columbia University Press, 2002). Reprinted with permission of the publisher.

2. A similar list, based on literature rather than media, can be found in Ronald L. Grimes, *Reading, Writing, and Ritualizing: Ritual in Fictive, Liturgical, and Public Places* (Washington, DC: Pastoral Press and Oregon Catholic Press, 1993).

3. The distinctions among rite, ritualization, and magic are worked out in Ronald L. Grimes, *Ritual Criticism: Case Studies in Its Practice, Essays on Its Theory,* ed. Frederick M. Denny, vol. 10, Studies in Comparative Religion (Columbia: University of South Carolina Press, 1990), 9ff., and in Ronald L. Grimes, *Beginnings in Ritual Studies,* rev. ed. (Columbia: University of South Carolina Press, 1994), chap. 3.

4. Erving Goffman, *Interaction Ritual: Essays on Face-to-Face Behavior* (Garden City, NY: Doubleday Anchor, 1967).

5. Pueblos themselves do not think of these as "corn" dances. The designation is an English ("Anglo") one.

6. "Prophetic" here obviously does not mean "predictive." It means "socially critical."

7. Gregor Goethals, *The TV Ritual: Worship at the Video Altar* (Boston: Beacon, 1981). Robbie Davis-Floyd assumes the same strategy; see Robbie E. Davis-Floyd, *Birth as an American Rite of Passage* (Berkeley: University of California Press, 1992). A critique of this position can be found in Ronald L. Grimes, *Deeply into the Bone: Re-inventing Rites of Passage* (Berkeley: University of California Press, 2000).

8. Janice Peck's discussion of ritual and television depends on Goethals for her understanding of ritual; see Janice Peck, "The Appeal of Form: Ritual, Rhetoric, and Televisual Framing," in *The Gods of Televangelism: The Crisis of Meaning and the Appeal of Religious Television* (Cresskill, NJ: Hampton, 1993). Also see Gregor Goethals, *The TV Ritual: Worship at the Video Altar* (Boston: Beacon, 1981).

9. Bobby C. Alexander, *Televangelism Reconsidered: Ritual in the Search for Human Community* (Atlanta, GA: Scholars Press, 1994), 4.

10. Vincent Crapanzano, "Rite of Return: Circumcision in Morocco," in *The Psychoanalytic Study of Society*, ed. Werner Muensterberger (New Haven, CT: Yale University Press, 1980).

11. James Carey, ed., *Media, Myths and Narratives: Television and the Press* (Newbury Park, CA: Sage, 1989).

12. Her understanding of ritual is borrowed from Roger Grainger, *The Language of the Rite* (London: Darton, Longman and Todd, 1974).

13. Vivian Sobchack, "Genre Film: Myth, Ritual, and Sociodrama," in *Film/Culture: Explorations of Cinema in Its Social Context*, ed. Sari Thomas (Metuchen, NJ: Scarecrow, 1982), 163.

14. Abelman borrows the distinction between ritualized and instrumental viewing from A. M. Rubin, "Ritualized and Instrumental Television Viewing," *Journal of Communication* 34, no. 3 (1984): 67–77.

15. Michael Schudson, "Advertising as Capitalist Realism," in *Advertising, the Uneasy Persuasion: Its Dubious Impact on American Society* (New York: Basic Books, 1984), 209–233, especially 214, 228.

16. Quentin J. Schultze, "Secular Television as Popular Religion," in *Religious Television: Controversies and Conclusions*, ed. Stewart M. Hoover and Robert Abelman (Norwood, NJ: Ablex, 1990), 20.

17. Ron Burnett, *Cultures of Vision: Images, Media, and the Imaginary* (Blooming-ton: Indiana University Press, 1995), 86.

18. Meyer Fortes warns, "It is a short step from the notion of ritual as communication to the non-existence of ritual *per se*." Meyer Fortes, "Religious Premises and Logical Technique in Divinatory Ritual," *Philosophical Transactions of the Royal Society of London* 251 (1966): 409–422.

19. Quentin J. Schultze, "Television Drama as Sacred Text," in *Channels of Belief: Religion and American Commercial Television*, ed. John P. Ferre (Ames: Iowa State University Press, 1990). Cf. Schultze, "Secular Television as Popular Religion."

20. Hoover's strategy is more restrained and precise. For him, television is "armchair pilgrimage." Stewart M. Hoover, "Television Myth and Ritual: The Role of Substantive Meaning and Spatiality," in *Media, Myth, and Narratives: Television and the Press*, ed. James W. Carey (Newbury Park, CA: Sage, 1988), 171.

21. M. E. Combs-Schilling, *Sacred Performances: Islam, Sexuality, Sacrifice* (New York: Columbia University Press, 1989), 29. Another definition similar in its emphasis on the multimedia nature of ritual is offered by Bruce Kapferer, who says it is "a multi-modal symbolic form, the practice of which is marked off (usually spatially and temporally) from, or within, the routine of everyday life, and which has specified, in advance of its enactment, a particular sequential ordering of acts, utterances and events, which are essential to the recognition of the ritual by cultural

members as being representative of a specific cultural type." Bruce Kapferer, *A Celebration of Demons: Exorcism and the Aesthetics of Healing in Sri Lanka* (Bloomington: Indiana University Press, 1983), 2.

22. Jonathan Z. Smith, "The Bare Facts of Ritual," *History of Religion* 20, nos. 1–2 (1980): 125.

23. A critique of Smith's theory can be found in chapter 8.

24. See Richard Schechner, *Between Theater & Anthropology* (Philadelphia: University of Pennsylvania Press, 1985).

25. Originally published as Ronald L. Grimes, "Consuming Ritual: A&E's *Sacred Rites and Rituals*," in *Contemporary Consumption Rituals: A Research Anthology*, ed. Cele C. Otnes and Tina M. Lowrey (Mawah, NJ: Erlbaum, 2003). Reprinted with permission of the publisher.

26. The Web site for Arts and Entertainment's *Ancient Mysteries* is http://www.aande.com/tv/shows/ancientmystery.html.

27. After undergoing several media interviews on ritual (with NPR, PRI, and BBC), I find it easy to anticipate the questions, since they are remarkably similar. The queries, desires, and fantasies bearing on ritual are clearly culture- and time-bound.

28. An interest in the negative sides of ritual did, however, show up in the final version of the film.

29. Richard Schechner, "Restoration of Behaviour," in *Readings in Ritual Studies*, ed. Ronald L. Grimes (Upper Saddle River, NJ: Prentice-Hall, 1996).

30. Richard Schechner, *Essays on Performance Theory, 1970–1976* (New York: Drama Book Specialists, 1977).

31. One of the scholars in the film, Vivian-Lee Nyitray, tries to head off the assumption of primitivity by saying that ritual performers are not "primitive," rather they exhibit "expanded plausibility structures."

32. Rite: sequences of action rendered special by virtue of their condensation, elevation, or stylization. Rites are distinct, socially recognized set of procedures. Often they are named, as well as enacted, in set-aside times and specially chosen places.

Ritual: the general idea of actions characterized by a certain "family" of qualities, for instance, that they are performed, formalized, patterned, condensed, and so on. No one or two of these qualities is definitive. Therefore, ritual is not "digital," that is, either on or off. Rather, all behavior is ritualized—some of it more, some of it less. The degree of ritualization increases as the number and intensity of these and other behavioral qualities increase.

Ritualization: (1) activities not normally viewed as rites but treated as if they were or might be, for instance, giving birth, house cleaning, canoeing, and TV watching—all have been regarded *as* ritual; (2) in ethology, ritual insofar as animals engage in it, actions usually associated with aggression or mating.

Ritualizing: the act of deliberately cultivating or constructing a new rite. The terms are more fully explained in Grimes, *Beginnings in Ritual Studies*. See also Grimes, *Ritual Criticism: Case Studies in Its Practice, Essays on Its Theory*.

33. One could use other terms. These are imperfect, and my investment in them is not high.

34. The aesthetic is similar to, but not identical with, that presented in Karl Heider, *Ethnographic Film* (Austin: University of Texas Press, 1976).

35. Neither term should be taken literally.

36. The first was "Reinventing Ritual," directed by Sonya Jampolsky and produced by Johanna Eliot, a three-part series by Ocean Entertainment of Halifax for Vision TV (first aired October 22, 2003). The second was "Human Rites," a pilot on coming of age, produced by Hamlin Grange and Cynthia Reyes of Pro Media International, Toronto, for CBC Television (2003, never aired).

37. Contact information: Jeanette DeBouzek, 413 10th St SW, Albuquerque, NM 87102, phone: 505-242-6198. E-mail: jd@alphavillevideo.com.

38. Available from the National Film Board of Canada at: http://cmm.onf.ca/E/titleinfo/index.epl?id=33029.

39. Available from Throughline Productions, 2080 Josyln Place, Boulder, CO, 80304, phone: 303-443-7588.

40. The original presentation, first delivered as the Kavanagh Lecture at the Institute of Sacred Music, Yale University, October 16, 2003, was illustrated with visual materials only described or merely alluded to here. The presentation, along with a video clip from it, was subsequently published as Ronald L. Grimes, "Shooting Rites," *Colloquium* 2 (2005). Revised versions were later presented at the University of Tilburg and the South Asia Institute of Heidelberg University. Reprinted with permission of the publisher.

41. *Work and Pray: Living the Psalms with the Nuns of Regina Laudis*. Margot Fassler, dir., U.S.A., 48 min, DVD, color, 2004.

42. See the series site at http://www.ucpress.edu/books/ROG.ser.html.

43. Ronald L. Grimes, *Symbol and Conquest: Public Ritual and Drama in Santa Fe, New Mexico* (Albuquerque: University of New Mexico Press, 1992; reprint, Cornell University Press, 1976).

44. *Gathering Up Again: Fiesta in Santa Fe.* Jeanette DeBouzek and Diane Reyna, dirs., 46 min., VHS, color, 1992.

45. Walter Edwards, *Modern Japan through Its Weddings: Gender, Person, and Society in Ritual Portrayal* (Stanford, CA: Stanford University Press, 1989).

46. Paul Adjin-Tetty.

47. First aired in December 1996.

48. James Van Der Zee and others, *The Harlem Book of the Dead* (Dobbs Ferry, NY: Morgan and Morgan, 1978).

49. In the foreword of Van Der Zee and others, *The Harlem Book of the Dead.*

50. Victor W. Turner, *Dramas, Fields and Metaphors: Symbolic Action in Human Society* (Ithaca, NY: Cornell University Press, 1974).

51. *Triumph of the Will*, Leni Riefenstahl, dir., 110 min., 16 mm. film, b&w, 1935.

52. *Olympiad Part 2: Festival of Beauty*, Leni Riefenstahl, dir., 85 min., VHS, b&w, 1938.

53. For an exploration of Riefenstahl's films and their behind-the-scenes dynamics, see *The Wonderful, Horrible Life of Leni Riefenstahl.* Ray Muller, dir., New York, 181 min., DVD, color, b&w, 1993.

54. Marita Sturken and Lisa Cartwright, *Practices of Looking: An Introduction to Visual Culture* (Oxford: Oxford University Press, 2001).

55. Lucy R. Lippard, ed., *Partial Recall* (New York: New Press, 1992).

56. Combs-Schilling, *Sacred Performances: Islam, Sexuality, Sacrifice.*

57. Since this lecture is named in his honor, one might, for example, try to imagine Aidan Kavanagh's response to such photos. See Aidan Kavanagh, *Elements of Rite: A Handbook of Liturgical Style* (New York: Pueblo, 1982).

58. Ronald L. Grimes, "Ritual and Performance," in *Encyclopedia of Religion and American Cultures*, ed. Gary Laderman and Luis León (Santa Barbara, CA: ABC Clio, 2003).

59. See especially chapters 2 and 4 in the bonus materials section called "The Journey of *The Apostle*," in *The Apostle*, Robert Duvall, dir., 124 min., DVD, color, 1998.

60. My profuse gratitude goes to several respondents: Norma Joseph, Faydra Shapiro, and Myra Soifer, along with several rabbis who contributed their reflections on "Sunrise, Sunset."

61. On the DVD version, the scene begins at title 1, chapter 17, hour 1, minute 30, second 10.

62. The method I pursue here is a further refinement and application of the one outlined in "Fictive Ritual" (see Grimes, *Reading, Writing, and Ritualizing: Ritual in Fictive, Liturgical, and Public Places*, pt. 3, especially p. 134.)

63. Ivan G. Marcus, *The Jewish Life Cycle: Rites of Passage from Biblical to Modern Times* (Seattle: University of Washington Press, 2004), 136.

64. This point is made by several reputable scholars in the field, e.g., Marcus, *The Jewish Life Cycle: Rites of Passage from Biblical to Modern Times*, 136.

65. The outline is an educated guess based on a few general resources. More detailed historical-ethnographic research would have to be done to produce a truly accurate reconstruction.

66. Marcus, *The Jewish Life Cycle: Rites of Passage from Biblical to Modern Times*, 166.

67. When visiting film-studies colleagues are of a postmodernist or post-colonialist persuasion, they sometimes deconstruct the film, that is, expose ways the film is constructed to serve vested social interests. Even though this kind of film-studies approach is not strictly formalist, it nevertheless attends to what actually occurs on the screen more tenaciously than a typical religious-studies approach does. Even when film-studies scholars are discussing socially important topics such as gender and ethnicity, they tend to root their interpretations in the ways these social processes are constructed in and by the film itself.

68. See Michael L. Satlow, *Jewish Marriage in Antiquity* (Princeton, NJ: Princeton University Press, 2001), 162–163.

69. For this reason I do not consider the song an encomium to tradition, as does Wolitz. Seth L. Wolitz, "The Americanization of Tevye, or Boarding the Jewish *Mayflower*," *American Quarterly* 40, no. 4 (1988): 527.

70. The terms are, of course, those of Victor W. Turner, *The Ritual Process* (Ithaca, NY: Cornell University Press, 1969). See also Turner, *Dramas, Fields and Metaphors: Symbolic Action in Human Society.*

71. The scene is based on the memories of an old Jewish couple who had emigrated from Russia to Israel, and Jewison takes it to be iconic of the entire film.

See Norman Jewison, *This Terrible Business Has Been Good to Me: An Autobiography* (Toronto: Key Porter, 2004), 178.

72. Northrop Frye calls this sort of criticism "archetypal," but he does not use the term in either a complimentary or a Jungian sense. Northrop Frye, *Anatomy of Criticism* (New York: Atheneum, 1968).

73. Cele Otnes and Elizabeth Pleck, *Cinderella Dreams: The Allure of the Lavish Wedding*, Life Passages (Berkeley: University of California Press, 2003), 2–3.

74. Otnes and Pleck, *Cinderella Dreams: The Allure of the Lavish Wedding*, 168.

75. For more on the importance of images in the formation of Jewish identity, see Michael Berkowitz, "Religious to Ethnic-National Identities: Political Mobilization through Jewish Images in the United States and Britain, 1881–1939," in *Practicing Religion in the Age of the Media: Explorations in Media, Religion, and Culture*, ed. Stewart M. Hoover and Lynn Schofield Clark (New York: Columbia University Press, 2002).

76. A superb article on this and other examples of the tension between Jewish and American culture is Barbara Kirshenblatt-Gimblett, "Imagining Europe: Popular Arts of American Jewish Ethnography," in *Divergent Centers: Shaping Cultures in Israel and America*, ed. Deborah Dash Moore and Ilan Troen (New Haven, CT: Yale University Press, 2001).

77. Sholom Aleichem, *Tevye's Daughters: Collected Stories of Sholom Aleichem*, trans. Frances Butwin (New York: Crown, 1949), 37.

78. Wolitz, "The Americanization of Tevye, or Boarding the Jewish *Mayflower.*"

79. Jewison talks as if there is (Jewison, *This Terrible Business Has Been Good to Me: An Autobiography*, 180), but Hillel Halkin says there is not (cited in Jan Lisa Huttner, *Everybody's Fiddler*, 2003, September 5. Available at http://www.forward .com/issues/2003/03.09.05/arts3.fiddler.html.

80. Huttner, *Everybody's Fiddler.*

81. Wolitz says the fiddler comes from Chagall's 1908 painting *The Dead Man.* See Wolitz, "The Americanization of Tevye, or Boarding the Jewish *Mayflower,*" 526. However, Huttner is certain that the source is the 1920 painting *Music* (Huttner, *Everybody's Fiddler.*)

82. Jewison, *This Terrible Business Has Been Good to Me: An Autobiography.*

83. The credits are as follows: from the Mirisch Production Company; produced and directed by Norman Jewison; screenplay by Joseph Stein, adapted from his stage play; music for stage play and film by Jerry Bock; lyrics for stage play and film by Sheldon Harnick; produced on the New York stage by Harold Prince; stage production directed and choreographed by Jerome Robbins; music adapted and conducted by John Williams; original choreography by Jerome Robbins; adapted for the screen by Tom Abbott; violin soloist Isaac Stern.

84. Jewison, *This Terrible Business Has Been Good to Me: An Autobiography*, 13.

85. Jewison, *This Terrible Business Has Been Good to Me: An Autobiography*, 178.

86. Jewison, *This Terrible Business Has Been Good to Me: An Autobiography*, 175. Jewison thinks one reason for his not having received an Academy Award until very late is that he was regarded as a "Canadian political dissident" (Jewison, *This Terrible Business Has Been Good to Me: An Autobiography*, 273.)

87. The view is Peter Stone's, cited in Wolitz, "The Americanization of Tevye, or Boarding the Jewish *Mayflower*," n. 44.

88. Eventually, director Norman, in good United Church fashion, starts sending money back to the village to pay for the support of Tevye's horse, lest he be sent to the glue factory.

89. Of United Jewish Communities, New York, New York. My thanks go to Rabbi Myra Soifer, who assisted me in querying the rabbis.

90. Jewison, *This Terrible Business Has Been Good to Me: An Autobiography*, 11.

91. Jewison got in trouble with Jews for making *Jesus Christ Superstar* and confesses that he was quite hurt by the criticism. Similar troubles would arise when it became known that he was being asked to direct *Malcolm X*. The firestorm was so great—no white director should make the film—that Spike Lee was given the job instead, even though it was Jewison who had convinced Denzel Washington to play the lead.

92. From the director's commentary on the bottle dance sequence (*Fiddler on the Roof*, Norman Jewison, dir., 180 min., DVD, color, 1971).

93. John Bush Jones, *Our Musicals, Ourselves: A Social History of the American Musical Theater* (Hanover, NH: Brandeis University Press, 2003), 212.

94. Richard Altman and Mervyn Kaufman, *The Making of a Musical: Fiddler on the Roof* (New York: Crown, 1971), 156.

95. Jewison, *This Terrible Business Has Been Good to Me: An Autobiography*, 183.

96. See Loring M. Danforth, *The Death Ritual of Rural Greece* (Princeton, NJ: Princeton University Press, 1982).

97. Regarding the connection of *Fiddler* with the Holocaust, see Kirshenblatt-Gimblett, "Imagining Europe: Popular Arts of American Jewish Ethnography," 2.

98. Alisa Solomon, *Can the Broadway Revival of Everyone's Favorite Jewish Musical Ignore Today's Radically Different Cultural Context?* January 21–27, 2004. Available at www.villagevoice.com/issues/0403/solomon.php.

99. Of Congregation Shaare Emeth, St. Louis, Missouri.

100. M. Darrol Bryant, "Cinema, Religion, and Popular Culture," in *Religion in Film*, ed. John R. May and Michael Bird (Knoxville: University of Tennessee Press, 1982), 101, 103, 106.

101. I have already raised a similar question about literary works. Here, my answer to the question is a revision of that one. See Grimes, *Ritual Criticism: Case Studies in Its Practice, Essays on Its Theory*, 140–141.

102. Originally published as Ronald L. Grimes, "Zen and the Art of Not Teaching Zen and the Arts: An Autopsy," in *Teaching Buddhism in the West: From the Wheel to the Web*, ed. Victor Sogen Hori, Richard P. Hayes, and James Mark Shields (London: RoutledgeCurzon, 2002). Reprinted with permission of the publisher.

103. Originally published as Ronald L. Grimes, "Ritualizing September 11," in *Disaster Ritual: Explorations of an Emerging Ritual Repertoire*, ed. Paul Post and others, *Liturgia Condenda* (Leuven, Belgium: Peeters, 2003). Reprinted with permission of the publisher. Parts of this chapter were presented in 2002 as "The Ritualization of North American Visual Culture, Post-9/11," a multimedia presentation for the American Academy of Religion's Religion and Media Workshop.

104. Originally delivered as Ronald L. Grimes, "Acts of Screening and Metaphoric Moves: Ritual Studies Reflections through a Sliding Glass Door" (paper presented at the Dumbarton Oaks Byzantine Symposium, "Sacred Screens: The Origins, Development, and Diffusion of the Byzantine Sanctuary Barrier," Washington, DC, 2003). A revised version was presented in 2004 at the University of Windsor (Canada) in the Humanities Research Group's Distinguished Speakers Series. It was subsequently published as Ronald L. Grimes, "Ritual, Performance, and the Sequestering of Sacred Space," in *Ritual Economies*, ed. Lorenzo Buj (Windsor, ON: University of Windsor Humanities Research Group, 2004). Reprinted with permission of the publisher.

105. The artistic director of the Sundance Playwright's Lab was David Kranes. The artistic director of WordBridge was Richard Rice.

106. The script was written by Marisa B. Wegrzyn.

107. A provocative treatment of the relationship between play, thus fictionality, and the sacred is Robert Neale, *In Praise of Play: Towards a Psychology of Religion* (New York: Harper and Row, 1969).

108. Regarding the relationship between ordinariness, ritual, and the sacred, consult Lynda Sexson, *Ordinarily Sacred* (New York: Crossroad, 1982), and Ronald L. Grimes, *Marrying & Burying: Rites of Passage in a Man's Life* (Boulder, CO: Westview, 1995). A more typical move among religious studies scholars would be to frame discussions of sacred screens in the rhetoric of sacred space as articulated by Mircea Eliade, *The Sacred and the Profane: The Nature of Religion* (San Diego: Harcourt Brace, 1959), and his critics, e.g., Jonathan Z. Smith, "The Wobbling Pivot," *Journal of Religion* 52(1972): 134–159. The most successful attempt by a religious studies scholar to tender a theory of religious architecture that is inspired by, but not enslaved to, Eliade is Lindsay Jones, *Hermeneutical Calisthenics: A Morphology of Ritual-Architectural Priorities*, vol. 2 of The Hermeneutics of Sacred Architecture: Experience, Interpretation, Comparison (Cambridge, MA: Harvard University Press for the Harvard University Center for the Study of World Religions, 2000); Lindsay Jones, *Monumental Occasions: Reflections on the Eventfulness of Religious Architecture*, vol. 1 of The Hermeneutics of Sacred Architecture: Experience, Interpretation, Comparison (Cambridge, MA: Harvard University Press for the Harvard University Center for the Study of World Religions, 2000).

109. In the past decade religious studies scholars have become more adept at studying items of material culture. See the May issue (vol. 18, no. 3) of *Spotlight on Teaching*, an insert in *Religious Studies News* (published by the American Academy of Religion). The entire issue is on teaching about material culture in religious studies. See also Mihaly Csikszentmihalyi, *The Meaning of Things: Domestic Symbols and the Self* (Cambridge: Cambridge University Press, 1981).

110. The master of the metaphor "framing" is Erving Goffman. See, for instance, Erving Goffman, *The Presentation of Self in Everyday Life* (Garden City, NY: Doubleday Anchor, 1959). Also see Erving Goffman, *Frame Analysis: An Essay on the Organization of Experience* (New York: Harper and Row, 1974).

111. John Damascene, for example, distinguishes between veneration and worship. One venerates icons but worships God. See George D. Dragas, "St. John Damascene's Teaching about Holy Icons," in *Icons, Windows on Eternity: Theology*

and Spirituality in Color (Geneva: WCC, 1990), 55. For St. Basil, the sacred image was transparent, a window that a worshiper looks through. See Leslie Brubaker, "Introduction: The Sacred Image," in *The Sacred Image East and West*, ed. Robert Ousterhout and Leslie Brubaker, *Illinois Byzantine Studies, 4* (Urbana: University of Illinois Press, 1995), 4.

112. Tom F. Driver, *Liberating Rites: Understanding the Transformative Power of Ritual* (Boulder, CO: Westview, 1998), 79–127. See also Grimes, "Ritual and Performance."

113. Women and laypeople were strictly forbidden to enter the Orthodox sanctuary.

114. Words and images in Byzantine churches served as a way to "enter" the sanctuary without physically entering it. See Sharon E. J. Gerstel, *Beholding the Sacred Mysteries: Programs of the Byzantine Sanctuary* (Seattle: College Art Association in association with University of Washington Press, 1999), 13. See p. 11, regarding other kinds of substitution.

115. Even art historians sometimes render "things" as "actors." For instance: "Decorated with saints who gesture across empty space and speak to each other by means of scrolls, the church need not be inhabited by people to be fully active. The sanctuary decoration participates in this idea of the living church by mirroring actual celebration. Momentarily joined by the priest, the painted celebrants included him in their prayers." Gerstel, *Beholding the Sacred Mysteries: Programs of the Byzantine Sanctuary*, 79; see also p. 48.

116. Sam D. Gill, "Disenchantment: A Religious Abduction," in *Native American Religious Action: A Performance Approach to Religion* (Columbia: University of South Carolina Press, 1977).

117. The full discussion is in Grimes, *Ritual Criticism: Case Studies in Its Practice, Essays on Its Theory*, 63–88.

118. Miguel de Unamuno, "Saint Immanuel the Good, Martyr," in *Abel Sanchez and Other Stories* (Chicago: Regnery, 1956).

119. Regarding proxemics, the study of social meanings encoded in spatial construction, see Edward T. Hall, *The Hidden Dimension* (New York: Anchor, 1973).

120. For more on the language of the body, see Ray L. Birdwhistell, *Kinesics and Context: Essays on Body Motion Communication* (Philadelphia: University of Pennsylvania Press, 1970).

121. On material culture studies, see Daniel Miller, *Home Possessions: Material Culture behind Closed Doors* (New York: Berg, 2001). Also see W. D. Kingery, *Learning from Things: Method and Theory of Material Culture Studies* (Washington, DC: Smithsonian, 1996).

122. This metaphoric equation is quite characteristic of Orthodox liturgy and a primary assumption of Orthodox theologians. Alexander Schmemann, for instance, describes symbolism in the liturgy as "eschatological," by which he means "the sign and that which it signifies are one and the same thing." See Alexander Schmemann, "Symbols and Symbolism in the Orthodox Liturgy," in *Orthodox Theology and Diakonia, Trends and Prospects*, ed. Demetrios J. Constantelos (Brookline, MA: Hellenic College Press, 1981), 100. For a more general view of metaphor as it is understood in religious studies, consult Mary Gerhart and Russell Allan, *Metaphoric*

Process: The Creation of Scientific and Religious Understanding (Fort Worth: Texas Christian University Press, 1984). A good general work on the topic is George Lakoff and Mark Johnson, *Metaphors We Live By* (Chicago: University of Chicago Press, 1980).

123. On classification in religion, see especially Jonathan Z. Smith, *Map Is Not Territory: Studies in the History of Religions* (Leiden: Brill, 1978). Also see Jonathan Z. Smith, *Imagining Religion: From Babylon to Jonestown* (Chicago: University of Chicago Press, 1988).

124. Mary Douglas, *Purity and Danger: An Analysis of Concepts of Pollution and Taboo* (London: Routledge and Kegan Paul, 1966). As well, see Mary Douglas, *Natural Symbols: Explorations in Cosmology* (New York: Vintage, 1973).

125. Since there is a feedback loop resulting in revisions of the script, there are more phases than this simplified summary suggests.

126. Studies of iconography could benefit enormously from current discussions of visual culture such as Sturken and Cartwright, *Practices of Looking: An Introduction to Visual Culture*. For an example of fieldwork-based, reception-oriented interpretation of religious elements in popular culture, see Lynn Schofield Clark, *From Angels to Aliens: Teenagers, the Media, and the Supernatural* (New York: Oxford University Press, 2003).

127. Inability to articulate meaning does not make something meaningless. A provocative discussion of ritual and symbolic meaning is Frits Staal, "The Meaninglessness of Ritual," *Numen* 26 (1979): 9–14. Another is Dan Sperber, ed., *Rethinking Symbolism* (Cambridge: Cambridge University Press, 1975).

128. For example, Maximus the Confessor imagines a church as a man: "Its soul is the sanctuary; the sacred altar, the mind; and the body the nave." Maximus the Confessor, *The Church, the Liturgy, and the Soul of Man: The Mystagogia of St. Maximus the Confessor*, trans. Julian Stead (Still River, MA: St. Bede's, 1982), 71.

129. James W. Fernandez, "The Mission of Metaphor in Expressive Culture," *Current Anthropology* 15, no. 2 (1974): 119–145. James W. Fernandez, "The Performance of Ritual Metaphors," in *The Social Use of Metaphor: Essays on the Anthropology of Rhetoric*, ed. J. David Sapir and J. Christopher Crocker. (Philadelphia: University of Pennsylvania Press, 1977); James W. Fernandez, "Persuasion and Performances," in *Myth, Symbol, and Culture*, ed. Clifford Geertz (New York: Norton, 1971); James W. Fernandez, *Persuasions and Performances: The Play of Tropes in Culture* (Bloomington: Indiana University Press, 1986).

130. Victor W. Turner, *The Anthropology of Performance* (New York: Performing Arts Journal Publications, 1987); Victor W. Turner, "Liminality and the Performative Genres," in *Rite, Drama, Festival, Spectacle: Rehearsals toward a Theory of Cultural Performance*, ed. John MacAloon (Philadelphia: ISHI, 1985); Arnold van Gennep, *The Rites of Passage* (Chicago: University of Chicago Press, 1960).

131. This case is argued more fully in Ronald L. Grimes, "Performance Is Currency in the Deep World's Gift Economy: An Incantatory Riff for a Global Medicine Show," *Interdisciplinary Studies in Literature and Environment* 9, no. 1 (2002): 149–164.

132. Part of this essay was originally delivered as a lecture at Princeton University in 1996. Later it was revised and published as Ronald L. Grimes, "Jonathan Z.

Smith's Theory of Ritual Space," *Religion* 29 (1999): 261–273. Reprinted with permission of Elsevier, publisher of the journal *Religion*.

133. See, e.g., David Chidester and Edward T. Linenthal, eds., *American Sacred Space* (Bloomington: Indiana University Press, 1995), 6, 15–16.

134. A critique of Eliade can be found in Smith, "The Wobbling Pivot."

135. Smith, "The Bare Facts of Ritual," 114.

136. Smith, "The Bare Facts of Ritual," 125.

137. At first, it seems that only the armchair scholar, resistant to entering the "cuckoo-land" (his term) of the primitive mentality, recognizes the contradiction between the ideals projected in ritual and the realities encountered in the bush. In the final analysis, however, Smith is unwilling to declare "primitives" to be some other kind of human being, so he suggests that ritualists themselves must recognize this incongruity; otherwise, they would not survive. He never provides evidence that this is the case.

138. Smith, "The Bare Facts of Ritual," 124.

139. Catherine Bell complains that this contradictory move is typical of many, if not most, theories of ritual; see Catherine Bell, *Ritual Theory, Ritual Practice* (New York: Oxford University Press, 1992), 6, 16.

140. Richard Huntington and Peter Metcalf, *Celebrations of Death: The Anthropology of Mortuary Rituals* (New York: Cambridge University Press, 1979), 99.

141. H. Dubois, *Monographie Des Betsileo* (Paris: Institut d'ethnologie, 1938). See also Huntington and Metcalf, *Celebrations of Death: The Anthropology of Mortuary Rituals*, 114.

142. Edward Schieffelin, *The Sorrow of the Lonely and the Burning of the Dancers* (New York: St. Martin's, 1976).

143. The ideal/real split is handled differently in Theodor Gaster's theory of ritual and myth. See my exposition of Gaster's theory in Grimes, *Ritual Criticism: Case Studies in Its Practice, Essays on Its Theory*, 142.

144. Grimes, *Ritual Criticism: Case Studies in Its Practice, Essays on Its Theory*, 44–45.

145. Smith, "The Bare Facts of Ritual," 116.

146. Jonathan Z. Smith, *To Take Place: Toward Theory in Ritual* (Chicago: University of Chicago Press, 1987), 96. The epigraph for the chapter, "To Take Place," is from Stéphane Mallarmé.

147. Smith, *To Take Place: Toward Theory in Ritual*, 104.

148. Smith, *To Take Place: Toward Theory in Ritual*, xii., quoting from Claude Lévi-Strauss.

149. A danger of this slippage is the overextended metaphor. For example, in *American Sacred Space*, Chidester and Linenthal conclude their introduction by brandishing an analogy with astonishing implications. "In an important sense," they claim, "the authors of the essays collected in this book have rediscovered America. Not content with the guidebooks, formulas, and comforts of academic tourism, the authors have risked the uncharted dangers of exploration to see America new" (Chidester and Linenthal, *American Sacred Space*, 31). A reader's "itinerary" through the book is construed as the equivalent of a pilgrimage to sacred sites.

150. Smith, *To Take Place: Toward Theory in Ritual*, 112.

151. Smith, *To Take Place: Toward Theory in Ritual*, 108.

152. Smith, *To Take Place: Toward Theory in Ritual*, 109.

153. My *Ritual Criticism* is devoted to arguing that ritual action and intellectual critique are not polar opposites.

154. Smith, *To Take Place: Toward Theory in Ritual*, 109.

155. This point is most fully developed in Sperber, *Rethinking Symbolism*.

156. Smith, *To Take Place: Toward Theory in Ritual*, 110.

157. Smith, *To Take Place: Toward Theory in Ritual*, 110

158. Burke's formulation of the synecdochic relation between scene (place) and agent (actor) is, in my opinion, more balanced and thus more acceptable. See Kenneth Burke, *Grammar of Motives* (Berkeley: University of California Press, 1969), chap. 1.

159. Smith, *To Take Place: Toward Theory in Ritual*, 45.

160. Smith, *To Take Place: Toward Theory in Ritual*, 110.

161. Lonnie Kliever, "Story and Space: The Forgotten Dimension," *Journal of the American Academy of Religion* 45, no. 2 (1977): 529–563.

162. Smith, *To Take Place: Toward Theory in Ritual*, 108.

163. Smith, *To Take Place: Toward Theory in Ritual*, 110.

164. Smith, *To Take Place: Toward Theory in Ritual*, 48.

165. Smith, *To Take Place: Toward Theory in Ritual*, 112. As early as 1969, Smith was portraying temple ritual as normative, but he was attributing the view to Rabbi Shmuel bar Nachman (who imagines the world as ritually constituted), not to himself as the basis for a theory of ritual (see Jonathan Z. Smith, "Earth and Gods," *Journal of Religion* 49, no. 2 [1969]: 117). A similar transposition—from being a specific example to becoming a major premise of his theory—can be found in Smith's definition of ritual as a kind of controlled perfection. The "requirement for ritual perfection" can also be found earlier, in "Earth and Gods" (p. 116), where it is much more culturally and religiously specific.

166. Smith, *To Take Place: Toward Theory in Ritual*, 103.

167. Smith, *To Take Place: Toward Theory in Ritual*, 1.

168. Lakoff and Johnson, *Metaphors We Live By*.

169. David Carrasco, "The Sacrifice of Tezcatlipoca: To Change Place," in *To Change Place: Aztec Ceremonial Landscapes*, ed. David Carrasco (Niwot: University Press of Colorado, 1991), 31–57. Carrasco worries that Smith, like Eliade, does not make sufficient allowance for change and movement through space, hence the subtitle of Carrasco's critique, "To Change Place." Carrasco offers a view of ritual space that takes account of circumferential (as opposed to central) space—something Eliade does not do—and that takes account of movement, change, transformation— something Smith, apparently, does not do well enough. Carrasco's notion of the "metamorphic vision of place" is a useful, though underdeveloped, alternative to Eliade's "sacred space" and Smith's "locative and utopian space." Carrasco's theoretical privileging of vision (much in the same way that Smith privileges space) renders his alternative somewhat problematic for ritual studies.

170. Tod D. Swanson, "To Prepare a Place: Johannine Christianity and the Collapse of Ethnic Territory," *Journal of the American Academy of Religion* 62, no. 2 (1994): 262.

171. Swanson, "To Prepare a Place: Johannine Christianity and the Collapse of Ethnic Territory," 257.

172. Susan L. Scott, a writer and educator based in Waterloo, Ontario, directs the Walkerton Water Stories Project, an environmental-arts response to a farm community's water crisis. She teaches writing and religious studies at Wilfrid Laurier University. Her writings have appeared in *Vox Feminarum* (1996), *The New Quarterly: New Directions in Canadian Writing* (2003), and *The Encyclopedia of Religion and Nature* (2005). Currently, she is writing *Domestic Mysticism: Ecologies of Place*. Our thanks to Gregory Caicco for his editorial assistance.

173. An account of earlier Lab activities appears in Grimes, *Beginnings in Ritual Studies*.

174. Local history, agrarian reform, and landscape architecture on the farm all dovetail in the evocative memoir Douglas Chambers, *Stonyground: The Making of a Canadian Garden* (Toronto: Knopf, 1996). The name "Stonyground" is after a line in Yeats. For Chambers's long-standing interest in landscape architecture, see Douglas Chambers, *The Planters of the English Landscape Garden: Botany, Trees, and the Georgics* (New Haven, CT: Yale University Press, 1993).

175. For the causes of the *E. coli* crisis, see the Honourable Dennis R. O'Connor, *Part One Report of the Walkerton Inquiry: The Events of May 2000 and Related Issues* (Toronto: Ontario Ministry of the Attorney General, 2002). Ensuing recommendations for safe water legislation appear in the Honourable Dennis R. O'Connor, *Part Two Report of the Walkerton Inquiry: A Strategy for Safe Drinking Water* (Toronto: Ontario Ministry of the Attorney General, 2002).

176. The terms "community restoration" and "stewardship of stories" are used throughout the Water Stories Project to signify the parallels between re-storying a place with local, indigenous knowledge and practicing ecological restoration. For a full analysis of the stewardship ethic and the broader cultural implications of restoration, see William R. Jordan III, *The Sunflower Forest: Ecological Restoration and the New Communion with Nature* (Berkeley: University of California Press, 2003). Dolores Hayden makes the connection between natural and cultural preservation explicit: "If environmental history is successful in its project, the story of how different peoples have lived and used the natural world will become one of the most basic and fundamental narratives in all of history." See Dolores Hayden, "Urban Landscape History: The Sense of Space and the Politics of Space," in *Understanding Ordinary Landscapes*, ed. Paul Groth and Todd W. Bressi (New Haven, CT: Yale University Press, 1997), 112. To decipher cultural stories inscribed in natural histories and vice versa, see Anne Whiston Spirn, *The Language of Landscape* (New Haven, CT: Yale University Press, 1998).

177. Many local stories are preserved in a weekly column in the *Walkerton Herald-Times* called "The Cordwainer," by retired shoemaker and raconteur Lloyd Cartwright.

178. The first, nontouring phase of the Water Stories Project is documented in *The New Quarterly: New Directions in Canadian Writing* 87(Summer 2003): 13–73.

179. See Kenneth P. Feit, "The Priestly Fool," *Anglican Theological Review* 5 (1975): 97–108. Also see Kenneth P. Feit and Matthew Fox, "The Story-Teller as Prophet," *Bear & Company* 1981, 6–7.

180. See also Grimes, *Marrying & Burying: Rites of Passage in a Man's Life.*

181. For farming in this historic region, see Jon Radojkovic, *Barns of the Queen's Bush* (Port Elgin, ON: Brucedale Press, 2001). For reflections on the pioneer era when the great timber-frame barns were first built, see Norman Robertson, *The History of the County of Bruce*, 4th ed. (Wiarton, ON: Bruce County Historical Society, 1960). Barn bees are recalled in Anonymous, *Bruce Township: Tales and Trails from Early Days to 1983* (Tiverton, ON: Bruce Township Historical Society, 1984). See also excerpts from N. E. Leeder, "Daybook," in *Roots and Branches of Saugeen 1854–1984: A History of Saugeen Township* (Owen Sound, ON: Saugeen History Hunters, 1984).

182. The list, from a bee in Normanby Township, goes on to include: "300 light rolls, beet pickles, pickled eggs, 6 pounds dried prunes, 1 large crock stewed raisins, 5 gallon stone jar white potatoes, 5 gallon stone jar sweet potatoes, and cucumber pickles" (Radojkovic, *Barns of the Queen's Bush*, 11).

183. With gross annual sales of $6.8 billion, farming is Ontario's second-largest economic sector, yet rural communities continue to suffer outmigration, cultural marginalization, and economic decline. For an eloquent analysis of the denigration of rural, see Norman Wirzba, ed., *The Art of the Commonplace: The Agrarian Essays of Wendell Berry* (Washington, DC: Shoemaker and Hoard, 2002). For a less elegiac view of agriculture, see Hugh Brody, *The Other Side of Eden: Hunters, Farmers and the Shaping of the World* (Vancouver: Douglas and McIntyre, 2000). See also David Lowenthal, "European Landscape Transformations: The Rural Residue," in *Understanding Ordinary Landscapes*, ed. Paul Groth and Todd W. Bressi (New Haven, CT: Yale University Press, 1997).

184. Richard Schechner and Lisa Wolford, eds., *The Grotowski Sourcebook* (London: Routledge, 1997).

185. See, for example, Caroline Humphrey and James Laidlaw, *The Archetypal Actions of Ritual: A Theory of Ritual Illustrated by the Jain Rite of Worship* (Oxford: Clarendon, 1994), 263, 268, n. 262.

186. Grimes, *Ritual Criticism: Case Studies in Its Practice, Essays on Its Theory.*

187. Members of the University of Heidelberg's *Dynamics of Ritual* Project, especially those working on ritual mistakes and ritual failure, have demonstrated how widespread is the awareness of ritual error. See http://www.ritualdynamik.uni-hd.de/en/index.htm; also see http://www.sai.uni-heidelberg.de/abt/IND/index/mitarbe/huesken/fehler.pdf.

188. Driver, *Liberating Rites: Understanding the Transformative Power of Ritual.*

189. Douglas, *Purity and Danger: An Analysis of Concepts of Pollution and Taboo.*

190. Jordan, *The Sunflower Forest: Ecological Restoration and the New Communion with Nature.*

191. Originally published as Ronald L. Grimes, "Ritual Theory and the Environment," in *Nature Performed: Environment, Culture, Performance*, ed. Bronislaw Szerszynski and others (London: Blackwell, 2003). Reprinted with permission of the publisher.

192. Brian Swimme and Thomas Berry, *The Universe Story from the Primordial Flaring Forth to the Ecozoic Era: A Celebration of the Unfolding of the Cosmos* (San Francisco: HarperSanFrancisco, 1992).

193. William R. Jordan III, "Restoration and the Reentry of Nature," in *Finding Home: Writing on Nature and Culture from Orion Magazine*, ed. Peter Sauer (Boston: Beacon, 1992); William R. Jordan III, "Rituals of Restoration," *The Humanist*, November/December 1993; Jordan, *The Sunflower Forest: Ecological Restoration and the New Communion with Nature*.

194. Beatrice Briggs, "Help Wanted," *Restoration and Management Notes* 12, no. 2 (1994): 124.

195. Elizabeth Bragg. *The Council of All Beings Workshop Manual: A Step by Step Guide*, 1998. Available at *http://forests.org/ric/deep-eco/cabcont.htm;* John Seed and others, *Thinking Like a Mountain: Towards a Council of All Beings* (Philadelphia: New Society, 1988).

196. Susan M. Darlington, "The Ordination of a Tree: The Buddhist Ecology Movement in Thailand," *Ethnology* 37, no. 1 (1998): 1–15.

197. R. Murray Schafer, "The Theatre of Confluence, 1," *Descant* 22, no. 2 (1991: 27–45); R. Murray Schafer, "The Theatre of Confluence, 2," *Descant* 22, no. 2 (1991): 87–103.

198. Schafer, "The Theatre of Confluence, 2," 97.

199. The Earth Charter Web site is located at http://www.earthcharter.org/. See also J. Baird Callicott, ed., *Earth's Insights: A Multicultural Survey of Ecological Ethics from the Mediterranean Basin to the Australian Outback* (Berkeley: University of California Press, 1994).

200. Stanley J. Tambiah, "A Performative Approach to Ritual," *Proceedings of the British Academy* 65 (1979): 119.

201. S. G. F. Brandon, "Religious Ritual," in *Dictionary of the History of Ideas*, ed. Philip Wiener (New York: Scribner's, 1973), 99.

202. Schechner, *Essays on Performance Theory, 1970–1976*.

203. Julian Huxley, "A Discussion on Ritualization of Behaviour in Animals and Man," *Philosophical Transactions of the Royal Society of London, Series B* 251 (1966): 409–422.

204. Huxley, "A Discussion on Ritualization of Behaviour in Animals and Man," 250.

205. Huxley, "A Discussion on Ritualization of Behaviour in Animals and Man," 258.

206. See, for example, Driver, *Liberating Rites: Understanding the Transformative Power of Ritual*.

207. Eugene d'Aquili and Andrew B. Newberg, *The Mystical Mind: Probing the Biology of Religious Experience* (Minneapolis, MN: Fortress, 1999).

208. Roy A. Rappaport, *Pigs for the Ancestors: Ritual in the Ecology of a New Guinea People*, new, enlarged ed. (New Haven, CT: Yale University Press, 1984), 358.

209. Roy A. Rappaport, *Ritual and Religion in the Making of Humanity* (Cambridge: Cambridge University Press, 1999), 27.

210. Rappaport, *Ritual and Religion in the Making of Humanity*, 125.

211. Roy A. Rappaport, *Ecology, Meaning, and Religion* (Berkeley, CA: North Atlantic, 1979), 194.

212. Rappaport, *Ecology, Meaning, and Religion*, 197.

213. Rappaport, *Ecology, Meaning, and Religion*, 228.

214. Rappaport, *Ecology, Meaning, and Religion*, 215.

215. Rappaport, *Ecology, Meaning, and Religion*, 216.

216. Rappaport, *Ecology, Meaning, and Religion*, 216.

217. Rappaport, *Ecology, Meaning, and Religion*, 158.

218. Rappaport, *Ritual and Religion in the Making of Humanity*, 453.

219. Rappaport, *Ecology, Meaning, and Religion*.

220. Frederick Turner, *Natural Classicism: Essays on Literature and Science* (New York: Paragon House, 1985). Turner attributes to ritual a conserving role, comparing it with the role of genes in conserving patterns. He also attributes to it a transforming role.

221. Rappaport, *Ritual and Religion in the Making of Humanity*, 452.

222. Rappaport, *Ritual and Religion in the Making of Humanity*, 460.

223. Rappaport, *Ritual and Religion in the Making of Humanity*, 469.

224. Rappaport, *Ritual and Religion in the Making of Humanity*, 461.

225. Rappaport served as president of the American Anthropological Association.

226. See, for instance, Steve Jones, *Darwin's Ghost* (n.p.: Doubleday Canada, 1999); Steven Pinker, *How the Mind Works* (New York: Norton, 1997).

227. Theodor H. Gaster, "Ancient Near Eastern Ritual Drama," in *The Encyclopedia of Religion*, ed. Mircea Eliade (New York: Macmillan, 1987).

228. My thanks to Gary Snyder for his generous encouragement and support and for not wincing at being riprapped off. This presentation was performed several times: first at St. Thomas University in Fredericton, New Brunswick, Canada; then at "Between Nature," a conference on ecology and performance at Lancaster University in England; and finally at the 2001 annual meeting of the Eastern International Region of the American Academy of Religion at Ithaca College in New York. Financial support for this research included a grant partly funded by Wilfrid Laurier University operating funds and by an institutional grant from the Social Sciences and Humanities Research Council of Canada. The chapter was originally published as Grimes, "Performance Is Currency in the Deep World's Gift Economy: An Incantatory Riff for a Global Medicine Show." Reprinted with permission of the publisher.

229. Gary Snyder, *The Practice of the Wild* (San Francisco: North Point, 1990), 75.

230. Paul Erlich cited in Swimme and Berry, *The Universe Story from the Primordial Flaring Forth to the Ecozoic Era: A Celebration of the Unfolding of the Cosmos*, 247.

231. Swimme and Berry, *The Universe Story from the Primordial Flaring Forth to the Ecozoic Era: A Celebration of the Unfolding of the Cosmos*, 246.

232. Wes Jackson, "Becoming Native to This Place," in *People, Land, and Community: Collected E. F. Schumacher Society Lectures*, ed. Hildegarde Hannum (New Haven, CT: Yale University Press, 1997), 158.

233. Carol Kaesuk Yoon, *Study Jolts Views on Recovery from Extinctions*, 2000. Available at http://www.nytimes.com/library/national/science/030900sci-environ-wildlife.html.

234. Forum on Religion and Ecology Web site: http://environment.harvard.edu/religion.

235. Harvard's Center for the Study of Values in Public Life sponsors an environmental ethics and public policy program. Like the Forum, the Center places its emphasis almost exclusively on ethics, policy, and justice issues. The Boston Research Center for the 21st Century sponsors consultations on the Earth Charter and publishes a series of books on war, peace, and the earth. In a presentation entitled "The Earth Charter and the Culture of Peace," sociologist Elise Boulding, one of the key participants, offers a formal definition of "peace culture," which she takes to be essential for generating a transformation of consciousness that will permit planetary survival. "Peace culture," she says, "is a mosaic of identities, attitudes, values, beliefs, and institutional patterns that lead people to live nurturantly with one another and with the earth itself without the aid of structured power differentials. That mosaic," she says, "enables humans to deal creatively with their differences and to share their resources." From Elise Boulding, "The Earth Charter and the Culture of Peace," in *Women's Views on the Earth Charter*, ed. Helen Casey and Amy Morgante (Boston: Boston Research Center for the 21st Century, 1997), 32.

236. Earth Charter Web site: http://www.earthcharter.org/.

237. Rita Gross, "Personal Transformation and the Earth Charter," in Boston Research Center, ed., *Buddhist Perspectives on the Earth Charter* (Boston: Boston Research Center for the 21st Century, 1977), 54.

238. Darlington, "The Ordination of a Tree: The Buddhist Ecology Movement in Thailand," 10.

Sources Cited

Aleichem, Sholom. *Tevye's Daughters: Collected Stories of Sholom Aleichem*. Translated by Frances Butwin. New York: Crown, 1949.

Alexander, Bobby C. *Televangelism Reconsidered: Ritual in the Search for Human Community*. Atlanta, GA: Scholars Press, 1994.

Altman, Richard, and Mervyn Kaufman. *The Making of a Musical: Fiddler on the Roof*. New York: Crown, 1971.

Anonymous. *Bruce Township: Tales and Trails from Early Days to 1983*. Tiverton, ON: Bruce Township Historical Society, 1984.

Bell, Catherine. *Ritual Theory, Ritual Practice*. New York: Oxford University Press, 1992.

Berkowitz, Michael. "Religious to Ethnic-National Identities: Political Mobilization through Jewish Images in the United States and Britain, 1881–1939." In *Practicing Religion in the Age of the Media: Explorations in Media, Religion, and Culture*, edited by Stewart M. Hoover and Lynn Schofield Clark, 305–327. New York: Columbia University Press, 2002.

Birdwhistell, Ray L. *Kinesics and Context: Essays on Body Motion Communication*. Philadelphia: University of Pennsylvania Press, 1970.

Boulding, Elise. "The Earth Charter and the Culture of Peace." In *Women's Views on the Earth Charter*, 31–35. Boston: Boston Research Center for the 21st Century, 1997.

Bragg, Elizabeth. *The Council of All Beings Workshop Manual: A Step by Step Guide*. 1998. Available at http://forests.org/ric/deep-eco/cabcont.htm.

Brandon, S. G. F. "Religious Ritual." In *Dictionary of the History of Ideas*, edited by Philip Wiener, 99. New York: Scribner's, 1973.

Briggs, Beatrice. "Help Wanted." *Restoration and Management Notes* 12, no. 2 (1994): 124.

Brody, Hugh. *The Other Side of Eden: Hunters, Farmers and the Shaping of the World*. Vancouver: Douglas and McIntyre, 2000.

Brubaker, Leslie. "Introduction: The Sacred Image." In *The Sacred Image East and West*, edited by Robert Ousterhout and Leslie Brubaker, 1–24, Illinois Byzantine Studies, 4. Urbana: University of Illinois Press, 1995.

Bryant, M. Darrol. "Cinema, Religion, and Popular Culture." In *Religion in Film*, edited by John R. May and Michael Bird, 101–114. Knoxville: University of Tennessee Press, 1982.

Burke, Kenneth. *Grammar of Motives*. Berkeley: University of California Press, 1969.

Burnett, Ron. *Cultures of Vision: Images, Media, and the Imaginary*. Bloomington: Indiana University Press, 1995.

Callicott, J. Baird, ed. *Earth's Insights: A Multicultural Survey of Ecological Ethics from the Mediterranean Basin to the Australian Outback*. Berkeley: University of California Press, 1994.

Carey, James, ed. *Media, Myths and Narratives: Television and the Press*. Newbury Park, CA: Sage, 1989.

Carrasco, David. "The Sacrifice of Tezcatlipoca: To Change Place." In *To Change Place: Aztec Ceremonial Landscapes*, edited by David Carrasco, 31–57. Niwot: University Press of Colorado, 1991.

Chambers, Douglas. *The Planters of the English Landscape Garden: Botany, Trees, and the Georgics*. New Haven, CT: Yale University Press, 1993.

Chambers, Douglas. *Stonyground: The Making of a Canadian Garden*. Toronto, ON: Alfred A. Knopf, 1996.

Chidester, David, and Edward T. Linenthal, eds. *American Sacred Space*. Bloomington: Indiana University Press, 1995.

Clark, Lynn Schofield. *From Angels to Aliens: Teenagers, the Media, and the Supernatural*. New York: Oxford University Press, 2003.

Combs-Schilling, M. E. *Sacred Performances: Islam, Sexuality, Sacrifice*. New York: Columbia University Press, 1989.

Confessor, Maximus the. *The Church, the Liturgy, and the Soul of Man: The Mystagogia of St. Maximus the Confessor*. Translated by Julian Stead. Still River, MA: St. Bede's, 1982.

Crapanzano, Vincent. "Rite of Return: Circumcision in Morocco." In *The Psychoanalytic Study of Society*, edited by Werner Muensterberger, 9:15–36. New Haven, CT: Yale University Press, 1980.

Csikszentmihalyi, Mihaly. *The Meaning of Things: Domestic Symbols and the Self*. Cambridge: Cambridge University Press, 1981.

Danforth, Loring M. *The Death Ritual of Rural Greece*. Princeton, NJ: Princeton University Press, 1982.

d'Aquili, Eugene, and Andrew B. Newberg. *The Mystical Mind: Probing the Biology of Religious Experience*. Minneapolis, MN: Fortress, 1999.

Darlington, Susan M. "The Ordination of a Tree: The Buddhist Ecology Movement in Thailand." *Ethnology* 37, no. 1 (1998): 1–15.

Davis-Floyd, Robbie E. *Birth as an American Rite of Passage*. Berkeley: University of California Press, 1992.

DeBouzek, Jeanette, and Diane Reyna, dirs. *Gathering Up Again: Fiesta in Santa Fe*. 46 min., VHS, color. 1992.

Douglas, Mary. *Natural Symbols: Explorations in Cosmology*. New York: Vintage, 1973.

————. *Purity and Danger: An Analysis of Concepts of Pollution and Taboo*. London: Routledge and Kegan Paul, 1966.

Dragas, George D. "St. John Damascene's Teaching about Holy Icons." In *Icons, Windows on Eternity: Theology and Spirituality in Color*, 53–72. Geneva: WCC, 1990.

Driver, Tom F. *Liberating Rites: Understanding the Transformative Power of Ritual*. Boulder, CO: Westview, 1998.

Dubois, H. *Monographie Des Betsileo*. Paris: Institut d'ethnologie, 1938.

Duvall, Robert, dir. *The Apostle*. 124 min., DVD, color. 1998.

Edwards, Walter. *Modern Japan through Its Weddings: Gender, Person, and Society in Ritual Portrayal*. Stanford, CA: Stanford University Press, 1989.

Eliade, Mircea. *The Sacred and the Profane: The Nature of Religion*. San Diego: Harcourt Brace, 1959.

Fassler, Margot, dir. *Work and Pray: Living the Psalms with the Nuns of Regina Laudis*. 48 min, DVD, color. U.S.A., English, 2004.

Feit, Kenneth P. "The Priestly Fool." *Anglican Theological Review* 5 (1975): 97–108.

Feit, Kenneth P., and Matthew Fox. "The Story-Teller as Prophet." *Bear & Company* 1981, 6–7.

Fernandez, James W. "The Mission of Metaphor in Expressive Culture." *Current Anthropology* 15, no. 2 (1974): 119–145.

————. "The Performance of Ritual Metaphors." In *The Social Use of Metaphor: Essays on the Anthropology of Rhetoric*, edited by J. David Sapir and J. Christopher Crocker, 100–131. Philadelphia: University of Pennsylvania Press, 1977.

————. "Persuasion and Performances." In *Myth, Symbol, and Culture*, edited by Clifford Geertz, 39–60. New York: Norton, 1971.

————. *Persuasions and Performances: The Play of Tropes in Culture*. Bloomington: Indiana University Press, 1986.

Fortes, Meyer. "Religious Premises and Logical Technique in Divinatory Ritual." *Philosophical Transactions of the Royal Society of London* 251 (1966): 409–422.

Frye, Northrop. *Anatomy of Criticism*. New York: Atheneum, 1968.

Gaster, Theodor H. "Ancient Near Eastern Ritual Drama." In *The Encyclopedia of Religion*, edited by Mircea Eliade, 446–450. New York: Macmillan, 1987.

Gerhart, Mary, and Russell Allan. *Metaphoric Process: The Creation of Scientific and Religious Understanding*. Fort Worth: Texas Christian University Press, 1984.

Gerstel, Sharon E. J. *Beholding the Sacred Mysteries: Programs of the Byzantine Sanctuary*. Seattle: College Art Association in association with University of Washington Press, 1999.

Gill, Sam D. "Disenchantment: A Religious Abduction." In *Native American Religious Action: A Performance Approach to Religion*, 58–75. Columbia: University of South Carolina Press, 1977.

Goethals, Gregor. *The TV Ritual: Worship at the Video Altar*. Boston: Beacon, 1981.

Goffman, Erving. *Frame Analysis: An Essay on the Organization of Experience*. New York: Harper and Row, 1974.

————. *Interaction Ritual: Essays on Face-to-Face Behavior*. Garden City, NY: Doubleday Anchor, 1967.

————. *The Presentation of Self in Everyday Life*. Garden City, NY: Doubleday Anchor, 1959.

Grainger, Roger. *The Language of the Rite*. London: Darton, Longman and Todd, 1974.

Grimes, Ronald L. "Acts of Screening and Metaphoric Moves: Ritual Studies Reflections through a Sliding Glass Door." Paper presented at the Dumbarton Oaks Byzantine Symposium, "Sacred Screens: The Origins, Development, and Diffusion of the Byzantine Sanctuary Barrier," Washington, DC, 2003.

———. *Beginnings in Ritual Studies*. Rev. ed. Columbia: University of South Carolina Press, 1994.

———. "Consuming Ritual: A&E's *Sacred Rites and Rituals*." In *Contemporary Consumption Rituals: A Research Anthology*, edited by Cele C. Otnes and Tina M. Lowrey, 21–36. Mawah, NJ: Erlbaum, 2003.

———. *Deeply into the Bone: Re-inventing Rites of Passage*. Berkeley: University of California Press, 2000.

———. "Jonathan Z. Smith's Theory of Ritual Space." *Religion* 29 (1999): 261–273.

———. *Marrying & Burying: Rites of Passage in a Man's Life*. Boulder, CO: Westview, 1995.

———. "Performance Is Currency in the Deep World's Gift Economy: An Incantatory Riff for a Global Medicine Show." *Interdisciplinary Studies in Literature and Environment* 9, no. 1 (2002): 149–164.

———. *Reading, Writing, and Ritualizing: Ritual in Fictive, Liturgical, and Public Places*. Washington, DC: Pastoral Press and Oregon Catholic Press, 1993.

———. "Ritual and Performance." In *Encyclopedia of Religion and American Cultures*, edited by Gary Laderman and Luis León, 2:515–528. Santa Barbara, CA: ABC Clio, 2003.

———. "Ritual and the Media." In *Practicing Religion in the Age of the Media. Explorations in Media, Religion and Culture*, edited by Stewart Hoover and Lynn Schofield Clark, 219–234. New York: Columbia University Press, 2002.

———. *Ritual Criticism: Case Studies in Its Practice, Essays on Its Theory*. Edited by Frederick M. Denny. Vol. 10, Studies in Comparative Religion. Columbia: University of South Carolina Press, 1990.

———. "Ritual Theory and the Environment." In *Nature Performed: Environment, Culture, Performance*, edited by Bronislaw Szerszynski and others, 31–45. London: Blackwell, 2003.

———. "Ritual, Performance, and the Sequestering of Sacred Space." In *Ritual Economies*, edited by Lorenzo Buj, 1–20. Windsor, ON: University of Windsor Humanities Research Group, 2004.

———. "Ritualizing September 11." In *Disaster Ritual: Explorations of an Emerging Ritual Repertoire*, edited by Paul Post and others, 199–213, Liturgia Condenda. Leuven, Belgium: Peeters, 2003.

———. "Shooting Rites." *Colloquium* 2 (2005): 1–10.

———. *Symbol and Conquest: Public Ritual and Drama in Santa Fe, New Mexico*. Albuquerque: University of New Mexico Press, 1992. Reprint, Cornell University Press.

———. "Zen and the Art of Not Teaching Zen and the Arts: An Autopsy." In *Teaching Buddhism in the West: From the Wheel to the Web*, edited by Victor

Sogen Hori, Richard P. Hayes, and James Mark Shields, 155–169. London: RoutledgeCurzon, 2002.

Gross, Rita. "Personal Transformation and the Earth Charter." In *Buddhist Perspectives on the Earth Charter*, 53–58. Boston: Boston Research Center for the 21st Century, 1977.

Hall, Edward T. *The Hidden Dimension*. New York: Anchor, 1973.

Hayden, Dolores. "Urban Landscape History: The Sense of Space and the Politics of Space." In *Understanding Ordinary Landscapes*, edited by Paul Groth and Todd W. Bressi, 111–133. New Haven, CT: Yale University Press, 1997.

Heider, Karl. *Ethnographic Film*. Austin: University of Texas Press, 1976.

Hoover, Stewart M. "Television Myth and Ritual: The Role of Substantive Meaning and Spatiality." In *Media, Myth, and Narratives: Television and the Press*, edited by James W. Carey, 161–178. Newbury Park, CA: Sage, 1988.

Humphrey, Caroline, and James Laidlaw. *The Archetypal Actions of Ritual: A Theory of Ritual Illustrated by the Jain Rite of Worship*. Oxford: Clarendon, 1994.

Huntington, Richard, and Peter Metcalf. *Celebrations of Death: The Anthropology of Mortuary Rituals*. New York: Cambridge University Press, 1979.

Huttner, Jan Lisa. *Everybody's Fiddler*, 2003, September 5. Available at http://www.forward.com/issues/2003/03.09.05/arts3.fiddler.html.

Huxley, Julian. "A Discussion on Ritualization of Behaviour in Animals and Man." *Philosophical Transactions of the Royal Society of London, Series B* 251 (1966): 409–422.

Jackson, Wes. "Becoming Native to This Place." In *People, Land, and Community: Collected E. F. Schumacher Society Lectures*, edited by Hildegarde Hannum, 154–167. New Haven, CT: Yale University Press, 1997.

Jewison, Norman, dir. *Fiddler on the Roof*. 180 min., DVD, color. English, 1971.

———. *This Terrible Business Has Been Good to Me: An Autobiography*. Toronto: Key Porter, 2004.

Jones, John Bush. *Our Musicals, Ourselves: A Social History of the American Musical Theater*. Hanover, NH: Brandeis University Press, 2003.

Jones, Lindsay. *Hermeneutical Calisthenics: A Morphology of Ritual-Architectural Priorities*. Vol. 2 of The Hermeneutics of Sacred Architecture: Experience, Interpretation, Comparison. Cambridge, MA: Harvard University Press for the Harvard University Center for the Study of World Religions, 2000.

———. *Monumental Occasions: Reflections on the Eventfulness of Religious Architecture*. Vol. 1 of The Hermeneutics of Sacred Architecture: Experience, Interpretation, Comparison. Cambridge, MA: Harvard University Press for the Harvard University Center for the Study of World Religions, 2000.

Jones, Steve. *Darwin's Ghost*. N.p.: Doubleday Canada, 1999.

Jordan, William R., III. "Restoration and the Reentry of Nature." In *Finding Home: Writing on Nature and Culture from Orion Magazine*, edited by Peter Sauer, 98–115. Boston: Beacon, 1992.

———. "Rituals of Restoration." *The Humanist*, November/December 1993: 23–26.

———. *The Sunflower Forest: Ecological Restoration and the New Communion with Nature*. Berkeley: University of California Press, 2003.

Kapferer, Bruce. *A Celebration of Demons: Exorcism and the Aesthetics of Healing in Sri Lanka*. Bloomington: Indiana University Press, 1983.

Kavanagh, Aidan. *Elements of Rite: A Handbook of Liturgical Style*. New York: Pueblo, 1982.

Kingery, W. D. *Learning from Things: Method and Theory of Material Culture Studies*. Washington, DC: Smithsonian, 1996.

Kirshenblatt-Gimblett, Barbara. "Imagining Europe: Popular Arts of American Jewish Ethnography." In *Divergent Centers: Shaping Cultures in Israel and America*, edited by Deborah Dash Moore and Ilan Troen, 155–191. New Haven, CT: Yale University Press, 2001.

Kliever, Lonnie. "Story and Space: The Forgotten Dimension." *Journal of the American Academy of Religion* 45, no. 2 (1977): 529–563.

Lakoff, George, and Mark Johnson. *Metaphors We Live By*. Chicago: University of Chicago Press, 1980.

Leeder, N. E. "Daybook." In *Roots and Branches of Saugeen 1854–1984: A History of Saugeen Township*. Owen Sound, ON: Saugeen History Hunters, 1984.

Lippard, Lucy R., ed. *Partial Recall*. New York: New Press, 1992.

Lowenthal, David. "European Landscape Transformations: The Rural Residue." In *Understanding Ordinary Landscapes*, edited by Paul Groth and Todd W. Bressi, 180–188. New Haven, CT: Yale University Press, 1997.

Marcus, Ivan G. *The Jewish Life Cycle: Rites of Passage from Biblical to Modern Times*. Seattle: University of Washington Press, 2004.

Maximus the Confessor. *The Church, the Liturgy, and the Soul of Man: The Mystagogia of St. Maximus the Confessor*. Translated by Julian Stead. Still River, MA: St. Bede's, 1982.

Miller, Daniel. *Home Possessions: Material Culture behind Closed Doors*. New York: Berg, 2001.

Muller, Ray, dir. *The Wonderful, Horrible Life of Leni Riefenstahl*. 181 min., DVD, color, b&w. New York, 1993.

Neale, Robert. *In Praise of Play: Towards a Psychology of Religion*. New York: Harper and Row, 1969.

O'Connor, the Honourable Dennis R. *Part One Report of the Walkerton Inquiry: The Events of May 2000 and Related Issues*. Toronto: Ontario Ministry of the Attorney General, 2002.

———. *Part Two Report of the Walkerton Inquiry: A Strategy for Safe Drinking Water*. Toronto: Ontario Ministry of the Attorney General, 2002.

Otnes, Cele, and Elizabeth Pleck. *Cinderella Dreams: The Allure of the Lavish Wedding*, Life Passages. Berkeley: University of California Press, 2003.

Peck, Janice. "The Appeal of Form: Ritual, Rhetoric, and Televisual Framing." In *The Gods of Televangelism: The Crisis of Meaning and the Appeal of Religious Television*, 197–221. Cresskill, NJ: Hampton, 1993.

Pinker, Steven. *How the Mind Works*. New York: Norton, 1997.

Radojkovic, Jon. *Barns of the Queen's Bush*. Port Elgin, ON: Brucedale Press, 2001.

Rappaport, Roy A. *Ecology, Meaning, and Religion*. Berkeley, CA: North Atlantic, 1979.

———. *Pigs for the Ancestors: Ritual in the Ecology of a New Guinea People*. New, enlarged ed. New Haven, CT: Yale University Press, 1984.

———. *Ritual and Religion in the Making of Humanity*. Cambridge: Cambridge University Press, 1999.

Riefenstahl, Leni, dir. *Olympiad Part 2: Festival of Beauty*. 85 min., VHS, b&w. 1938.

———, dir. *Triumph of the Will*. 110 min., 16 mm. film, b&w. 1935.

Robertson, Norman. *The History of the County of Bruce*. 4th ed. Wiarton, ON: Bruce County Historical Society, 1960.

Rubin, A. M. "Ritualized and Instrumental Television Viewing." *Journal of Communication* 34, no. 3 (1984): 67–77.

Satlow, Michael L. *Jewish Marriage in Antiquity*. Princeton, NJ: Princeton University Press, 2001.

Schafer, R. Murray. "The Theatre of Confluence, 1." *Descant* 22, no. 2 (1991): 27–45.

———. "The Theatre of Confluence, 2." *Descant* 22, no. 2 (1991): 87–103.

Schechner, Richard. *Between Theater & Anthropology*. Philadelphia: University of Pennsylvania Press, 1985.

———. *Essays on Performance Theory, 1970–1976*. New York: Drama Book, 1977.

———. "Restoration of Behaviour." In *Readings in Ritual Studies*, edited by Ronald L. Grimes, 441–458. Upper Saddle River, NJ: Prentice-Hall, 1996.

Schechner, Richard, and Lisa Wolford, eds. *The Grotowski Sourcebook*. London: Routledge, 1997.

Schieffelin, Edward. *The Sorrow of the Lonely and the Burning of the Dancers*. New York: St. Martin's, 1976.

Schmemann, Alexander. "Symbols and Symbolism in the Orthodox Liturgy." In *Orthodox Theology and Diakonia, Trends and Prospects*, edited by Demetrios J. Constantelos, 90–102. Brookline, MA: Hellenic College Press, 1981.

Schudson, Michael. "Advertising as Capitalist Realism." In *Advertising, the Uneasy Persuasion: Its Dubious Impact on American Society*, 209–233. New York: Basic Books, 1984.

Schultze, Quentin J. "Secular Television as Popular Religion." In *Religious Television: Controversies and Conclusions*, edited by Stewart M. Hoover and Robert Abelman, 239–248. Norwood, NJ: Ablex, 1990.

———. "Television Drama as Sacred Text." In *Channels of Belief: Religion and American Commercial Television*, edited by John P. Ferre, 3–27. Ames: Iowa State University Press, 1990.

Seed, John, and others. *Thinking Like a Mountain: Towards a Council of All Beings*. Philadelphia: New Society, 1988.

Sexson, Lynda. *Ordinarily Sacred*. New York: Crossroad, 1982.

Smith, Jonathan Z. "The Bare Facts of Ritual." *History of Religion* 20, nos. 1–2 (1980): 112–127.

Smith, Jonathan Z. "Earth and Gods." *Journal of Religion* 49, no. 2 (1969): 102–127.

———. *Imagining Religion: From Babylon to Jonestown*. Chicago: University of Chicago Press, 1988.

———. *Map Is Not Territory: Studies in the History of Religions*. Leiden: Brill, 1978.

———. *To Take Place: Toward Theory in Ritual*. Chicago: University of Chicago Press, 1987.

———. "The Wobbling Pivot." *Journal of Religion* 52(1972): 134–159.

Snyder, Gary. *The Practice of the Wild*. San Francisco: North Point, 1990.

Sobchack, Vivian. "Genre Film: Myth, Ritual, and Sociodrama." In *Film/Culture: Explorations of Cinema in Its Social Context*, edited by Sari Thomas, 147–165. Metuchen, NJ: Scarecrow, 1982.

Solomon, Alisa. *Can the Broadway Revival of Everyone's Favorite Jewish Musical Ignore Today's Radically Different Cultural Context?* January 21–27, 2004. Available at www.villagevoice.com/issues/0403/solomon.php.

Sperber, Dan, ed. *Rethinking Symbolism*. Cambridge: Cambridge University Press, 1975.

Spirn, Anne Whiston. *The Language of Landscape*. New Haven, CT: Yale University Press, 1998.

Staal, Frits. "The Meaninglessness of Ritual." *Numen* 26 (1979): 9–14.

Sturken, Marita, and Lisa Cartwright. *Practices of Looking: An Introduction to Visual Culture*. Oxford: Oxford University Press, 2001.

Swanson, Tod D. "To Prepare a Place: Johannine Christianity and the Collapse of Ethnic Territory." *Journal of the American Academy of Religion* 62, no. 2 (1994): 241–263.

Swimme, Brian, and Thomas Berry. *The Universe Story from the Primordial Flaring Forth to the Ecozoic Era: A Celebration of the Unfolding of the Cosmos*. San Francisco: HarperSanFrancisco, 1992.

Tambiah, Stanley J. "A Performative Approach to Ritual." *Proceedings of the British Academy* 65 (1979): 113–169.

Turner, Frederick. *Natural Classicism: Essays on Literature and Science*. New York: Paragon House, 1985.

Turner, Victor W. *The Anthropology of Performance*. New York: Performing Arts Journal Publications, 1987.

———. *Dramas, Fields and Metaphors: Symbolic Action in Human Society*. Ithaca, NY: Cornell University Press, 1974.

———. "Liminality and the Performative Genres." In *Rite, Drama, Festival, Spectacle: Rehearsals toward a Theory of Cultural Performance*, edited by John MacAloon, 19–41. Philadelphia: ISHI, 1985.

———. *The Ritual Process*. Ithaca, NY: Cornell University Press, 1969.

Unamuno, Miguel de. "Saint Immanuel the Good, Martyr." In *Abel Sanchez and Other Stories*, 207–267. Chicago: Regnery, 1956.

Van Der Zee, James, and others. *The Harlem Book of the Dead*. Dobbs Ferry, NY: Morgan and Morgan, 1978.

van Gennep, Arnold. *The Rites of Passage*. Chicago: University of Chicago Press, 1960.

Wirzba, Norman, ed. *The Art of the Commonplace: The Agrarian Essays of Wendell Berry*. Washington, DC: Shoemaker and Hoard, 2002.

Wolitz, Seth L. "The Americanization of Tevye, or Boarding the Jewish *Mayflower*." *American Quarterly* 40, no. 4 (1988): 514–536.

Yoon, Carol Kaesuk. *Study Jolts Views on Recovery from Extinctions*, 2000. Available at http://www.nytimes.com/library/national/science/030900sci-environ-wildlife.html.

Index

CPSIA information can be obtained
at www.ICGtesting.com
Printed in the USA
FSOW04n1726010816
23289FS